Formal Approaches to Romance Morphosyntax

Linguistische Arbeiten

Edited by
Klaus von Heusinger, Agnes Jäger,
Gereon Müller, Ingo Plag,
Elisabeth Stark and Richard Wiese

Volume 576

Formal Approaches to Romance Morphosyntax

Edited by
Marc-Olivier Hinzelin, Natascha Pomino
and Eva-Maria Remberger

DE GRUYTER

ISBN 978-3-11-099526-8
e-ISBN (PDF) 978-3-11-071915-4
e-ISBN (EPUB) 978-3-11-071928-4
ISSN 0344-6727

Library of Congress Control Number: 2020947344

Bibliographic information published by the Deutsche Nationalbibliothek
The Deutsche Nationalbibliothek lists this publication in the Deutsche Nationalbibliografie;
detailed bibliographic data are available on the Internet at http://dnb.dnb.de.

© 2022 Walter de Gruyter GmbH, Berlin/Boston
This volume is text- and page-identical with the hardback published in 2021.
Printing and binding: CPI books GmbH, Leck
Printed in Germany

www.degruyter.com

Contents

Marc-Olivier Hinzelin, Natascha Pomino and Eva-Maria Remberger
Romance Morphosyntax: Interpreting data from a theoretical perspective —— 1

Part 1: Agreement

Doreen Georgi and Elisabeth Stark
Past participle agreement in French – one or two rules? —— 19

Thom Westveer, Petra Sleeman and Enoch O. Aboh
Competing genders: French partitive constructions between grammatical and semantic gender —— 49

Part 2: Clitics and Null Subjects

Antonio Fábregas and Teresa Cabré
Towards a syntactic account of ungrammatical clitic sequences and their repairs —— 91

Michael Zimmermann
Investigating the setting of the null-subject parameter in Early Classical French —— 117

Part 3: Functional Categories and the Verb

Silvio Cruschina and Andrea Calabrese
Fifty shades of morphosyntactic microvariation —— 145

Dalina Kallulli
Issues in the morpho-syntax and semantics of Voice in Romance and beyond —— 199

Barbara Schirakowski
What constrains the formation of Spanish nominalized infinitives? —— 225

Lena Baunaz and Genoveva Puskás
Complementizer functional sequence: the contribution of Italo-Romance —— 251

Marc-Olivier Hinzelin, Natascha Pomino and
Eva-Maria Remberger

Romance Morphosyntax: Interpreting data from a theoretical perspective

Introduction

Abstract: This volume comprises a selection of contributions presented at a workshop entitled *The Morphosyntax of the Romance Languages and its Formal Analysis*, part of the XXXV Romanistentag 'Dynamics, Encounter, and Migration' in Zurich in 2017. The single chapters offer elaboration and revision of existing theoretical approaches as well as new formal analytical methods to Romance morphosyntax together with a comparative perspective on a range of data from the Romance languages, much of it novel in substance. They draw on approaches developed in recent grammatical theorizing, particularly in Generative Grammar; theoretical frameworks complementary to Generative Syntax, such as Distributed Morphology and Nanosyntax, are successfully adopted in order to analyse a vast range of Romance data not only from major Romance languages but also from non-standard, diatopic, and diachronic varieties.

Keywords: Romance, Morphosyntax, Distributed Morphology, Nanosyntax

1 The Interaction of Morphology and Syntax

This book aims to contribute to the discussion surrounding words and word structure and their interaction in phrasal and clausal syntax from a Romance perspective, using different formal mechanisms embedded in the framework of Distributed Morphology, Nanosyntax and Minimalist Syntax. Recent years have witnessed a resurfacing of interest in the interaction of morphology and syntax, from

---

Marc-Olivier Hinzelin: Universität Hamburg, Überseering 35, 22297 Hamburg, Germany, marc.hinzelin@uni-hamburg.de
Natascha Pomino: Bergische Universität Wuppertal, Gaußstraße 20, 42119 Wuppertal, Germany, pomino@uni-wuppertal.de
Eva-Maria Remberger: Universität Wien, Spitalgasse 2 (Campus, Hof 8), 1090 Wien, Austria, eva-maria.remberger@univie.ac.at

https://doi.org/10.1515/9783110719154-001

both a metatheoretical and a phenomenon-based perspective. This volume comprises both perspectives: some of the papers have a special focus on which theoretical architecture is appropriate to explain a grammatical phenomenon, whereas other authors examine the question of which factors or features impinge on the morphosyntactic phenomenon at issue and how this effect can be accounted for.

Morphosyntax can be understood as the comprehensive study of morphological and syntactic properties of linguistic units or as the analysis of the interaction of morphology and syntax at the interface only. There are certain phenomena where we wouldn't want to separate sentence and word level, and part of the key to understanding the architecture of grammar is working out what those phenomena are. Possible answers are hence very much dependent on the perspective taken: the grammatical theory chosen steers us in a certain direction; a typological exploration may give us deeper insights into language variation and the possible grammatical paths; a synchronic analysis relying on native speaker judgements provides us with answers that are quite different to those that might arise from a historical-comparative study meticulously investigating the structures available in manuscripts from a bygone era. Studying language change can help us to answer the question of whether both components of grammar are really balanced in the sense that one takes over the job of the other, or whether we are in fact simply dealing with one and the same component, as argued by many scholars within the generative tradition (this question is discussed extensively in Carstairs-McCarthy 2010).

For many grammatical phenomena, especially for agreement phenomena where syntactic relations are realized morpho(phono)logically, it is not easy to draw a dividing line between syntactic and morphological structure. From the perspective of syntax-driven models, this has led to the assumption that syntax is the module responsible not only for deriving syntactically complex phrases but also for deriving morphologically complex items, both in inflection and in word formation. The core assumption of so-called non-lexicalist realizational models is that syntax generates hierarchical structures based on abstract features and morphology maps those features (and structures) onto phonological material.

From a theoretical perspective, there are thus ongoing discussions and conflicting assumptions concerning the relationship between syntax and morphology. The question is whether morphology should be conceived as an autonomous component of grammar or whether it simply belongs to syntax. The *Strong* vs. *Weak Lexicalist Hypothesis* discusses whether derivation forms part of syntax (cf. Chomsky 1970, Williams 1981a, b, Selkirk 1982, Lieber 1983, 1992). A similar question addresses the role of inflection: the generative account of "Auxiliary Transformation" (Chomsky 1957: 38–42, 113), later termed 'Affix Hopping', treats inflectional morphology as syntactic derivation. If morphology is conceived as autonomous, the question of where it takes place within the grammatical architecture (pre-syntactically, post-syntactically or parallel to syntax) remains unanswered.

One main open question to be considered is the one whether there is a difference between morphological and syntactic processes. If this is the case, then we need to establish what creates this difference and on which basic units (features, morphemes, words, etc.) syntax operates. Under the theoretical perspective, there are at least three different approaches to morphology: within the Strong Lexicalist approach, syntax and morphology (i.e. inflection and derivation) are two different components. In these frameworks, morphosyntax is reduced more or less to interface phenomena in the sense that information has to be transferred or percolates from one component to the other. For instance, in the Feature Checking approach of early Minimalism (Chomsky 1995) (as well as in other unification-based approaches) lexical elements enter the syntactic derivation fully inflected, i.e. with prespecified grammatical feature values. The syntactic checking mechanism verifies whether or not these values match those encoded within the functional makeup of the corresponding phrase (e.g. AgrS for subject-verb agreement). In contrast, the weak version of lexicalism states that derivation is part of the lexicon, but inflection belongs to syntax. In Chomsky (2000, 2001) a checking mechanism AGREE is introduced which is compatible with this view: Only interpretable features are fully specified (or valued) in the lexicon, non-interpretable features are conceived as unvalued features (e.g. the person-number feature of verbs). Heads with unvalued features (= PROBES) acquire the corresponding values during the syntactic derivation. For this, the probe (e.g. T(ense) with unvalued person-number features) searches for a constituent with the corresponding interpretable feature (= GOAL; e.g. the subject DP) and the operation AGREE copies the values from the GOAL onto the PROBE (= feature valuation). After this valuation process the features of the PROBE are now accessible for post-syntactic processes, e.g. for Vocabulary Insertion, but they remain invisible for purposes of LF (cf. Chomsky 2000, 2001). In this approach, all inflectional phenomena are thus understood as morphosyntax, i.e. as cases where we cannot divide the two levels. And finally, syntactic approaches to morphology (e.g. Distributed Morphology) argue in favour of syntax being the only structure-generating device.

In early *Distributed Morphology* (DM; Halle & Marantz 1993, 1994), one of the most articulated non-lexicalist realizational models, a set of post-syntactic operations can alter or rearrange the syntactic output before the list of form-meaning correspondences (= Vocabulary Items in DM) is accessed. Since the early works in DM, a considerable number of different post-syntactic operations have been proposed, such as *fusion, fission, impoverishment, local dislocation, pruning*, etc. Some of these processes are considered necessary to cope with different mismatches between syntax and morphology:

- *Fusion* is assumed, for example, for portmanteau morphemes (e.g. French *du*, instead of **de le* 'of the') and other cases where the syntactic output is more complex than the morphological formatives (e.g. the present tense forms of the Romance verb; cf. Oltra Massuet 1991).
- *Fission*, on the other hand, is proposed to account for more or less the opposite situation i.e. for those cases where the form is more complex than the syntactic output, as e.g. in Tamazight Berber where the agreement morpheme (= one terminal node) can be exponed by one, two or three Vocabulary Items which may appear as prefixes and/or suffixes (cf. Noyer 1997).
- *Impoverishment* is an operation that does not alter the number of syntactic terminal nodes but only the features contained there, and has been used to explain, for instance, repairs of Romance Clitic Clusters (e.g. Spanish *se lo* for **le lo*) (cf. Bonet 1991).
- *Local dislocation* has been proposed for the analysis of clitics, and specifically for the linear ordering of special clitics: second-position clitics (e.g. Latin *-que* 'and') are inserted, for example, in a terminal node that has to be dislocated post-syntactically due to the 'intrinsic' need of the corresponding Vocabulary Item.
- Another process introduced to account for locality effects (on allomorphy) is *pruning*: nodes that are not exponed with phonological material are removed from the structure directly after Vocabulary Insertion with a direct effect on (linear) adjacency (Embick 2010): $\sqrt{root}\frown[x,-\emptyset], [x,-\emptyset]\frown Y \rightarrow \sqrt{root}\frown Y$ ('if x – which is linearly adjacent to $\sqrt{root}$ and to Y – is not realized, it is pruned so that $\sqrt{root}$ and Y become linearly adjacent to each other'). Whereas, according to Embick, pruning is sensitive to the phonological null status of the pruned category, Calabrese (2019) extends this process in assuming that diacritic features (e.g. [+suppletive]) may also trigger pruning before Vocabulary Insertion takes place.

However, the assumption of the multiple post-syntactic processes above has met with some criticism on the basis of the principle that (given equal explanatory adequacy) a smaller number of processes is preferable to a larger number; several efforts have thus been made to eliminate these processes (cf. Haugen & Siddiqi's 2016 arguments in favour of a Vocabulary-Insertion-only programme for non-lexicalist realizational models of morphology). *Fission* can be avoided, for example, by allowing insertion into one and the same syntactic node more than once (cf. Halle 1997); *impoverishment* is not necessary, if insertion of zero exponents is allowed (cf. Trommer 1999), and *fusion* as well as *pruning* can be avoided, if Vocabulary Insertion is not limited to terminal elements, as in the non-terminal spell-out of Nanosyntax (cf. Starke 2009, 2011) and the spanning approach of Svenonius (2012), among others.

The nanosyntactic approach in particular constitutes an attempt to resolve the contradiction between complex syntactic structures and their often syncretic or portmanteau morphophonological realizations. In nanosyntax, terminal nodes can be 'sub-morphemic', i.e. just featural, and the logical consequence of the missing one-to-one correspondence between syntactic input and morphological output is the possibility not only of realizing terminal nodes, whether they are features or categories, but also of allowing sub-trees to be part of the vocabulary. That is, Vocabulary Items come in "different syntactic sizes" and are thus internally – nanosyntactically – structured (Starke 2009: 2). Nanosyntax, however, then needs to assume novel mechanisms, such as cyclic overriding, and the superset principle, in order to avoid the insertion of e.g. It. *?più buono* '[literally] more good' instead of *meglio* 'better' for the syntactic sub-tree [COMPARATIVE [POSITIVE]] (for a comparison between Distributed Morphology and Nanosyntax, cf. e.g. Caha 2016).

The articles in this volume also examine the general question of which morphological operations impinge on syntax and how these effects can be accounted for in an appropriate way. The issues discussed concern the morphological encoding of syntactic relations and their alteration by morphological means. Core examples of morphosyntactic properties examined are mood, aspect, tense, gender, number, diathesis and agreement. All the contributions in this volume model the dynamics observable in generating well-formed morphosyntactic structures, paying particular attention to the localization of interface conditions. With regard to the technical modelling of the processes that express the dynamics when several submodules of grammar interact at interface level, it is clear that most of the morphosyntactic processes can be described and modelled by feature interaction, be it in the form of inherent lexical or functional features (e.g. when morphophonological realization is feature-driven, i.e. by contextual features) or in the migration of the latter from one node to the other. Consequently, the interac-

for a discrete treatment of French PPA according to the context (auxiliary *être/avoir* 'be/have') are presented. Two different analyses are required to account for the behaviour of PPA in French, i.e. with *avoir* a movement analysis is successful, but with *être* only an *in-situ* treatment makes sense. The two divergent analyses are also of theoretical interest as PPA with *avoir* may be considered as a differential marking of arguments, thus showing similarities to DOM.

Thom Westveer, Petra Sleeman, and Enoch Aboh ('Competing genders: French partitive constructions between grammatical and semantic gender') shed light on grammatical and semantic agreement in French partitive constructions; specifically, they discuss how gender mismatches are related to the type of partitive and the type of animate noun. Four noun classes are distinguished in French animate nouns according to the formal relationship between the masculine and the feminine noun used to express natural gender. Some nouns show a gender distinction by using completely unrelated words from a formal point of view (class A, e.g. *un frère/une sœur* 'a brother/sister'), whereas in another class the feminine word is morphologically derived from the masculine one (class B, e.g. *un étudiant/une étudiante* 'a student'). The two other classes use the same noun for both genders: in class C with epicene nouns only the determiner distinguishes between masculine and feminine (e.g. *un/une ministre* 'a minister'), whereas in class D the noun has a fixed gender but may refer to both sexes (e.g. *un personnage* 'a character'). Gender mismatches may arise in classes B and C if in a superlative construction one referent out of a group of persons of different sex is highlighted and the gender used in the determiner referring to the actual sex of one person clashes with the default masculine gender of the plural noun referring to the mixed group as whole. Using test sentences judged by native speakers, Westveer, Sleeman, and Aboh compare the acceptability of grammatical vs. semantic gender agreement.

The two contributions in the second section (*Clitics and Null Subjects*; Antonio Fábregas & Teresa Cabré 'Towards a syntactic account of ungrammatical clitic sequences and their repairs' and Michael Zimmermann 'Investigating the setting of the null subject parameter in Early Classical French. Insights from diaries') discuss two much-debated issues in Romance linguistics: clitics and null subjects. Many aspects of ungrammatical clitic sequences in Romance and their repairs by substitution or deletion (e.g. Spanish **le lo > se lo*, Italian **si si > ci si*) have often been explained on morphological grounds while the positioning of the clitics themselves is, at least in many approaches, syntactically motivated (e.g. Perlmutter 1971, Bonet 1991, 1993, 1995, Grimshaw 1997, Pescarini 2007, Rivero 2008, Nevins 2012). Clitic sequences are thus understood as a clear morphosyntactic

tion of various submodules of grammar is a relevant issue for all the topics discussed in this book: agreement (articles by Georgi & Stark and Westveer, Sleeman & Aboh) is one of the central areas where morphology and syntax typically interact. Characteristic Romance phenomena, such as clitic pronouns and null subjects (contributions by Fábregas & Cabré and Zimmermann), are equally relevant for this interface; they also introduce the topic of pronominal referentiality, i.e. a semantico-pragmatic perspective. Functional meaning as expressed by aspectual periphrases (chapter by Cruschina & Calabrese) and voice distinctions (cf. Kallulli's article) not only targets the interface between syntax and morphology but at the same time the resulting meaning of verbal forms, i.e. their interpretation at the level of semantics, dependent on the morphosyntactic structure. The morphosyntactic make-up of nominalized infinitives (article by Schirakowski) on the one hand, and mood phenomena, such as the operator-driven selection of the subjunctive mediated by particular complementizers (contribution by Baunaz & Pustkás) on the other are again related to interface conditions. This time, however, the interaction takes place at the level of event structure, *Aktionsart*, argument structure, and semantics of predicates – and, thus, also affects the access to the lexicon.

2 Interpreting Romance Data

The book is divided into three thematic sections consisting of two to four articles each. The first section (*Agreement*; Doreen Georgi & Elisabeth Stark 'Past participle agreement in French – one or two rules?' and Thom Westveer, Petra Sleeman & Enoch O. Aboh 'Competing genders: French partitive constructions between grammatical and semantic gender') is dedicated to different agreement phenomena in (non-normative) French and what these agreement facts tell us about the corresponding syntactic structure: Doreen Georgi and Elisabeth Stark ('Past participle agreement in French – one or two rules?') take a fresh look at past participle agreement (PPA), a well-known brainteaser for every student of French but also for native speakers as errors abound in written and oral performance. The intriguing question regarding this intricate phenomenon is why these rules are so hard to master and why they are so fundamentally different from those found in other Romance languages. Georgi and Stark show, based on differences in error rates, that at least in some constructions, past participle agreement obeys rules invented by normative grammar which are therefore artificial and incompatible with the syntax of natural languages. Eliminating these instances, they propose a novel analysis for French past participle agreement. Strong arguments

phenomenon where the output of syntax is 'repaired' by post-syntactic morpho(phono)logical processes as for example in the framework of *Distributed Morphology* (Halle & Marantz 1993).

Antonio Fábregas and Teresa Cabré ('Towards a syntactic account of ungrammatical clitic sequences and their repairs') cast doubt on this morphosyntactic view of ungrammatical clitic sequences and their repairs. In their very innovative analysis, they show that morphosyntactic treatments can be naturally restated in purely syntactic terms and that their syntactic analysis is in fact superior to any morphological or morphosyntactic account. A major example of a Romance morphosyntactic phenomenon thus turns out to be purely syntactic. Apart from presenting new theoretical insights, this paper shows that at least some phenomena are not *per se* morphosyntactic. In doing so, the dividing line between syntax and morphology is redrawn. Fábregas and Cabré start from two central assumptions: first, that the functional structure (= the extended projections of verbs, nouns, adjectives, etc. encoding grammatical information as e.g. T(P), C(P), Asp(P), D(P), Num(P), Gen(P)) is to be split into ontological domains (cf. Wiltschko 2014, Ramchand & Svenonius 2014) and, second, that within this functional structure there is a clitic area with hierarchically ordered subdomains for different types of clitics. Whenever there is a clash of two clitics of the same type, the repair applies to the leftmost clitic in the concerned Clitic Phrase (subdomain) and, according to the *Burning House Principle*, replaces them with a clitic from the hierarchically higher type. While earlier morphological approaches relate to the surface and can explain most, but not all, of the replacements or deletions (cf. e.g. Bonet 1991), the syntactic approach is argued to offer a crucial advantage: it takes into account the different properties (i.e. feature bundles) of the different clitic types, integrates semantic and syntactic functions, and is compatible with the principle of syntactic movement towards higher positions. In sum, the proposed analysis overcomes problems that have so far been unresolved and shows that repairs of Romance clitic clusters are better explained by a purely syntactic approach.

From a diachronic perspective, Michael Zimmermann ('Investigating the setting of the null subject parameter in Early Classical French. Insights from diaries') investigates French diaries from the early classical period with respect to subject pronoun usage, offering insights into what language change can tell us about the interaction of syntax and morphology. The null subject status is a much-debated issue in the history of French, as old French was a null subject language, although with some peculiarities, while modern French clearly no longer is. The exact point in time when the change in null subject status occurred remains an open issue, as does the interpretation of constructions that still show absence of subjects after this point. These are marginally encountered even in different varieties of contemporary French, ranging from colloquial omissions with *falloir* 'must' in *faut que...* '(it) is necessary that...', which is also found in many Oïl varieties as documented in Gilliéron & Edmont's (1902–1910) *Atlas linguistique de la France*, to fossilized expressions in archaizing written registers of standard French. The situation becomes even more complex when we have to interpret written texts from earlier periods without having access to native speakers and their judgements. Zimmermann presents strong arguments for a non-null subject analysis of the manuscripts examined from the first half of the 17th c. despite the presence of subject omission in specific constructions. In finite declarative root clauses, the omission is a peculiarity of the diary register, as also found in modern English and French. Finite subordinate clauses, however, show only very few cases of subject omission. The apparent counterexamples to a non-null subject analysis found in the finite subordinate clauses in Zimmermann's corpus are shown to be signs of a different writing style imitating earlier texts.

The third section (*Functional Categories and the Verb*; Silvio Cruschina & Andrea Calabrese 'Fifty shades of morphosyntactic microvariation: Motion verb constructions in southern Italian dialects'; Dalina Kallulli 'Issues in the morpho-syntax and semantics of Voice in Romance and beyond'; Barbara Schirakowski 'What constrains the formation of Spanish nominalized infinitives? A case study on transitive base verbs and event interpretations' and Lena Baunaz & Genoveva Puskas 'Complementizer functional sequence: the contribution of Italo-Romance') covers the relationship within the verbal functional domain. The article by Silvio Cruschina and Andrea Calabrese ('Fifty shades of morphosyntactic microvariation: Motion verb constructions in southern Italian dialects') focuses on the grammaticalization of motion verbs resulting in different Romance verbal periphrases. Since GO-periphrases have a wide range of manifestations and are thus a widely discussed topic in Romance linguistic theory, the investigated phenomena present an excellent testing ground for the interaction of syntax and morphology and, in anticipation of future research, also for the modelling of diachronic cycles. The main topic is the analysis of different types of verbal periphrases in southern Italian dialects, where GO-periphrases show different morphological realizations, but the same aspectual meaning. In several dialects, GO works as a functional restructuring verb, whereas in other dialects we find a doubly inflected periphrasis where the functional GO-verb and the lexical main verb agree (in a kind of concord) with each other. Further cases of morphosyntactic microvariation are found in varieties where this agreement is restricted to only some cells of the paradigm (i.e. displaying defectiveness) or is entirely absent. This eventually leads to the development of a morphological prefix for the invariable GO-forms. In order to resolve this microvariational puzzle, which cannot be explained by syntactic structure alone, the authors combine the hierarchical structure of the syntactic aspect field devised by Cinque (1999, 2001) with the processes provided by Distributed Morphology (cf. Halle & Marantz 1993), the latter being complemented by a novel version of cyclic pruning of terminal nodes (Calabrese 2019). The article is an example of fruitful cooperation between different fields of expertise within generative grammar, i.e. the Generative syntax of southern Italian dialects at the interface (Cruschina 2012) and the application of Distributed Morphology to Italo-Romance data (cf. Calabrese 2015, 2019).

Dalina Kallulli ('Issues in the morpho-syntax and semantics of Voice in Romance and beyond') investigates the categories of voice from Latin to Romance in a highly comparative perspective, and particularly in the context of other phenomena of non-active marking. Voice-related syncretisms, as found in Albanian and Greek, where the same non-active morphology is used in reflexive, passive, and anticausative constructions, show that the morphosyntax of voice needs to be modelled using more fine-grained distinctions. Building on her earlier work in Kallulli (2007, 2013), specifically the idea that overt morphological voice markings reflect feature distinctions associated with the v° head in the syntax, she analyses non-active morphology as reflecting not just the absence of an external argument, but also the presence of an [+activity] feature on the little v° head in syntactic configurations lacking an external argument. This, she argues, also accounts for the derivation of so-called 'unmarked anticausatives' (i.e., anticausatives that do not bear non-active morphology but instead surface with active voice morphology), since unlike in the passive, in anticausatives v° lacks an [+activity] feature and only has [+cause]. Turning to deponent verbs, which are crosslinguistically largely denominal, Kallulli argues that, since nominals lack external arguments, non-active morphology with this class of verbs is actually the expected, canonical form (for a diachronic explanation within Indo-European linguistics, see also Grestenberger 2014, 2018, which is discussed in detail in Kallulli's article). In Romance, the morphological correspondent of the non-active morphology of Albanian, Greek, and Latin deponents is the reflexive clitic *se*, as in inherent reflexives such as Italian *vergognarsi* 'be ashamed' or *meravigliarsi* 'be amazed'. That is, the v° with the feature [-external argument] in deponents and inherent reflexives serves as a verbalizer, which also explains the voice gaps (e.g. Italian **vergognare qualcuno* and the non-existence of active form deponents).

Barbara Schirakowski ('What constrains the formation of Spanish nominalized infinitives? A case study on transitive base verbs and event interpretations') analyses two types of Spanish nominalized infinitives, which are at the border between verbal clausality and deverbal nominalization. She adopts Ramchand's

(2008) *First Phase Syntax*, a highly appropriate approach for the analysis of phenomena related to verbal argument structure and word formation. The different types of nominalized infinitives (NI) – e.g. *el cantar de los pájaros* 'the singing of the birds' (NI + *de*-phrase; the most nominal of the NIs) vs. *el cantar una copla* 'the copla-singing' (verbal NI; NI + direct object) vs. *el cantar yo La Traviata* 'my singing of La Traviata' (sentential; the most verbal of the NIs) – are another instance of morphosyntax, since, based on the assumption of mixed extended projections, they can be understood as a means of syntactic nominalization. In order to capture the nominal and verbal properties of NIs, it has been proposed in the literature that the syntactic derivation begins with the projection of the verbal phrase / verbal predicate – which can be decomposed into subevental components (cf. Ramchand 2008) – and (other) verbal functional projections (e.g. voice, aspect) which are then at one point in the derivation embedded under nominal functional projections in order to become nominal. The different types of NI are usually explained by different *loci* at which the verbal structure is nominalized and by the category of the nominalizer (e.g. n° or D°). Recent discussions in the literature have therefore focussed primarily on using syntactic projections to account for various nominal and verbal properties of various types of NIs. In this spirit, Schirakowski devotes her paper to the question of which factors of the verbal base and possible verbal arguments constrain the formation of Spanish nominalized infinitives. Her main argument is that the formation of NI does not solely depend on the verbal bases, but that the interaction between two factors, argument realization and event interpretation, is the leading force. Based on a critical literature review which suggests that event interpretation plays a central role, and an empirical investigation relativizing this factor, Schirakowski convincingly shows that argument realization is another important factor, where generic interpretation is preferred. With regard to event interpretation, Schirakowski demonstrates that proper atelicity is not required but an open, atelic interpretation must be somehow available – if the verb itself is telic, coercion towards an unbounded reading via adverbials must be realized.

Lena Baunaz and Genoveva Puskás ('Complementizer functional sequence: the contribution of Italo-Romance') study the selection of subjunctive embedded clauses in Italo-Romance, which they claim to be local and mediated by a complementizer. In their analysis, which is based on Nanosyntax (cf. Starke 2009, 2011, Caha 2009, and others), complementizers are hierarchically structured sets of features. Since in Nanosyntax Vocabulary Insertion is not limited to terminal elements, it can apply to sub-trees of the structures derived by syntax. This idea is confirmed by the morphological syncretism found in languages like French, where one and the same item, *que*, serves as a complementizer, a relative pronoun and a *wh*-item and can thus be represented by the nested structure [Comp [Rel [Wh]]]. The insertion of the corresponding Vocabulary Items available for these structures is further conditioned by featural components. A complementizer selecting a subjunctive clause is licensed by a bouletic operator, which is conditioned by the featural composition of the matrix predicate: the matrix predicate is emotive (which includes sentient) and has an emotive external argument. Purely sentient, non-emotive predicates instead select an indicative inducing complementizer. This explains why the same verb can have a subjunctive and an indicative complement clause, but with a different interpretation as far as the emotive property of the external argument is concerned. Standard French and Italian have syncretic complementizers for both functions, as well as for the function of a relative and an interrogative pronoun, whereas many southern Italian dialects, Romanian as well as Greek have two distinct complementizers, depending on the presence of the bouletic operator in the matrix verb.

3 Summary

This volume fills a gap within Romance linguistics, where morphosyntax is still understudied in general and even more so going beyond a mere descriptive approach. The recently published *Manual of Romance Morphosyntax and Syntax* by Dufter & Stark (eds) (2017) follows aims similar to our volume: it also discusses, under a formal perspective, different morphosyntactic phenomena found in Romance. Yet, in contrast to our volume, it is a manual that gives a broad overview over selected grammatical areas and has, as manuals do, a highly introductory character. The articles in our volume present, in contrast, in-depth formal analyses of the phenomena at issue based on current research. Our volume aims at focusing more in detail on particular problems and special cases in Romance morphosyntax, in order to develop appropriate formal analyses that contribute to the further advancement of linguistic theory. The overall goal is thus to investigate what the analysed phenomena tell us about their structural make-up and the grammatical processes involved.

All the contributions in this volume draw on approaches developed in recent grammatical theorizing, particularly in Generative Grammar: theoretical frameworks complementary to Generative Syntax, as Distributed Morphology and Nanosyntax, are successfully adopted in order to analyse the vast range of Romance data which stem not only from major Romance languages but also from non-standard, diatopic, and diachronic varieties. Interestingly, all the contributions have argued for or are at least compatible with realizational models of morphology. We leave it for further discussion whether there are morphosyntactic phenomena which cannot be implemented based on a realizational approach.

Acknowledgements: We are deeply grateful to the anonymous peer reviewers as well as the series' editors for their helpful comments and evaluations, which substantially improved the quality and coherence of the volume. We would also like to thank the contributors of this volume for their efficient cooperation, and sometimes also patience, with us. And finally, many thanks go to Pamela Goryczka (University of Vienna) for organizing and carrying out the final formatting process together with Marike Hollinderbäumer and Tim Diaubalick (both University of Wuppertal).

4 References

Bonet, Eulàlia. 1991. *Morphology after syntax.* Ph.D. dissertation. Cambridge, MA: MIT Press.
Bonet, Eulàlia. 1993. 3rd person pronominal clitics in dialects of Catalan. *Catalan Working Papers in Linguistics* 3(1). 85–111.
Bonet, Eulàlia. 1995. Feature structure of Romance clitics. *Natural Language and Linguistic Theory* 13. 607–647.
Caha, Pavel. 2009. The nanosyntax of case. Ph.D. dissertation. Tromsø: University of Tromsø.
Caha, Pavel. 2016. Note on insertion in Distributed Morphology and Nanosyntax. Manuscript [available online: https://ling.auf.net/lingbuzz/002855 (1 August, 2020)].
Calabrese, Andrea. 2012. Allomorphy in the Italian passato remoto: A Distributed Morphology analysis. *Language and Information Society* (Sogang University, Korea), 1–75.
Calabrese, Andrea. 2019. *Morphophonological investigations: A theory of PF. From syntax to phonology in Italian and Sanskrit verb forms.* Manuscript, University of Connecticut.
Carstairs-McCarthy, Andrew. 2010. *The evolution of morphology* [Studies in the Evolution of Language 14]. Oxford: Oxford University Press.
Chomsky, Noam. 1957. *Syntactic structures* [Janua Linguarum: Series Minor 4]. Fourteenth printing 1985. The Hague: Mouton.
Chomsky, Noam. 1970. Remarks on nominalization. In Roderick A. Jacobs & Peter S. Rosenbaum (eds.), *Readings in English Transformational Grammar,* 184–221. Waltham, MA: Ginn.
Chomsky, Noam. 2000. Minimalist Inquiries: The Framework. In Roger Martin, David Michaels & Juan Uriagereka (eds.), *Step by Step. Essays on Minimalist Syntax in Honor of Howard Lasnik,* 89–156. Cambridge, MA: The MIT Press.
Chomsky, Noam. 2001. Derivation by phase. In Michael Kenstowic (ed.), *Ken Hale: A life in language,* 1–52. Cambridge, MA: The MIT Press.
Cinque, Guglielmo. 1999. *Adverbs and functional heads.* Oxford/New York: Oxford University Press.

Cinque, Guglielmo. 2001. 'Restructuring' and functional structure. *University of Venice Working Papers in Linguistics* 11. 45–127.
Cruschina, Silvio. 2012. *Discourse-related features and functional projections*. Oxford/New York: Oxford University Press.
Dufter, Andreas & Elisabeth Stark (eds.). 2017. *Manual of Romance Morphosyntax and Syntax*. Berlin: De Gruyter.
Embick, David 2010. *Localism versus globalism in morphology and phonology*. Cambridge, MA: MIT Press.
Gilliéron, Jules & Edmond Edmont (1902-1910): *Atlas linguistique de la France*. Paris: Honoré Champion.
Grestenberger, Laura. 2014. *Feature mismatch: Deponency in Indo-European*. Doctoral dissertation. Cambridge, MA: Harvard University.
Grestenberger, Laura. 2018. Deponency in finite and non-finite contexts. *Language* 94(3). 487–526.
Grimshaw, Jane. 1997. The best clitic: constraint interaction in morphosyntax. In Liliane Haegeman (ed.), *Elements of grammar*, 169–196. Dordrecht: Kluwer.
Halle, Morris. 1997. Distributed Morphology: Impoverishment and fission. *MIT Working Papers in Linguistics* 30. 425–449.
Halle, Morris & Alec Marantz. 1993. Distributed Morphology and the pieces of inflection. In Kenneth Hale & Samuel J. Keyser (eds.), *The view from building* 20, 111–176. Cambridge, MA: MIT Press.
Halle, Morris & Alec Marantz. 1994. Some key features of Distributed Morphology. In Andrew Carnie & Heidi Harley (eds.), *Papers on Phonology and Morphology* [MIT Working Papers in Linguistics 21], 275–288. Cambridge, MA: The MIT Press.
Haugen, Jason & Daniel Siddiqi. 2016. Towards a restricted realization theory: Multimorphemic monolistemicity, portmanteaux, and post-linearization spanning. In Daniel Siddiqi & Heidi Harley (eds.), *Morphological Metatheory*, 343–385. Amsterdam/Philadelphia: John Benjamins.
Kallulli, Dalina. 2007. Rethinking the passive/anticausative distinction. *Linguistic Inquiry* 38(4). 770–780.
Kallulli, Dalina. 2013. (Non-)canonical passives and reflexives: deponents and their like. In Artemis Alexiadou & Florian Schäfer (eds.), *Non-Canonical Passives*, 337–358. Amsterdam/Philadelphia: John Benjamins.
Lieber, Rochelle. 1983. Argument linking and compounds in English. *Linguistic Inquiry* 14(2). 251–285.
Lieber, Rochelle. 1992. *Deconstructing morphology: Word formation in syntactic theory*. Chicago: The University of Chicago Press.
Nevins, Andrew. 2012. Haplological dissimilation at distinct stages of exponence. In Jochen Trommer (ed.), *The morphology and phonology of exponence*, 84–116. Oxford: Oxford University Press.
Noyer, Rolf. 1997. *Features, positions and affixes in autonomous morphological structure*. New York: Garland Publishing.
Oltra Massuet, M. Isabel. 1999. *On the notion of theme vowel: A new approach to Catalan verbal morphology*. MA thesis. Cambridge, MA: MIT.
Perlmutter, David. 1971. *Deep and surface structure constraints in syntax*. New York: Holt, Rinehart and Winston.

Pescarini, Diego. 2007. Types of syncretism in the clitic systems of Romance. *Anuario del Seminario de filología vasca Julio de Urquijo* 41. 285–300.
Ramchand, Gillian C. 2008. *Verb meaning and the lexicon. A first-phase syntax*. Cambridge: Cambridge University Press.
Ramchand, Gillian & Peter Svenonius. 2014. Deriving the functional hierarchy. *Language Sciences* 46. 152–174.
Rivero, María Luisa. 2008. Oblique subjects and person restrictions in Spanish: a morphological approach. In Susann Fischer, Roberta D'Alessandro & Gunnar Hrafnbjargarson (eds.), *Agreement restrictions*, 215–250. Berlin: De Gruyter.
Selkirk, Elisabeth O. 1982. *The syntax of words* [Linguistic Inquiry Monographs 7]. Cambridge, MA: The MIT Press.
Starke, Michal. 2009. Nanosyntax. A short primer to a new approach to language. *Nordlyd* 36(1) [Special issue on Nanosyntax]. 1–6. [available online: https://septentrio.uit.no/index.php/nordlyd/article/view/213/205 (1 August, 2020)].
Starke, Michal. 2011. Towards an elegant solution to language variation: Variation reduces to the size of lexically stored trees. Unpublished Manuscript. Barcelona, Spain.
Svenonius, Peter. 2012. Spanning. Manuscript. CASTL: University of Tromsø.
Trommer, Jochen. 1999. Morphology consuming syntax's resources: Generation and parsing in a minimalist version of Distributed Morphology. Manuscript [available online: https://ling.auf.net/lingbuzz/000116 (1 August, 2020)].
Williams, Edwin. 1981a. On the notions 'lexically related' and 'head of a word'. *Linguistic Inquiry* 12(2). 245–274.
Williams, Edwin. 1981b. Argument structure and morphology. *The Linguistic Review* 1(1). 81–114.
Wiltschko, Martina. 2014. *The universal structure of categories*. Cambridge: Cambridge University Press.

Part 1: **Agreement**

Doreen Georgi and Elisabeth Stark
Past participle agreement in French – one or two rules?

Abstract: Past participle agreement in French has been taken to be conditioned (among other factors) by movement of the internal argument out of the VP, i.e. as a reflex of movement. However, drawing on data that have been neglected so far in the formal literature on the topic (Lahousse 2011), we show that this characterization is in part misguided: past participle agreement is also possible with *in-situ* internal arguments of unaccusative/passive verbs (that combine with the perfect auxiliary *être*), and hence cannot generally be considered a reflex of movement. We argue that a unified analysis of all past participle contexts in French is not only difficult – the sole attempt at a uniform analysis of a very similar pattern in Italian by D'Alessandro and Roberts (2008) cannot be extended to French – but also undesirable, because past participle agreement in contexts with the auxiliary *avoir* differs in a number of properties compared to past participle agreement in contexts that require the auxiliary *être*. We thus argue that past participle agreement in French is in fact not a homogeneous phenomenon but results from two different mechanisms: agreement between the past participle and the internal argument in its base position (not in a Spec-head configuration as is usually assumed), or from resumption (following a suggestion by Boeckx 2003).

Keywords: past participle agreement, French, agreement in-situ, resumption, reflexes of movement

1 Introduction

A well-studied phenomenon in the morphosyntax of Romance languages is past participle agreement (PPA): in sentences with a perfect or passive auxiliary, the past participle can (and sometimes must) agree in (a subset of) *phi*-features with

---

Doreen Georgi: Universität Potsdam, Karl-Liebknecht-Strasse 24-25, 14476 Potsdam, Germany, doreen.georgi@uni-potsdam.de
Elisabeth Stark: Universität Zürich, Zürichbergstrasse 8, 8032 Zürich, Switzerland, estark@rom.uzh.ch

an argument. In this paper, we will reconsider PPA in French and argue that despite the intensive research on this phenomenon, a comprehensive integration even of the basic facts in a formal analysis is still lacking. In particular, we will argue that a unified analysis of PPA under the auxiliaries *avoir* and *être* is not only difficult, but actually undesirable, since PPA has different properties in these contexts. Hence, we claim that PPA under *avoir* has a different status / source than PPA under *être*.

The paper is structured as follows: in the remainder of section 1 we will remind the reader of the distribution of PPA in French. Furthermore, we show that important facts in the context of the auxiliary *être*, though available in the descriptive literature, have not been considered in formal analyses of PPA; in fact, these data are unexpected in previous approaches. Section 2 summarizes the main ideas of existing analyses and points out their shortcomings. In section 3 we argue, based on a whole series of corpus facts, why, in our view, PPA in French is not a unified phenomenon and should be considered the result of two different syntactic mechanisms. In section 4 we present a formal implementation of these ideas. Finally, section 5 concludes.

From a descriptive point of view, the rules of PPA in standard French can be formulated as follows, in the terminology of Relational Grammar (following e.g. Perlmutter & Postal 1983):

> Accordo del PP in francese
> Sia *b* una proposizione, *a* un nominale di *b* e *p* un participio passato di una forma verbale perifrastica di *b*. *p* si accorda in genere e numero con *a* se e solo se:
> I. la proposizione è finalemente intransitiva [= internal argument is not in its post-verbal base position].
> II. *a è legittimato al controllo dell'accordo*.
> Un nominale è legittimato al controllo dell'accordo sse:
> (a) non è chômeur [= *a* is in an argument position]
> (b) è il 2 inizializzato da *p* [= is the internal argument of *p*].
> (Loporcaro 1998: 53)[1]

---

[1] 'Past participle agreement in French
With *b* being a clause, *a* a nominal in *b* and *p* a past participle as part of a periphrastic verb form of *b*, *p* agrees in gender and number with *a* if and only if:
i. the clause is intransitive [...].
ii. *a* is entitled to control the agreement.
   a nominal is entitled to control the agreement if:
   (a) it is not a *chômeur* [...]
   (b) it is the initial 2 of *p* [...].' (our translation).'

II(a) in the Italian quote above can be translated as "*a* is in an argument position" and II(b) as "*a* is the internal argument of *p*". Generally, in a pan-Romance perspective and still following the observations in Loporcaro (1998), two factors determine past participle agreement in Romance: auxiliary selection (*être*, 'to be', with unaccusatives (3), passives (2a), reflexive constructions; *avoir*, 'to have', with unergative verbs and active-transitive constructions), and, in the case of active-transitive constructions, *linear order* between past participle and internal argument (DP_{int}). In French, PPA is only possible in this context when DP_{int} linearly precedes the past participle, i.e. when DP_{int} has left its base position inside the VP because it has undergone cliticization, *wh*-movement, or relativization ((3b), (3c), (4a) vs. (1) and (4b)). Moreover, whenever there is agreement with the subject, *être* is chosen in standard French (cf. Stark & Riedel 2013: 119).

(1) Pierre a donné la pomme à Jean.
    Pierre has given the apple to John
                        (active-trans., DP_{int} in-situ, no PPA)

(2) a. La pomme a été donné-**e** à Jean.
       the apple has been given.FEM.SG to John
                        (passive, PPA with preposed DP_{int})
    b. Pierre a donné la pomme à Jean.
       Pierre has given the apple to John
                        (active-trans., DP_{int} in-situ, no PPA)

(3) a. Marie est arrivé-**e**.
       Marie is arrived.FEM.SG   (unaccusative, PPA with preposed DP_{int})
    b. Pierre l'a donné-**e** à Jean.
       Pierre it-has given.FEM.SG to John
                        (active-trans., PPA with cliticized DP_{int})
    c. La pomme que Pierre a donné-**e** à Jean.
       the apple that Pierre has given.FEM.SG to John
                        (active-trans., PPA with relativized DP_{int})

(4) a. Combien de pommes Pierre a-t-il pesé-es?
       how.many of apples Pierre has-L-he weighed.FEM.PL
                        (active-trans., PPA with ex-situ wh-DP_{int})
    b. Pierre a pesé combien de pommes?
       Pierre has weighed how.many of apples
                        (active-trans., no PPA with in-situ wh-DP_{int})

Looking for a potential 'function', in semantic-pragmatic terms, of past participle agreement in Romance and especially standard French (cf. Stark 2013), one might assume that this kind of agreement functions as a 'signal' for reduced transitivity (cf. Kayne 1989: internal argument in Spec Agr$_o$P = 'object conjugation', Blanche-Benveniste 2006, Loporcaro's 1998 first condition). This could be so since the subject of a sentence with past participle agreement is very often a theme (patient), not of a higher thematic role (e.g. agent), i.e. there is no DP externally merged in Spec$v$P (cf. examples (2a), (3) against (1) and (2b), also Belletti 2017: chapter 5.1). However, that evidently only holds for past participle agreement in constructions with *être*. Subjects in past participle agreement constructions with *avoir* are agents (examples (4a) and (4b)), and still, we have agreement (not with the subject, but with the *preceding, never the following*, internal argument).

It is indisputable that linear order plays a role in the presence/absence of PPA in contexts with the auxiliary *avoir* in French. However, for some reason, the linear order factor has also been taken to be operative in cases where the auxiliary is *être*. Looking at the relevant passive and unaccusative examples in (2a) and (3) above, we can see that the PPA controlling argument, an underlying internal argument, has undergone movement and thus precedes the past participle. Indeed, this reordering of DP_{int} takes place in the vast majority of contexts where the auxiliary *être* is used. This is because there is only a single argument in the structure with unaccusative/passive verbs, and since French has the EPP-property (the derived subject position SpecT must be filled), this sole argument is often the only candidate to fulfill the EPP, and it thus moves out of the VP. But the reason for this displacement of DP_{Int} is the EPP, it is not in any way triggered by the choice of the auxiliary or the presence of PPA. Nevertheless, in virtually all formal analyses of French PPA, the phenomenon is assumed to be conditioned by the preposing of DP_{Int} – regardless of the choice of the auxiliary. Indeed, PPA is mostly treated as a *reflex* of DP_{int}-movement (see among others Kayne 1985, Déprez 1998, Belletti 2006). Put differently, movement of DP_{Int} is considered a necessary factor for PPA to occur (though not always a sufficient condition), and this is what unifies PPA-contexts with *avoir* and *être*.

However, this is not true. The generalization holds for cases with the auxiliary *avoir*, but not for contexts that require *être*. As shown in Fender (2002) and Lahousse (2011: 184,186), there are contexts (called inversion constructions) in which DP_{Int} of passive / unaccusative v can actually stay *in-situ* because the EPP-property is satisfied by a different XP or is not satisfied at all (on the surface), and still there must be PPA with DP_{Int}, see (5) and (6):

(5) a. Une épreuve   sera   présenté-e   à   chaque candidat.
         a   test   be.FUT.3sg   presented.FEM.SG   to   each   candidate
         'A test will be presented to each candidate.'
     b. A chaque candidat   sera   présenté-e   une épreuve.
         to each   candidate be.FUT.3SG   presented.FEM.SG   a   test
         'Each candidate will be presented a test.'

(6) a. Je voudrais   que soient   inscrit-s   tous les enfants de Marie.
         I would like that be.SUBJ.3PL enrolled.PL   all the children of Marie
     b. *Je voudrais que soient   tous inscrit-s   les enfants de Marie.
         I would like that be.SUBJ.3PL all enrolled.PL   the children of Marie
         'I would like that all children of Marie are enrolled.'

Crucially, Lahousse (2006, 2011) provides evidence that DP$_{Int}$ in the inversion constructions (5b) and (6a) is indeed in its base position: for example, this is suggested by the fact that quantifier float is impossible in (6b), and that the preferred reading in (5b) is a narrow scope reading of the existential quantifier in the scope of the universal quantifier in the indirect object *A chaque candidat* – which follows naturally if *une épreuve* is positioned lower in the syntactic structure. The latter observation also renders implausible a generalized assumption of right dislocation with a null clitic for these structures as sketched in Kayne (1989, Belletti 2017) for PPA with *avere* with *in-situ* direct objects in some Italian dialects. These facts show that displacement of DP$_{Int}$ (the linear order factor) is *not* a necessary condition for PPA (with the auxiliary *être*). Consequently, PPA in French cannot in general be described and analyzed as a reflex of movement; at least, the connection to movement of DP$_{Int}$ only holds for contexts with the auxiliary *avoir*.[2] For some reason, these facts have not been considered in the formal literature on PPA in French (see section 2 for further discussion).

Finally, note that the difference between *avoir*- and *être*-contexts with respect to the importance of the linear order factor leads us to the preliminary conclusion (to be expanded in section 3) that we are in fact dealing with two different rules which underlie standard French PPA: one is based on linear order (agreement in constructions with *avoir* with preceding clitics or *wh*-marked elements), some-

---

[2] In earlier stages of French (Old French, see Dupuis 1992) and Italian as well as in some modern Romance varieties (e.g. in Catalan, Brown 1988) one can also find PPA with an *in-situ* internal argument of an active transitive verb. See Legendre (2017) for an overview of PPA-patterns in Romance.

thing that is not in itself exotic (Corbett 2006: 199–200, see the remarks on subject-verb vs. verb-subject agreement in number in Slavonic, a phenomenon also found in many Romance varieties, e.g. non-standard Brazilian Portuguese), while the other one is not. The aim of our paper is to provide more arguments that PPA with *avoir* and *être* is not a unified phenomenon since the two constructions at issue differ in a number of properties, and to provide a formal analysis for both subtypes of PPA that derives these properties.

2 Previous analyses of (French) PPA

Most existing formal analyses of PPA (Kayne 1985, 1989, Bouchard 1987, Lefebvre 1988, Lois 1990, Branigan 1992, Obenauer 1992, Friedemann & Siloni 1997, Déprez 1998, Drijkoningen 1999 and Belletti 2006) are formulated on the assumption that PPA only occurs when an internal argument undergoes movement out of VP. Thus, they mostly take PPA to be a reflex of movement.[3] As we have seen, this does not describe the whole pattern since it ignores the fact that PPA is possible with an *in-situ* DP_{Int} of an unaccusative v in French (and Italian). As already noted in Bouchard (1987), Sportiche (1990), Déprez (1998), and Boeckx (2003), this pattern is totally unexpected in existing analyses which basically treat PPA as the consequence of a Spec-head-agreement relation between the participle head (a functional verbal projection) and DP_{Int}, following the seminal analysis by Kayne (1989). Furthermore, even in the *avoir*-contexts where PPA co-occurs with DP_{Int}-movement, it cannot simply be equated with a reflex of movement as noted in Branigan (1992) and Boeckx (2003). Reflexes of XP-movement have been shown to exhibit three patterns cross-linguistically with respect to their distribution across clauses under long-distance movement of an argument (see Georgi 2014, 2017): they occur in all clauses of the dependency, only in the clause in which the moved XP surfaces, or only in the clauses crossed by XP but in which XP does not surface. However, French PPA shows a different pattern: if DP_{Int} undergoes long

---

[3] More recent Minimalist approaches to PPA do not consider PPA to be directly triggered by movement, viz. the result of Spec-head-agreement. Rather, they postulate a downward Agree relation (in strict parallel to subject-verb agreement) where the participle head probes for its goal (the internal argument) inside the VP, see Chomsky (2001), D'Alessandro & Roberts (2008, see below), Belletti (2017: ch.3), Longenbaugh (2019). Thus, past participle agreement with *avoir* needs, as opposed to past participle agreement with *être*, additional or different conditions, i.e. independently motivated preposing of the object DP (because of *wh*-movement or its clitic status, Kayne 1989, Belletti 2006).

extraction, PPA can only occur in the lowest clause of the dependency, viz. in the clause in which DP_{int} has its θ-position, see (7).

(7) a. La lettre qu'-il   a   dit(*-e)   que Pierre lui a
       the letter which-he has   said.FEM.SG that Pierre him has
       envoyé*(-e).
       sent.FEM.SG
       (Chomsky 1995: 325)
    b. Quelles chaises as-tu   dit(*-es)   qu'-il   a   *repeint*(-es)*.
       which   chairs have-you   said.FEM.PL that-he has repeint*(-es)
       (Grohmann 2003: 287)
    c. Combien de fautes   Jean a-t-il   dit(*-es)   que Paul a
       how-many of mistakes John has-L-he said.FEM.PL that Paul has
       fait(-es)?
       done.FEM.PL
       (Boeckx 2003: 60)

This is another argument for not treating PPA as a reflex of movement even in contexts with *avoir*.[4]

The only comprehensive analysis of PPA that aims to cover both PPA with *avoir* (requires movement of DP_{int}) and *être* (independent of DP_{int}-movement) by the same mechanism is proposed in D'Alessandro & Roberts (2008, henceforth D&R) for standard Italian (with a very similar PPA-split). In their analysis, D&R adopt the clause structure in (8) for clauses with periphrastic tenses, illustrated for a transitive verb (p. 481):

(8) $[_{vP} V_{Aux} [_{vPrtP} DP_{ext} [_{vPrt'} V_{Prt} [_{vP} V DP_{int}]]]]$

---

4 Several analyses of the special French PPA-pattern under long movement have been proposed. Two main ideas are pursued: (a) there is no movement to the relevant specifier (Specv / SpecAgrO) in clauses other than the one where DP_{int} has its base position and hence no Spechead-agreement (see Branigan 1992, Grohmann 2003); instead, cross-clausal movement proceeds from SpecC of the embedded clause directly to SpecC of the next higher clause. (b) DP_{int} targets Specv / SpecAgrO only in the lowest clause of the dependency, while in higher clauses it adjoins to the projection of the participle head (an A'-position), and agreement (an A-relation) is impossible with adjuncts (cf. Chomsky 1995: 325f., following a suggestion in Kayne 1989). The latter is a pure stipulation to get the facts right, while the first is dubious given the ever-growing body of literature on movement reflexes that occur in the vP-domain (see among others Urk forthcoming and Korsah & Murphy 2019 for recent overviews). See also Georgi (2014: ch. 4.3.) for a more detailed discussion of previous approaches to the long-movement PPA-pattern in French.

The head v_{Prt} merges with VP and introduces the external argument (DP_{ext}). The auxiliary is hosted by v_{Aux}, a raising predicate that attracts the structurally closest argument to its specifier. D&R (2008) assume that active transitive V in Italian moves to v_{Prt} to pick up the inflectional features on the latter. Evidence for this movement comes from the placement of certain manner adverbs and floated quantifiers attached to the VP that follow the past participle, see the examples in (10) and (11). For unaccusative/passive contexts, the movement of V is optional (cf. Cinque 1999, Guasti & Rizzi 2000). For D&R (2008), PPA is the result of a downward Agree relation between v_{Prt} (the probe) and DP_{int} (the goal) in the syntax. v_{Prt} bears an unvalued *phi*-probe that seeks gender and number values on DP_{int}. This Agree relation always takes place. Whether the valued features on v_{Prt} are morphophonologically realized (= PPA) or not (= absence of PPA) is regulated in the postsyntactic morphological component by the condition in (9).

(9) Given an Agree relation A between probe P and goal G, morphophonological agreement between P and G is realized if P and G are contained in the complement of the minimal phase head H. XP is the complement of a minimal phase head H if there is no distinct phase head H^0 contained in XP whose complement YP contains P and G.

According to (9), PPA (= the valued *phi*-features on v_{Prt}) is only realized on v_{Prt} if the probe (= v_{Prt}) and the goal (= DP_{int}) are contained in the same spell-out domain of the minimal phase head. Phase heads are transitive active v and C (but no other heads, especially not unaccusative/passive v). They trigger the spell-out of their complements once they have projected a phrase (Chomsky 2000, 2001). Combined with the aforementioned assumptions, the PPA-pattern of Italian is derived as follows: (i) Active transitive verb, DP_{int} stays *in-situ*: V raises to v_{Prt}, v_{Prt} is a phase head, and DP_{int} stays inside VP. Hence, the probe v_{Prt} and the goal DP_{int} are not in the same spell-out domain: the complement of the minimal phase head v_{Prt} is the VP, but VP only contains the goal, not the probe. Thus, the *phi*-features on v_{Prt} remain unpronounced, there is no PPA. (ii) Active transitive verb, DP_{int} undergoes movement (e.g. cliticization): again, V raises to v_{Prt} and v_{Prt} is a phase head. But crucially, DP_{int} leaves its base position and attaches to v_{Aux} (= cliticization). As a consequence of DP_{int}-movement, the probe v_{Prt} and the goal are in the same spell-out domain, viz. in the complement of the next higher phase head C. Transitive v_{Prt} is always in C's spell-out domain, DP_{int} becomes part of it when it moves out of VP. As a consequence, the *phi*-features of v_{Prt} are morphologically realized as PPA. (iii) Unaccusative/passive verb: V optionally moves to v_{Prt}. Crucially, unaccusative v_{Prt} is not a phase head – the next higher phase head is C. Thus, whether DP_int undergoes movement or not, both the probe v_Prt and the goal are part of the same spell-out domain (= TP, complement of C). As a result, the *phi*-features on v_Prt are morphologically realized (= PPA).

There are several aspects of this approach to PPA in Italian that strike us as problematic, either in general or with respect to extending the proposal to French PPA: (a) phase status of unaccusative v: Legate (2003) provides a number of empirical arguments (reconstruction, quantifier raising, parasitic gaps) that show that the specifier of unaccusative v serves as an intermediate landing site for movement, just like the specifier of transitive active v. Hence, unaccusative v must also be a phase head (see also the references in Richards 2011 for more work that comes to the same conclusion). But if v_Prt is always a phase head, we should not see PPA with an *in-situ* DP_int of an unaccusative verb in D'Alessandro & Roberts' analysis (2008) (only the goal is in the complement domain of v_Prt), contrary to the facts.

(b) V-movement: in D&R's (2008) account of PPA, (at least active transitive) V has to move to v_Prt to pick up the inflection (PPA). However, in French no such movement takes place; the participle always follows the crucial class of manner adverbs, unlike in Italian, see examples (10) and (11) as opposed to (12) and (13). If V does not move in French, we should never see PPA show up on V (unless one postulates additional postsyntactic operations to bring the inflection and V together, e.g. Local Dislocation à la Embick & Noyer 2001).

(10) a. Hanno   accolto   bene   il   suo   spettacolo.
        have.3PL   received well   the his   performance
     b. *Hanno   bene   accolto   il   suo   spettacolo.
        have.3PL   well   received the his   performance

(11) a. Questo   genere di spettacoli   è   sempre stato bene accolto.
        this   kind   of performances be.3SG   always been well received
     b. Questo   genere di spettacoli   è   sempre stato accolto bene.
        this   kind   of performances be.3SG   always been received well

(12) a. Ils   ont   bien   accueilli son   spectacle.
        they   have.3PL   well   received   his   performance
     b. *Ils   ont   accueilli bien   son   spectacle.
        they   have.3PL   received well   his   performance

(13) a. Ce   genre de spectacle   a   toujours été bien   accueilli.
        this kind of performance have.3SG   always   been well   received

b. *Ce genre de spectacle a toujours été accueilli bien.
  this kind of performance have.3SG always been received well
  (cf. Cinque 1999: 102–103)

(c) A'-movement of DP_{Int}: D&R (2008) illustrate PPA triggered by DP_{Int} movement with cliticization (A-movement) to the relatively low position v_{Aux}. This leads to PPA since DP_{Int} moves to the same spell-out domain in which v_{Prt} is located (= TP, domain of the phase head C). If, however, DP_{Int} undergoes A'-movement to SpecC, it is no longer in C's spell-out domain, unlike v_{Prt}. Hence, A'-movement (*wh*-movement, relativization) should *never* trigger PPA in D&R's account. In fact, this is true for Italian. However, it is not for (standard) French, where A'-movement of DP_{Int} can trigger PPA, see (3c) and (4a).

(d) the role of copies/traces: a way to avoid this problem in French and to have A'-movement trigger PPA in D&R's approach would be to take into account not the terminal landing site of the moved DP_{Int} (SpecC) but rather intermediate landing sites of successive-cyclic movement (cf. Chomsky 1986 et seq.). The intermediate landing site of A'-movement would be in Specv$_{Prt}$. The intermediate copy in Specv$_{Prt}$ is in the same spell-out domain as v_{Prt}, viz. in TP, and could thus trigger realization of PPA. The same logic could be used to solve another problem in D&R's system that the authors themselves mention: subject-verb-agreement (SV-Agr) should be suspended when the subject undergoes (local or long-distance) A'-movement since the subject in its landing site SpecC is no longer in the same minimal spell-out domain as the probe on the head T (domain = TP). This unwelcome result for Italian (and French) could also be avoided by considering the intermediate landing site of the subject in SpecT (inside C's spell-out domain) for the calculation of morphological realization of probe features. However, this solution leads to an overgeneration problem elsewhere: under long-distance movement of DP_{Int} in French, we should see PPA in all clauses of the dependency. This is because the intermediate trace of the moving DP_{Int} in Specv of the higher clauses (viz. the clauses in which DP_{Int} is not base-generated) is in the same spell-out domain as the probe v_{Prt} of the respective clauses in a long-distance A'-dependency (assuming that these v_{Prt}-heads have access to the moving DP_{Int} in its intermediate landing site at the edge SpecC of the embedded clauses, which is the case given standard phase theory, see Chomsky 2001). However, this is not the case in French long-distance dependencies, PPA can only surface in the clause in which DP$_{Int}$ originates (see examples in (7) above).[5] So taking into account intermediate copies cannot be the solution for French. In fact, D&R provide a different solution to the SV-Agr problem. Following Chomsky (2008), they assume that subject A'-extraction involves both an A- and an A'-chain. Then they propose that only A-chains (as in the context of cliticization) are subject to the realization condition in (9). Put differently, A'-positions are ignored for the algorithm in (9). Of course, this alternative solution cannot be used for French either, since this would wrongly exclude PPA triggered by A'-movement in French (the only A-position in such chains is the base position of DP$_{Int}$, which is, however, not in the same spell-out domain as the probe v$_{Prt}$). Thus, it does not help to consider only a subset of positions (only A- or A'-chains, or only intermediate or terminal copies in movement chains) – under none of these assumptions can the French PPA-pattern be captured in D&R's system, as it either leads to over- or undergeneration of PPA. (e) Finally, problems arise in the morphological component when the morphological agreement rule in (9), only provided in prose in D&R, is technically implemented. The rule is relational in nature, viz. two elements need to interact to determine whether agreement is possible. This requires a memory device (e.g. a shared index) such that the PF component "knows" which elements have entered into Agree in the syntax. However, such empty devices are to be banned from the syntactic computation in the Minimalist Program (cf. Chomsky 1995 et seq.), the framework that D&R adopt (see also Rezac 2004: ch.3 for a critical discussion of derivational memory). For all of these reasons, we do not adopt (a version of) D&R's attempt at a uniform analysis of PPA-contexts for French.

3 Against a unified treatment of PPA with *avoir* and *être* in standard French

At this stage the central question that arises is whether it is actually adequate and useful to try to unify the occurrences of PPA with *avoir* and *être*. In this section, we provide arguments for a separate treatment of the *avoir*- and *être*-contexts. The argumentation is based on the observation that these contexts differ in several ways (each of which has individually been mentioned before in the literature on French PPA). We have already discussed the first one, viz. the role of linear

---

[5] Note that past participle agreement can occur in every clause of a long-distance dependency e.g. in the Algonquian language Passamaquoddy (Bruening 2001: ch.4), so the absence of PPA in higher clauses in French is not a general property of participle agreement.

order: movement of DP_{int} is only a necessary condition for PPA with *avoir*, but not with *être* (see section 1).

Second, PPA with *avoir* and *être* differ in their robustness. It has often been noticed that PPA with *être* is basically obligatory and indeed very robustly used in spontaneous spoken and written varieties of French, while the usage of PPA with *avoir* in the contexts where it is possible is (more or less) variable (Sportiche 1992, Branigan 1992, Friedeman & Siloni 1997, Guasti & Rizzi 2000, Boeckx 2003, Vega Vilanova 2018). More precisely, PPA with *avoir* is neglected in particular in A'-movement constructions (*wh*-movement, relativization of DP_{int}), but less so under DP_{int}-cliticization; PPA with *avoir* has been characterized as a phenomenon of (normed) written standard French but not of spontaneous spoken varieties. This split between PPA uses with *avoir* and *être* can also be corroborated by corpus data (Stark & Riedel 2013, Stark 2015a, b). While PPA is realized in about 90 percent of the cases in French text messages (corpus *sms4science.ch*), spoken French in Switzerland (corpus *OFROM*), spoken French in France (corpus *C-ORAL-ROM*) and spoken French from Switzerland and France (corpus *PFC*, Stark 2015a), a closer look at the distribution of unrealized PPA in these four corpora shows that the constructions with *avoir* differ from those with *être* in a significant way:

Tab. 1: Past participle agreement in *sms4science.ch* according to the construction

	Not realized	Realized	Total
Avoir	25	82	107
	23.4%	76.6%	100%
Être	32	377	409
	7.8%	92.2%	100%
Elliptical constructions	15	179	194
	7.7%	92.3%	100%
Total	72	638	710
	10.1%	89.9%	100%

Tab. 2: Past participle agreement in OFROM (only consonantal, i.e. 'audible', phonetically realized agreement)

	Not realized	Realized	Total
Avoir	7 46.67%	8 53.33%	15 100%
Être	7 11.29%	55 88.7%	62 100%
Elliptical constructions	0 0%	20 100%	20 100%
Total	14 14.58%	82 85.42%	97 100%

Tab. 3: Past participle agreement in C-ORAL-ROM (only consonantal agreement)

	Not realized	Realized	Total
Avoir	9 45.0%	11 55.0%	20 100%
Être	7 10.6%	59 89.39%	66 100%
Elliptical constructions	0 0%	24 100%	24 100%
Total	16 14.55%	94 85.45%	110 100%

Tab. 4: Past participle agreement in the French and Swiss parts of PFC (only consonantal agreement)

	Not realized	Realized	Total
Avoir	5 (F) + 1 (CH) 35.71% – 33.3%	9 (F) + 2 (CH) 64.29% - 66.7%	14 (F) + 3 (CH) 100%
Être	2 (F) + 0 (CH) 8% - 0%	23 (F) + 6 (CH) 92% - 100%	25 (F) + 6 (CH) 100%
Elliptical constructions	0 (F) + 0 (CH) 0%	13 (F) + 2 (CH) 100%	13 (F) + 2 (CH) 100%
Total	7 (F) + 1 (CH) 13.46% - 9.1%	45 (F) + 10 (CH) 86.54% – 90.9%	52 (F) + 11 (CH) 100%

(14) En fait c'est c- **la géographie je l**$_{\text{FEM.SG}}$**'avais découvert**$_{\text{(MASC.SG)}}$ en | _ | en pendant mon année de sciences sociales (OFROM)
'For real it's c- the geography I it-had discovered in /_ / during my year of sciences social.'

(15) C'est vraiment une destination complètement différente / de **celle**$_{\text{FEM}}$**-s**$_{\text{PL}}$ **que j'avais fait-e**$_{\text{FEM}}$**-s**$_{\text{PL}}$ avant (C-ORAL-ROM)
'It's really a destination completely different / from the-one that I-had done.FEM.PL.'

(16) **La retraite** [...] [...] [...] parce que je **l**$_{\text{FEM.SG}}$**'ai pris**$_{\text{(MASC.SG)}}$ un peu plus tôt que, que prévu (PFC France)
'The retirement [...] [...] [...] because I it-have taken a bit sooner than, than foreseen.'

(17) **Une amie** [...] Donc au début ils, **ils l**$_{\text{FEM.SG}}$**'ont mis-e**$_{\text{FEM.SG}}$ (PFC France)
'A friend [...] Thus at-the beginning they, they her-have put.FEM.SG.'

Examples (14) to (17) illustrate varying PPA with *avoir*. (15) and (17), with highly specific referents, show PPA, while (14) and (16) represent abstract referents as internal arguments, with a generic flavour – and without PPA.

In all four corpora the lack of normative obligatory PPA with *avoir* is considerably higher than the one for *être* (the absolute numbers for the oral corpora being very low, we could not run statistical tests, but the descriptive quantitative difference is evident). PPA with *avoir* seems more or less randomly applied in these data.

A further difference between PPA with *avoir* and *être* concerns its interpretative effects. As discussed at length in Déprez (1998) for a variety of contexts, the use of PPA with *avoir* obligatorily leads to a specific/definite (also referred to as "referential") interpretation of DP$_{\text{int}}$, while the absence of PPA leads to ambiguity: in this case DP$_{\text{int}}$ can be interpreted either as specific/definite or as non-specific/indefinite (Déprez 1998: 12, see also Rizzi 2001, Boeckx 2003). The basic observation goes back to Obenauer (1992). Consider example (18):

(18) Combien de fautes a-t-elle fait(**-es**)?
how.many of mistakes has-L-she made.FEM.PL
'How many (amongst a known set of) mistakes has she made?'
(with PPA)

'What is the number of things that are mistakes and that she has made?'
(without PPA)
(Déprez 1998: 10)

If PPA is used, we are talking about a specific, contextually presupposed set of mistakes; if PPA is absent, there is no such presupposition. Thus, PPA with *avoir* instantiates the cross-linguistically (and also in Romance languages) widespread phenomenon of differential argument encoding (cf. Bossong 1985, Enç 1991, Aissen 2003), which is always associated with interpretational differences of this kind (though it can also correlate with other dimensions than definiteness, e.g. animacy). Where French differs from most other Romance languages in this respect is that the split manifests itself as head-marking (viz. on the verb, also attested in other languages, e.g. in Persian) instead of dependent-marking (on an argument DP). In contexts with *être*, however, PPA is simply obligatory, regardless of the interpretation of the internal argument as specific or non-specific.

Finally, PPA with *avoir* and *être* differ in their "naturalness". Inside the Romance family, the normative rules for French PPA with *avoir* are rarely found. Ibero-Romance (except Catalan), Romanian, Sicilian and the Walloon dialect of Liège do not know PPA with *avoir* and its equivalents. Older stages of French show that this type of PPA was largely disappearing as early as the 12th and 13th century (cf. e.g. Brunot 1899: 523–524, Jensen 1990: 336). There are many Romance varieties that show a generalized PPA with internal arguments, regardless of word order (e.g. Languedocian Occitan), Friulian, Central and Southern Italian dialects, also some archaic registers of Italian (La Fauci 1988: 81–82); there are many others that show generalized agreement with (third person) object clitics, again irrespective of word-order (i.e. with pro- or enclisis), e.g. standard Italian, Provençal and Auvergnat (Occitan), Catalan, Ladin, some Rhaeto-Romance varieties, Northern Italian dialects (cf. Loporcaro 2010: 151–153). According to Loporcaro (1998: 13, but he doubts the dialectal data), only standard French, one Oïl variety and Aosta Valley Francoprovençal know PPA with *avoir* based on linear order. Furthermore, PPA with *avoir* in standard French meets all five criteria of "grammatical virus theory" (cf. MacKenzie 2013), and the variability of PPA with *avoir* correlates with lower socioeducative status of the speakers – it seems to be a learned rule (cf. Brissaud & Cogis 2008, Stark & Riedel 2013 for evidence from *sms4science.ch*). This is not the case for PPA with *être* corresponding to the parallel predicative construction and the historical adnominal origin of PPA (*elle est morte* meaning 'she died' as well as 'she is dead'). In fact, the complex rules of PPA with *avoir* were allegedly formulated by the 16th century poet Clément Marot (cf. Levitt 1973), copying and maybe partially misinterpreting the contemporaneous Italian facts.

We take all these differences between PPA with *avoir* and *être* in French to suggest *a non-uniform analysis* of the phenomenon, i.e. the source of *être*-PPA is different from that of *avoir*-PPA. Nevertheless, the two occurrences of PPA also have something in common: in French, PPA never targets the external argument (agent) as an agreement controller, the locus of PPA is always the past participle (never any other form of the verb, e.g. not the verb in simple present tense), and there is only a single set of exponents for PPA (the same suffixes are used, regardless of the form of the auxiliary). In addition, PPA is generally impossible in impersonal constructions (see Kayne 1989, Déprez 1998: 2: *Les chaleurs tropicales qu'il a fait-*es.* / *Qui sait [combien d'erreurs] il sera fait-*es?*), regardless of the auxiliary. Any analysis of PPA in French must explain both the differences as well as the similarities of PPA with *avoir* and *être*. In the next section, we will propose such an analysis.

4 An alternative proposal

In a nutshell, we propose that PPA under *être* results from *phi*-agreement between past participle v and the internal argument in its base position, while PPA under *avoir* is an instance of resumption, where the resumptive pronoun (RP) that resumes the internal argument is incorporated into past participle v. Reanalyzing PPA in *avoir*-contexts as resumption derives its sensitivity to linear order (movement of DP_{int}) and its restriction to the minimal clause under long movement. We couch our analysis within the Minimalist Program (Chomsky 1995 et seq.). Syntactic structure unfolds step-by-step from bottom to top by alternating application of the operations *Merge* (external or internal), which combines two elements, and *Agree*, which establishes feature transfer between a head and a phrase in its c-command domain. In Minimalism, syntactic operations are triggered by uninterpretable features [uF] that need to be discharged in the course of the derivation. These features occur in an ordered set on heads: Merge is triggered by a c-selection feature [uX] (where X ranges over category values) and is satisfied by combining the head that bears [uX] with an element of the matching category [X]; Agree is triggered by an unvalued probe feature [uX:__] that is valued by the corresponding valued features on a goal XP. We adopt the following functional sequence of verbal heads: V-v-Aux-T-C. The internal argument is merged as the sister of V; v is the head that introduces the external argument (this is triggered by the feature $[uD_\theta]$ on v, which states that v requires a DP in its specifier and assigns a thematic role to it). V moves to v to pick up the inflection in v. Perfect auxiliaries are generated between v and T in the head Aux. The form of Aux (*avoir* vs. *être*) is morphologically conditioned by the argument structure of V/v: if v introduces a thematic (agentive) external argument (unergative/transitive-active verb), viz. if it has a [uD$_\theta$]-feature, Aux is realized as *avoir*, in all other cases Aux is realized as *être*.[6] Movement (internal Merge) is subject to locality constraints such as the Phase Impenetrability Condition (PIC, Chomsky 2000, 2001), which enforces successive-cyclic movement through the edge (viz. the specifier) of every phase head on the way to the terminal landing site. As is standardly assumed, we take v and C to be phase heads (see Urk 2015 for recent discussion). As a consequence of the PIC, an internal argument that is to undergo A'-movement or cliticization needs to make an intermediate stop-over in an outer specifier of the vP. Following the aforementioned literature on phases, we take intermediate movement steps to phase edges to be triggered by edge features, rendered as [uEF]; edge features can optionally be added to phase heads when necessary (i.e. if the internal argument is to move out of the vP to the the TP- or CP-domain).[7]

We take PPA to be the phonological realization of *phi*-features, which represent the internal argument, located on past participle v (represented as [v, status: PP]). The difference is how these phi-features come to be on v: via agreement or incorporation of a resumptive pronoun. In the cases where PPA is obligatory and independent of movement (i.e. contexts with the auxiliary *être*), we assume that v agrees in phi-features with the internal argument in its base position (the complement of V). What these *être*-contexts have in common is that the head v does not introduce an externally merged DP in its specifier (unaccusative v does not select an external argument to begin with, and passive v is deprived of this ability e.g. by a lexical operation that deletes the relevant feature [uD$_\theta$] on v prior to the

---

6 We adopt a post-syntactic realizational model of morphology. The choice between *avoir* and *être* can thus be modeled as a purely morphological phenomenon, viz. as contextual allomorphy (though nothing crucial hinges on this for present purposes): there is only a single Aux-head in perfect and passive clauses; what varies is the phonological realization of this Aux-head in the post-syntactic component. The choice is sensitive to the locally accessible features of the head v, the head of Aux's sister node. Either v (or vP, which also bears the features due to projection) bears a (discharged) [uD$_\theta$]-feature (unergative/active-transitive v) or not (unaccusative v). In the former case, Aux is realized as *avoir*, in the latter as *être*.

7 In French, Specv can only serve as an intermediate landing site, not as a terminal landing site since French has neither scrambling nor object shift. Hence, with respect to internal Merge-triggering features, v can only bear edge features, but not criterial features (in Rizzi's 2006 sense). When exactly edge features can be added to phase heads is a controversial issue, since this seems to involve look-ahead; we will ignore this issue here since it is orthogonal to our main questions; see Georgi (2014) for an overview of the debate.

syntactic computation, see Chomsky 1981). The connection between v's inability to introduce a DP in Specv and its ability to trigger phi-agreement with DP$_{int}$ can be formally expressed by the (language-specific) negative feature cooccurrence restriction (FCR, Gazdar et al. 1985) in (19). This FCR states that the head v bears a phi-probe (to Agree with DP$_{int}$) only if it does not have a [uD]-feature, i.e. if it does not trigger Merge of an external DP in Specv. (20) shows the full set of features an unaccusative/passive v-head can thus bear: [uV] (triggers Merge of v with the VP), a phi-probe [uphi: __] (given the FCR in (19)) that seeks a value that is provided by Agree with a DP, and finally v can optionally bear an edge feature [uEF] (triggers an intermediate movement step of DP$_{int}$ to an outer Specv position, if DP$_{int}$ is to undergo movement to the TP or CP-domain). These features on v are ordered (indicated by `>'). i.e. they are discharged one after the other from left to right.

(19) ¬ [uD] ⊃ [uphi: __]
(20) unaccusative/passive v: [uV > uphi:__ (> uEF)]

The derivation for such contexts proceeds as follows: V merges with the internal argument DP$_{int}$; v merges with the VP (satisfying [uV]), attracts V and probes in its c-command domain for valued phi-features. It finds those of DP$_{int}$ and copies them to v (valuing the probe: ~~u~~phi: *value*). Next, if DP$_{int}$ is to undergo movement, v bears an edge feature that triggers an inter-mediate movement step of DP$_{int}$ to SpecvP, see (21). vP will then be selected by Aux, AuxP by T, etc.

(21) structure of unaccusative/passive vP (with DP$_{int}$-movement):
    [$_{vP}$ DP$_{int}$ [$_{v'}$ v+V [$_{VP}$ t$_V$ t$_{DPInt}$]]]

The phi-values on v are morphologically realized, which gives rise to PPA. We assume a postsyntactic realizational model of morphology à la Distributed Morphology (DM, Halle & Marantz 1993, 1994) in which the abstract morphosyntactic features are paired with phonological features (viz. exponents) only after the syntax. The exponents, called vocabulary items (VIs) in DM, for phi-features on past participle v are provided in (22):[8]

---

[8] The phonetic realization of PPA in (feminine) gender is dependent on the lexical item; participles such as *mis*, 'put', or *écrit*, 'written', show overt PPA-marking, participles ending in [-e] do not. The context restriction in (23) states that these exponents realize phi-features only if they are located on v and if v is in its past participle (PP) form (or status). This is a strictly local instance of allomorphy (all relevant features are on the same head). We assume that the form of v

(22) VIs for PPA (phonic code, applies only to some lexically restricted PPs):
 a. /_C/ ↔ [fem] / [v ___, [status:PP]]
 b. /V/ ↔ [masc] / [v ___, [status:PP]]

PPA in *être*-contexts surfaces independently of whether the internal argument undergoes movement or stays *in-situ* (as in the inversion constructions under (5) and (6) discussed in section 2) because phi-Agree between v and this argument applies *before* DP_{int} (possibly) undergoes movement; subsequent DP_{int}-movement out of v's probing domain can thus not bleed agreement. We have thereby derived that PPA in *être*-contexts is obligatory (otherwise the phi-probe on v would remain unvalued, leading to the crash of the derivation) and independent of whether DP_{int} undergoes movement or stays *in-situ*.

We now turn to the second case, *avoir*-contexts, where PPA is sensitive to linear order and exhibits DOM-effects. Aux is realized as *avoir* when v selects an external argument, viz. if it has [uD_θ]-feature (unergative + active-transitive verbs). Given the FCR in (19), such a v-head does not bear a phi-probe, and hence, PPA under *avoir* cannot be the result of agreement between v and the internal argument.[9] Instead, we argue that PPA results from resumption + incorporation. The idea that PPA in these contexts is related to resumption goes back to Boeckx (2003). He draws the connection because of two facts: (i) same interpretative effects: in dependencies that involve resumption (usually relative clauses), the DP associated to the resumptive pronoun (RP) is interpreted as specific/definite, and PPA under *avoir* leads to the same interpretation of the moved DP_{int}; (ii) island amelioration: just as resumptives do in many languages, PPA ameliorates island violations caused by DP_{int} in French (Boeckx 2003: 60). There are different approaches to resumption in the literature (see Salzmann 2017: ch.3 for a recent

---

(viz. its status: infinitive, past participle, etc.) is determined by the closest c-commanding verbal head, here Aux; this is a case of status government. One can model this e.g. as an Agree relation between Aux and v where Aux values the unvalued status feature of v (which probes upwards, unlike the *phi*-probe on v). Please note that in the orthographic code the VIs can be formulated as follows:
 a. <-e> ↔ [fem] / [v ___, [status:PP]]
 b. <-∅₁> ↔ [masc] / [v ___, [status:PP]]
 c. <-s> ↔ [pl] / [v ___, [status:PP]]
 d. <-∅₂> ↔ [sg] / [v ___, [status:PP]]

9 In Romance varieties in which PPA is possible with *in-situ* internal arguments under *avoir*, e.g. in Languedocian Occitan, v would always bear a phi-probe that probes for phi-features in its c-command domain, regardless of the context (viz. the argument structure of the verb). Thus, the (language-specific) FCR in (20) would not be active and PPA has only one source, viz. phi-agreement, in these varieties, not two different sources under *avoir* vs. *être*, as we claim for French.

overview). We will adopt the widely-assumed stranding / BigDP-approach (see Aoun et al. 2001, Belletti 2006, Boeckx 2003, Donati & Cecchetto 2011). According to this approach, the resumptive and its associate DP start out as one constituent, i.e. nominal arguments have an additional layer, a head that combines with the DP. We will call this head H. H bears the phi-features of its sister DP due to a phi-Agree relation between H (bearing a phi-probe) and the DP. By assumption, when the nominal argument is to undergo movement, either the whole HP can move or the DP subextracts and strands the head H. A stranded head H (adjacent to a gap) is realized as a resumptive pronoun; if H moves along with the DP and is thus adjacent to DP, this pronoun remains phonologically silent if we postulate a VI as in (23):

(23) /Ø/ ↔ [H] / ___ DP

We will adopt the stranding/BigDP-analyis to resumption but add the assumption that a stranded head H incorporates into the closest c-commanding head, viz. into v (to have a host for the affixes that spell-out H's features). Since H bears its associated DP's phi-features, these are located on v after incorporation and are phonologically realized there by the VIs in (22) (these VIs do not care about where the phi-features on the past participle in v come from: Agree or incorporation). Thus, PPA in *avoir*-contexts is basically the head-marking equivalent of resumption. The stranding/BigDP-approach also offers an explanation for why PPA with *avoir* requires movement of DP_{int} and for the distribution of PPA under long-distance DP_{int}-movement. We will illustrate this in what follows for an active-transitive verb. In this context, the v-head bears the ordered set of features in (24) ([uD] is replaced by [uH] since nominal arguments are assumed to be HPs now, but this feature still triggers Merge of the external argument). As before with unaccusative v, v first triggers Merge with the VP, then it assigns accusative case to DP_{int} (triggered by the feature [ucase:acc]). Afterwards, v triggers Merge of the external argument (of category HP now due to the H-layer above the DP) and assigns the agent theta-role to this argument.

(24) transitive-active v: [uV > ucase:acc > uHθ (> uEF)]

What is of interest is whether DP_{int} undergoes movement out of the vP. If it does, v must bear an edge feature [uEF] to trigger an intermediate movement step of HP_{int} to Specv; if DP_{int} stays *in-situ*, v does not bear [uEF]. There are three scenarios to consider: in the first, the internal argument HP_{int} does not undergo movement (v does not bear [uEF]). We do not see PPA in this context with an *in-situ* internal argument because H cannot be stranded (and hence cannot incorporate into v) if no movement of HP$_{int}$ is triggered in the first place. In the second and third scenario, the internal argument HP$_{int}$ does undergo movement; thus, v bears the feature [uEF]. Let us first assume that the whole HP$_{int}$ moves to SpecvP and then further to a higher position (= second scenario). Since the head H is not stranded but is still adjacent to the DP, it does not incorporate but is realized as zero (cf. (23)); hence, there is no PPA with a moved internal argument. In the third scenario, only the DP-part of HP$_{int}$ moves to its intermediate landing site SpecvP. In this case, H is stranded, incorporates into v and gives rise to PPA when its phi-features are phonologically realized (by the VIs in (22)). Hence, we have a case in which movement of the internal argument cooccurs with PPA. Since resumption (and other doubling phenomena), of which PPA is considered a subcase here, gives rise to a specific/definite reading of the associated DP and since resumption presupposes movement in the stranding analysis of resumption, we have derived Déprez' (1998) DOM-generalization: if there is PPA, the internal argument receives a specific/definite reading (because the DP-part of it must have moved out of the VP); if there is no PPA, there is ambiguity – the internal argument can have a specific reading (scenario two where the whole HP moves out of the VP) or a non-specific reading (HP does not move at all and stays inside VP, the domain of existential closure, cf. Diesing's 1992 Mapping hypothesis). Furthermore, we have also implemented in our analysis the generalization that PPA in French never targets the external argument, but only internal arguments. In *être*-contexts, this is because the probe on v probes downwards into its c-command domain of which the external argument is never a part.[10] In *avoir*-contexts, PPA results from incorporation of a stranded head and we know independently (see Baker 1988) that incorporation targets higher (c-commanding) heads, but cannot involve lowering of the head to a c-commanded host. PPA on v triggered by the external argument would, however, require lowering of the stranded H to v (since HP$_{ext}$ is base-merged in Specv). Finally, the resumption / stranding analysis of PPA also offers an explanation for the distribution of PPA under long-distance movement of the internal argument in active-transitive constructions (cf. Boeckx 2003: 60): stranding is impossible in positions other than the base position of HP.

---

10 The probing direction of [uphi:__] on v is of course just a stipulation, but it is suggested by the fact that only internal arguments trigger PPA. There is a consensus in the agreement literature that languages, and even individual heads in a given language, can differ in the direction of probing (upwards or downwards, see Baker 2008); the probing direction must be learned and is not predictable. In varieties in which PPA is triggered by (some) external arguments (e.g. in Abruzzese cf. D'Alessandro & Roberts 2010), the probe searches upwards for a goal.

In higher positions it would involve extraction from a moved phrase, but moved phrases are islands for subextraction. This is a general constraint on movement dependencies known as the Freezing Principle (Wexler & Culicover 1980), a subcase of the even more general condition on extraction Domains (Huang 1982).[11][12]

What is still missing in our analysis is a discussion of cases where PPA is impossible, viz. impersonal constructions. How can this be explained? Recent results from the research on expletives as we find them in impersonal constructions lead to the conclusion that expletives are base-merged in SpecvP (and not in SpecTP); hence, they occupy the same position as external arguments. The only difference to external arguments is that expletives do not receive a theta-role from v, but both compete for the same position (at least in languages without transitive-expletive constructions like French). Expletives are thus only possible when v does not select a thematic external argument (cf. Richards & Biberauer 2005, Deal 2009, Alexiadou & Schäfer 2012). We can thus say that v that does not select an external argument, viz. passive/unaccusative v, can still have a c-selection feature [uH], but one that is not associated with a theta-role (unlike the feature [uH$_\theta$] of unergative/active-transitive v). This non-thematic [uH]-feature can be

---

11 Boeckx's (2003) resumption analysis of French PPA differs from the one presented here (which follows more closely his general analysis of resumption in other languages) in that he postulates a silent resumptive; this resumptive does not incorporate into v, rather, v agrees in *phi*-features with the resumptive element in its *in-situ* position. We do not adopt this view because French is not a pro-drop language, so we would have to stipulate that pronouns can be zero only in this special case. Furthermore, we do not see how this agreement with the silent resumptive is blocked when the internal argument does not undergo movement at all, viz. why there is no agreement with *in-situ* internal arguments – the resumptive could still be present in the BigDP-structure. Boeckx does not say anything about the analysis of cases where PPA is obligatory or impossible.

12 Once we say that arguments are HPs and not just DPs, this holds in general, and thus also in the *être*-contexts with unaccusative/passive v – the sole argument must be an HP here, too. This requires a few amendments to the derivation in *être*-contexts. If the sole (internal) argument undergoes movement, either the whole HP moves (corresponding to the derivation sketched in (22), if we replace DP by HP), or the DP subextracts – a possibility not considered above for these contexts. As a consequence, H is stranded and incorporates into v. Thus, v bears the *phi*-features of its internal argument twice, once via Agree and once via incorporation. However, this does not lead to a double spell-out of these features, viz. double PPA. The reason is that the features of an element form a set, and for sets it holds that {a,a} = {a}. Hence, the two instances of the same *phi*-features are reduced to a single instance, and we see PPA only once. Thus, the extension required for the *avoir*-contexts (arguments are HPs) does not have any undesired consequences for the *être*-contexts.

discharged by external merge of an expletive.[13] Now recall the FCR in (19): it says that only v-heads that do not have an externally merged specifier (external Merge triggered by [uD], which is now [uH] given our new assumptions) bear a phi-probe. The [uH]-feature in the FCR is underspecified for theta-roles, so it holds for heads with [uH] regardless of whether discharge of [uH] goes hand in hand with theta-role assignment (active-transitive v) or not (as in impersonal constructions). Since in an impersonal construction v also bears [uH], it cannot bear a phi-probe by (19). As a consequence, there cannot be PPA as a result of Agree with HP_{int} in impersonal constructions. What would technically remain as a source of PPA is thus resumption + incorporation. Syntactically, nothing rules out such a derivation (scenario 3 above). We follow Déprez's (1998) insight that this derivation is excluded for semantic reasons. Recall that PPA under *avoir* leads to a specific/definite interpretation of the internal argument (because it involves movement of a subpart of the argument out of the VP, the domain of existential closure). However, impersonal constructions are subject to a definiteness restriction, viz. the associate of the expletive (= the internal argument of the verb) must be indefinite/non-specific. This clashes with the required interpretation of PPA (or resumption more generally) as definite/specific. Hence, the structure can only be interpreted if HP_{int} stays *in-situ* and thus necessarily receives a non-specific interpretation. To conclude, the two sources of PPA that we have proposed for French (downward Agree and resumption) are not available in impersonal constructions, and hence PPA is excluded.

To summarize, we have presented two different mechanisms that give rise to PPA in French, run-of-the-mill agreement and resumption. The choice of the strategy is connected to the argument structure of the verb (more precisely, the existence of an externally merged specifier in SpecvP). The different properties of PPA under *avoir* and *être* as well as the obligatoriness vs. optionality vs. impossibility of PPA in the various contexts fall out from general properties of the corresponding fairly standard formal implementations of these phenomena, viz. Agree (for agreement) and the stranding/BigDP-approach (for resumption).

---

[13] Obviously, the empirical observation that expletives are only possible in French (and many other languages) when the verb does not have a thematic external argument does not hold for languages with transitive expletive constructions (TECs). In such languages, external arguments and expletives do not compete for the same base-Merge position, but rather occupy different specifiers of v. This is also supported by the observation (= Bures's generalization) that TEC-languages have object shift/scrambling, and hence clearly an additional position available at the edge of vP (see e.g. Alexiadou & Schäfer 2012 for discussion).

5 Conclusion

In this paper, we have argued for two different analyses to account for PPA in standard French. While it is generally assumed that PPA in French is triggered or at least correlated with the absence of the internal argument in its original position (movement through a specific syntactic position), PPA with *in-situ* internal arguments is commonplace in constructions with the auxiliary *être*, as opposed to those with the auxiliary *avoir*. Auxiliary selection is related to argument structure, i.e. to the presence of an external argument in SpecvP. PPA in unaccusative, passive and related constructions (*être*), common in the history of and in modern varieties inside the Romance language family and robust also in production data, is analyzed as regular Agree operations between a probe in v and the goal, the internal argument, irrespective of any further movement operations. Contrary to PPA in these constructions with *être*, PPA in constructions with *avoir*, especially the standard French regularities (PPA with all kinds of moved internal arguments, including *wh*-elements, never with *in-situ* direct objects) are almost never attested in other Romance varieties. They were lost early in the history of French (before its normalization in the 17th century) and are not applied consistently by native speakers in French (neither in spoken nor in written corpora). As they seem to correlate with a certain specificity effect (cf. Déprez 1998), absent in the case of generalized PPA with *être*, they can be compared to the phenomenon of DOM, widespread in Romance, but usually realized as dependent-marking. We therefore argue that PPA with *avoir* can be assimilated to DOM, as a kind of differential head marking, and be analyzed as resumption and incorporation of the *phi*-features of the internal argument as subextraction (out of VP, see Diesing 1992) from the internal argument. This analysis also accounts for the unusual distribution of PPA under long-distance movement of the internal argument as well as for the impossibility of PPA in impersonal passive constructions. The fact that standard French possesses two different mechanisms that trigger PPA is maybe related to the origin of PPA with *avoir* as a kind of 'reinvented', originally artificial rule (cf. Stark 2015a) which became reinterpreted as a kind of differential argument marking device, otherwise absent in standard French. The optionality (or variation) in PPA with *avoir* observed in many speakers is due, we suggest, to the contradiction that the learned normative rule (generalized PPA with the moved internal argument in constructions with *avoir*) creates with the actual system (no PPA with non-specific internal arguments), leading to a conflict between the internal grammatical system and the prescriptive norm.

Acknowledgement: This research was partially funded by the Deutsche Forschungsgemeinschaft (DFG, German Research Foundation) – Project ID 317633480 – SFB 1287, Project C05 (Georgi).

6 References

6.1 Corpora

C-ORAL-ROM: Cresti, Emanuela & Massimo Moneglia. 2005. C-ORAL-ROM. Integrated Reference Corpora for Spoken Romance Languages. Amsterdam: Benjamins.

OFROM: *Corpus oral de français parlé en Suisse Romande.* http://www11.unine.ch (last consultation: 3 October 2018).

(cf. Avanzi, Matthieu, Béguelin, Marie-José & Federica Diémoz. 2012-2014. *Présentation du corpus OFROM – corpus oral de français de Suisse romande.* Université de Neuchâtel. http://www.unine.ch/ofrom (last consultation: 3 October 2018)).

PFC: *Phonologie du français contemporain.* http://www.projet-pfc.net (last consultation: 3 October 2018). By Durand, Jacques, Laks, Bernard & Chantal Lyche. 2002. La phonologie du français contemporain: usages, variétés et structure. In Claus Pusch & Wolfgang Raible (éds.), *Romanistische Korpuslinguistik- Korpora und gesprochene Sprache/Romance Corpus Linguistics – Corpora and Spoken Language.* Tübingen: Gunter Narr Verlag, 93-106. PDF (Durand/Laks/Lyche 2002).

www.sms4science.ch: Stark, Elisabeth, Ruef, Beni & Simone Ueberwasser. 2009-2014. Swiss SMS Corpus. University of Zurich. https://sms.linguistik.uzh.ch (last consultation: 3 October 2018).

6.2 Studies

Aissen, Judith. 2003. Differential object marking: Iconicity vs. economy. *Natural Language and Linguistic Theory* 21. 435–483.

Alexiadou, Artemis & Florian Schäfer. 2012. There-insertion and the unaccusativity hypothesis. In Gao Ming-le (ed.), *Universals and variation – Proceedings of Glow-in-Asia VIII*, 76–79. Beijing: Beijing Language and Culture University Press.

Aoun, Joseph, Choueiri, Lina & Norbert Hornstein. 2001. Resumption, movement, and derivational economy. *Linguistic Inquiry* 32(3). 371–403.

Baker, Mark C. 1988. *Incorporation: A theory of grammatical function changing.* Chicago: University of Chicago Press.

Baker, Mark C. 2008. *The syntax of agreement and concord.* Cambridge: Cambridge University Press.

Belletti, Adriana. 2006. (Past) participle agreement. In Martin Everaert & Henk C. van Riemsdijk (eds.), *The Blackwell Companion to syntax*, 1st edn, 493–521. Oxford: Blackwell.

Belletti, Adriana. 2017. (Past) participle Agreement. In Martin Everaert & Henk C. van Riemsdijk (eds.), *The Wiley Blackwell Companion to syntax*, 2nd edn, Vol. 1, 2972–3000. Oxford: Blackwell.
Blanche-Benveniste, Claire. 2006. L'accord des participes passés en français parlé contemporain. In Céline Guillot, Serge Heiden & Sophie Prévost (eds.), *À la quête du sens: études littéraires, historiques et linguistiques en hommage à Christiane Marchello-Nizia*, 33–49. Lyon: ENS.
Boeckx, Cedric. 2003. *Islands and chains: resumption as stranding*. Amsterdam/Philadelphia: Benjamins.
Bossong, Georg. 1985. *Differentielle Objektmarkierung in den neuiranischen Sprachen*. Tübingen: Narr.
Bouchard, Denis. 1987. A few remarks on past participle agreement. *Linguistics and Philosophy* 10(4). 449–474.
Branigan, Phil. 1992. *Subjects and complementizers*. Ph.D. dissertation. Cambridge, MA: MIT Manuscripts.
Brissaud, Catherine & Danièle Cogis. 2008. L'accord du participe passé. Reconsidération d'un problème ancien à la lumière de données récentes sur l'acquisition. In Jacques Durand, Benoît Habert & Bernard Laks (eds.), *Congrès mondial de linguistique française*, 413–424. Paris: 9–12 July 2008, Paris: Institut de Linguistique française.
Brown, Becky. 1988. Problems with past participle agreement in French and Italian dialects. In David Birdsong & Jean-Pierre Montreuil (eds.), *Advances in Romance linguistics*, 51–66. Dordrecht: Foris.
Brunot, Ferdinand. 1899. *Précis de grammaire historique de la langue française*. Paris: Masson et Cie.
Bruening, Benjamin. 2001. *Syntax at the edge: Cross-clausal phenomena and the syntax of passamaquoddy*. Cambridge, MA: MIT Press.
Chomsky, Noam. 1981. *Lectures on government and binding*. Dordrecht: Foris.
Chomsky, Noam. 1986. *Barriers*. Cambridge, MA: MIT Press.
Chomsky, Noam. 1995. *The minimalist program*. Cambridge, MA: MIT Press.
Chomsky, Noam. 2000. Minimalist inquiries: The framework. In Martin Roger, Michaels David & Juan Uriagereka (eds.), *Step by step*, 89–155. Cambridge, MA: MIT Press.
Chomsky, Noam. 2001. Derivation by phase. In Michael Kenstowicz & Ken Hale (eds.), *A Life in language*, 1–52. Cambridge, MA: MIT Press.
Chomsky, Noam. 2008. On phases. In Rorbert Freidin, Carlos Peregrín-Otero & Maria-Luisa Zubizarreta (eds.), *Foundational issues in linguistic theory. Essays in honor of Jean-Roger Vergnaud*, 133–166. Cambridge, MA: MIT Press.
Cinque, Guglielmo. 1999. *Adverbs and functional heads: A cross-linguistic perspective*. Oxford: Oxford University Press.
Corbett, Greville. 2006. *Agreement*. Cambridge: Cambridge University Press.
D'Alessandro, Roberta & Ian Roberts. 2008. Movement and agreement in Italian past participles and defective phases. *Linguistic Inquiry* 39(3). 477–491.
D'Alessandro, Roberta & Ian Roberts. 2010. Past participle agreement in Abruzzese: Split auxiliary selection and the null-subject parameter. *Natural Language and Linguistic Theory* 28. 41–72.
Deal, Amy Rose. 2009. The origin and content of expletives: Evidence from "Selection". *Syntax* 12(4). 285–323.

Déprez, Viviane. 1998. Semantic effects of agreement: The case of French past participle agreement. *Probus* 10. 1–65.
Diesing, Molly. 1992. *Indefinites*. Cambridge, MA: MIT Press.
Donati, Caterina & Carlo Cecchetto. 2011. Relabeling heads: A unified account for relativization structures. *Linguistic Inquiry* 42(4). 519–560.
Drijkoningen, Frank. 1999. Past participle agreement in French: Object-agreement? Adjective agreement. *Linguistics in the Netherlands* 16(1). 41–52.
Dupuis, Fernande. 1992. *L'expression du sujet dans les subordonnées en ancien français*. Ph.D. dissertation. Montréal: Université de Québec à Montréal.
Embick, David & Rolf Noyer. 2001. Movement operations after syntax. *Linguistic Inquiry* 32. 555–595.
Enç, Mürvet. 1991. The semantics of specificity. *Linguistic Inquiry* 22. 1–25.
Fender, Mary. 2002. Stylistic inversion in French. *Durham Working Papers in Linguistics* 8, 27–40.
Friedemann, Marc-Ariel & Tal Siloni. 1997. Agr$_{object}$ is not Agr$_{participle}$. *The Linguistic Review* 14. 69–96.
Gazdar, Gerald, Ewan Klein, Geoffrey Pullum & Ivan Sag. 1985. *Generalized phrase structure grammar*. Oxford: Blackwell.
Georgi, Doreen. 2014. *Opaque interactions of Merge and Agree: On the nature and order of elementary operations*. Ph.D. dissertation. Leipzig: University of Leipzig.
Georgi, Doreen. 2017. Patterns of movement reflexes as the result of the order of Merge and Agree. *Linguistic Inquiry* 48(4). 585–626.
Grohmann, Kleanthes. 2003. *Prolific domains: On the anti-locality of movement dependencies*. Amsterdam/Philadelphia: Benjamins.
Guasti, Maria Teresa & Luigi Rizzi. 2000. *Agreement and tense as distinct syntactic positions: evidence from acquisition*. Manuscript, University of Siena.
Halle, Morris & Alec Marantz. 1993. Distributed Morphology and the pieces of inflection. In Ken Hale & Samuel Jay Keyser (eds.), *The view from building 20*, 111–176. Cambridge, MA: MIT Press.
Halle, Morris & Alec Marantz. 1994. Some key features of Distributed Morphology. In Andrew Carnie, Heidi Harley and Tony Bures (eds.), *Papers on phonology and morphology*, MIT Working Papers in Linguistics (MITWPL), 21st edn, 275–288. Cambridge, MA: MIT Press.
Huang, C. T. James. 1982. *Logical relations in Chinese and the theory of grammar*. Ph.D. dissertation. Cambridge, MA: MIT Manuscripts.
Jensen, Frede. 1990. *Old French and comparative Gallo-Romance syntax*. Tübingen: Niemeyer.
Kayne, Richard. 1985. L'Accord du participe passé en français et en italien. *Modèles Linguistiques* 7. 73–90.
Kayne, Richard. 1989. Facets of Romance past participle agreement. In Paola Benincà (ed.), *Dialect variation and the theory of grammar*, 85–103. Dordrecht: Foris.
Korsah, Sampson & Andrew Murphy. 2019. Tonal reflexes of movement in Asante Twi. *Natural Language and Linguistic Theory* 38. 827–885.
La Fauci, Nunzio. 1988. *Oggetti e soggetti nella formazione della morfosintassi romanza*. Pisa: Giardini.
Lahousse, Karen. 2006. NP subject inversion in French: Two types, two configurations. *Lingua* 116. 424–461.
Lahousse, Karen. 2011. *Quand passent les cigognes? Le sujet nominal postverbal en français moderne*. Paris: Presses Universitaires de Vincennes.

Lefebvre, Claire. 1988. Past participle agreement in French: Agreement=Case. In David Birdsong & Jean-Perre Montreuil (eds.), *Advances in Romance linguistics*, 233–253. Dordrecht: Foris.
Legate, Julie Anne. 2003. Some interface properties of the phase. *Linguistic Inquiry* 34(3). 506–515.
Legendre, Géraldine. 2017. Auxiliaries. In Andreas Dufter & Elisabeth Stark (eds.), *Manual of Romance Morphosyntax and Syntax*, 272–298. Berlin/New York: De Gruyter.
Levitt, Jesse. 1973. The agreement of the past participle in modern French: Orthographic convention or linguistic fact? *Linguistics* 114. 25–41.
Lois, Ximena. 1990. Auxiliary selection and past participle agreement in Romance. *Probus* 2(2). 233–255.
Longenbaugh, Nicholas. 2019. On expletives and the agreement-movement correlation. Ph.D. dissertation. Cambridge, MA: MIT Manuscripts.
Loporcaro, Michele. 1998. *Sintassi comparata dell'accordo participiale romanzo*. Torino: Rosenberg e Sellier.
Loporcaro, Michele. 2010. The logic of Romance past participle agreement. In Roberta D'Alessandro, Adam Ledgeway & Ian Roberts (eds.), *Syntactic variation. The dialects of Italy*, 225–243. Cambridge: Cambridge University Press.
MacKenzie, Ian. 2013. Participle-object agreement in French and the theory of grammatical viruses. *Journal of Romance Studies* 13(1). 19–33.
Marandin, Jean-Marie. 2001. Unaccusative inversion in French. In Yves D'Hulst, Johan Rooryck & Jan Schroten (eds.), *Romance Languages and Linguistic Theory 1999, Selected papers from 'Going Romance' 1999, Leiden, 9–11 December 1999*, 195–222. Amsterdam/Philadelphia: Benjamins.
Obenauer, Hans-Georg. 1992. L'interprétation des structures wh et l'accord du participe passé. In Hans-Georg Obenauer & Anne Zribi-Hertz (eds.), *Structures de la phrase et théorie du liage*, 169–193. Vincennes: Presses Universitaires de Vincennes.
Perlmutter, David M. & Postal, Paul M. 1983. Some proposed laws of basic clause structure. In David M. Perlmutter (ed.), *Studies in relational grammar*, 1st edn, 81–128. Chicago and London: The Chicago University Press.
Rezac, Milan. 2004. *Elements of cyclic syntax: Agree and Merge*. Ph.D. dissertation. Toronto: University of Toronto.
Richards, Marc D. 2011. Deriving the Edge: What's in a Phase? *Syntax* 14(1). 74–95.
Richards, Marc D. & Theresa Biberauer. 2005. Explaining Expl. In Marcel den Dikken & Cristina Tortora (eds.), *The function of function words and functional categories*, 115–153. Amsterdam/New York: Benjamins.
Rizzi, Luigi. 2001. Reconstruction, weak island sensitivity, and agreement. In Carlo Cecchetto, Gennaro Chierchia & Maria-Teresa Guasti (eds.), *Semantic interfaces*, 145–176. Stanford, Calif.: CSLI.
Rizzi, Luigi. 2006. On the form of chains: criterial positions and ECP effects. In Lisa Cheng & Norbert Corver (eds.), *Wh-Movement: Moving on*, 97–134. Cambridge, MA: MIT Press.
Salzmann, Martin. 2017. *Reconstruction and resumption in indirect A'-dependencies. On the syntax of prolepsis and relativization in (Swiss) German and beyond*. Berlin/Boston: De Gruyter Mouton.
Sportiche, Dominique. 1990. *Movement, agreement and case*. Ms: UCLA.
Sportiche, Dominique. 1992. *Clitic constructions*. Ms: UCLA.

Stark, Elisabeth. 2013. *Le 'langage SMS' face à l'empirie – qu'en est-il de l'accord du participe passé?* Talk at the conférence au colloque international DIAII *La dia-variation en français actuel* at the Université de Sherbrooke, Sherbrooke, Québec, Canada, 29–31 May 2013.

Stark, Elisabeth. 2015a. *La grammaire normative face à la réalité d'usage – l'accord du participe passé dans les corpus oraux du français contemporain.* Keynote talk at the Journées PFC at the University of Vienna, 17–18 July 2015.

Stark, Elisabeth. 2015b. L'accord du participe passé dans la langue standard et en français vernaculaire. Notice FRACOV: http://www.univ-paris3.fr/index-des-fiches-227311.kjsp?RH=1373703153287 (last consultation: 3 October 2018).

Stark, Elisabeth & Isabelle Riedel. 2013. L'accord du participe passé dans les SMS francophones du corpus SMS Suisse. *Romanistisches Jahrbuch* 63(1). 116–138.

Urk, Coppe van. 2015. A uniform syntax for phrasal movement: A case study of Dinka Bor. Ph.D. dissertation. Cambridge, MA: MIT Manuscripts.

Urk, Coppe van (forthcoming): A taxonomy of successive cyclicity. In *Proceedings of BCGL 9: Phase Theory* (University of Brussels, Belgium, 13–14 December 2016).

Vega Vilanova, Jorge. 2018. Catalan participle agreement. On the interaction between syntactic features and language change. Ph.D. dissertation. Hamburg: University of Hamburg.

Wexler, Ken & Peter Culicover. 1980. *Formal principles of language acquisition*. Cambridge, MA: MIT Press.

Thom Westveer, Petra Sleeman and Enoch O. Aboh
Competing genders: French partitive constructions between grammatical and semantic gender

Abstract: In a study on the acceptance of semantic versus grammatical gender agreement in French, Sleeman & Ihsane (2016) argue that the acceptability of gender mismatches in partitive constructions is related to (i) the type of partitive construction and (ii) the type of animate noun involved. They base their argumentation on judgements of a limited number of (Swiss) French informants on a limited number of test sentences. The aim of the present study is to further explore gender agreement in partitive constructions in a more systematic way and with a larger sample of speakers, by means of a controlled grammaticality judgement task, administered to 62 native speakers of French. Our results are generally compatible with those of Sleeman & Ihsane and can be accounted for using their theoretical analysis. In addition this paper provides more insight into the linguistic factors that influence the acceptability of semantic agreement in French partitive constructions.

Keywords: partitive constructions, gender agreement, semantic vs. syntactic gender, gender mismatches, French

1 Introduction

This paper focusses on partitive constructions of the type X of Y (e.g. *the youngest of my children*), in which a subset X is selected from a set Y. We label X, referring

---

Thom Westveer: Department of Linguistics, University of Amsterdam, P.O. Box 1642, Spuistraat, 1000BP Amsterdam, Netherlands, T.J.T.Westveer@uva.nl
Petra Sleeman: Department of Linguistics, University of Amsterdam, P.O. Box 1642, Spuistraat, 1000BP Amsterdam, Netherlands, A.P.Sleeman@uva.nl
Enoch O. Aboh: Department of Linguistics, University of Amsterdam, P.O. Box 1642, Spuistraat, 1000BP Amsterdam, Netherlands, E.O.Aboh@uva.nlto

to the subset, as the outer DP and Y, referring to the set, as the inner DP. In languages overtly marking gender distinctions, such as French, these partitive constructions can present an interesting case of gender agreement: the outer DP and the inner DP may have different gender values, thus showing a gender mismatch. In the French example in (1a), the outer DP *la plus jeune* is feminine, while the inner DP *des anciens étudiants* referring to a mixed group of females and males, exhibits the masculine plural form.[1] This sentence presents a gender mismatch between the outer and the inner DP. In example (1b), however, the outer DP *le plus jeune* and the inner DP *des anciens étudiants* agree and both take the masculine form, even though the subset, to which the outer DP refers, is female.

(1) a. *La   plus   jeune   des   anciens   étudiants   s'appelle Hélène.*
       the.F   most   young   of.the   former.M.PL student.M.PL is.called Hélène
       'The youngest of the former students is called Hélène.'
    b. *Le   plus   jeune   des   anciens   étudiants   s'appelle Hélène.*
       the.M   most   young   of.the   former.M.PL student.M.PL is.called Hélène

Although these constructions are not specifically taught in school or discussed in grammar books, native speakers have intuitions about when a gender mismatch is acceptable or not. Sleeman & Ihsane (2016) investigated these intuitions with a limited number of informants and show that the acceptability of gender mismatches depends on the type of partitive construction and on the type of noun. Based on their results, they propose a theoretical analysis of gender agreement in partitive constructions, which we report on in section 2.

The aim of the present study is to further explore gender agreement in partitive constructions in a more systematic way and with a larger sample of speakers and test sentences. We submitted a questionnaire to 62 native speakers of French, enabling us to perform statistical analyses on our data, which was not possible in Sleeman & Ihsane's study, given the limited size of their sample. Our larger sample also enables us to check for influence of the factors sex and age of the participants, as the acceptability of gender mismatches may be influenced by the ongoing debate on feminisation and inclusive language use in French. Thus, younger speakers may accept gender mismatches more often than older speakers. Besides, several studies (e.g. Van Compernolle 2009) suggest a difference between female and male speakers when it comes to feminisation and inclusive language use, which may also impact the acceptability of gender mismatches. In

---

[1] In French, masculine gender serves as default gender for animate nouns if the referent's sex is unknown or irrelevant or if a noun refers to a mixed group of females and males.

addition, our more systematic test design, including a larger number of test sentences, allows us to investigate noun type differences. We formulate our research questions and discuss the methodology in section 3. Section 4 contains a detailed presentation of the results. In section 5, we discuss the results in more detail and compare them to those of Sleeman & Ihsane. We present some conclusions in section 6.

2 Gender agreement in French partitive constructions

In French, all nouns are assigned a grammatical gender, which can either be masculine or feminine. Nominal elements, such as pronouns, determiners, or adjectives, all agree in gender with the noun they combine with or refer to. For instance, the indefinite determiner and the adjective show masculine agreement with the masculine noun *chanteur* 'singer' in (2a) and feminine agreement with the feminine noun *chanteuse* 'female singer' in (2b).

(2) a. *Julien   Clerc   est   un/*une   chanteur   merveilleux/*merveilleuse.*
       Julien   Clerc   is   a.M/.F   singer.M.SG marvelous.M/.F
       'Julien Clerc is a marvelous singer.'
    b. *Françoise Hardy est   une/*un   chanteuse   merveilleuse/*merveilleux.*
       Françoise Hardy is   a.F/.M   singer.F.SG marvelous.F/.M
       'Françoise Hardy is a marvelous singer.'

With inanimate nouns, gender assignment is not semantically motivated and therefore arbitrary, even though a noun's gender is often predictable from its ending (cf. Lyster 2006): nouns that end in a vowel in spoken language tend to be masculine (e.g. *un palet* [palɛ] 'a.M puck'); those that end in a consonant tend to be feminine (*une palette* [palɛt] 'a.F palette').[2] Animate nouns, in contrast, usually exhibit a gender that matches with the biological sex of the noun's referent.

---

2 Please note that in spoken French, final consonants of nouns are not pronounced, except when followed by a vowel; in written French, masculine and feminine nouns present the opposite image: masculine nouns tend to end in a consonant, feminine nouns in a vowel.

Therefore, in (2a), *chanteur*.M refers to a male singer, while *chanteuse*.F (2b) designates a female.[3] However, some animate nouns – for instance the feminine noun *victime* 'victim' – have a fixed gender, even though they can refer to both females and males. Agreement with such nouns can be challenging. In the example in (3), the feminine noun *victime* refers to a male. The definite determiner and the adjective agree with the feminine gender of the noun. For the pronoun in the follow-up sentence, in contrast, there are two possible sources of gender agreement: the feminine noun *victime* or its male referent *Pierre*. If the pronoun shows agreement with the gender of the noun, it takes the feminine form. We refer to this type of agreement as syntactic agreement. If, on the other hand, the pronoun agrees with the biological sex of the referent, it will take the masculine form, an instance of semantic agreement (Corbett 2006).

(3)   *Pierre était la   seule/*le seul victime   ?Elle/?Il a   survécu.*
      Pierre   was   the.F only.F/.M   victim.F.SG She/He has survived
      'Peter was the only victim. He survived.'

Throughout this paper, we use the term agreement for sharing of gender features on all types of syntactic configurations. We do not distinguish between different syntactic configurations by using additional notions, such as concord or matching. Neither do we distinguish between valuation via a syntactic relationship between a valued and an unvalued feature, and semantic feature valuation from the non-linguistic context (following, e.g. Corbett 1991, Audring 2013, Kučerová 2018). Consequently, we do not use the term agreement in a technical sense.

Superlative partitives may also display competition between syntactic and semantic gender agreement, as is illustrated in (4). The agreement target in the outer DP in (4a-b) has two possible controllers: (i) the inner DP *des nouveaux professeurs* in the default masculine form or (ii) the NP *Hélène Manier*, referring to a female. In (4a), the default masculine form *le plus gentil* syntactically agrees with the default masculine gender of the noun *professeur*. In (4b), however, the feminine form *la plus gentille* agrees with its female referent, *Hélène Manier*, hence a case of semantic agreement.

---

[3] We leave aside the long-standing debate whether both the masculine form *chanteur* and the feminine form *chanteuse* are stored separately in the lexicon (full storage approach), or, instead, only the separate morphemes, that is, the stem *chant-* and the suffixes *-eur* and *-euse* (decomposition approach) (cf. Haspelmath & Sims 2010 and references therein). See Labbé Grunberg (2020) for a detailed investigation of cognitive processing of complex and non-complex words by native speakers of Dutch.

(4) a. *Le   plus gentil des   nouveaux professeurs   s'appelle Hélène Manier.*
      the.M most kind.M of.the new.M.PL teacher.PL   is.called Hélène Manier
   b. *La   plus gentille des   nouveaux professeurs   s'appelle Hélène Manier.*
      the.F most kind.F of.the new.M.PL teacher.PL   is.called Hélène Manier
   'The kindest of the new teachers is called Hélène Manier.'

Sleeman & Ihsane (2016) establish that the acceptability of gender mismatches depends on multiple factors. One such factor is the type of partitive construction: gender mismatches are accepted in superlative partitive constructions, as in (5), but not in quantified partitive constructions (6).

(5) *La/Le   plus jeune de mes nouveaux collègues   s'appelle Antoinette.*
    the.F/.M most young of my   new.M.PL colleague.PL is.called Antoinette
    'The youngest of my new colleagues is called Antoinette.'

(6) **Une/Un de mes   nouveaux collègues   s'appelle Antoinette.*
    one.F/.M of my   new.M.PL colleague.PL is.called Antoinette
    'One of my new colleagues is called Antoinette.'

In a quantified partitive, a quantifier, such as *un* 'one' in (6), heads the outer DP, whereas in a superlative partitive, the outer DP is headed by a definite determiner combined with a superlative adjective (5). Only in the latter case, speakers may accept a mismatch between inner and outer DP.

Another factor that appears to affect the acceptability of semantic agreement – only in superlative partitive constructions like (5) – is the type of (animate) noun involved in the sentence. Sleeman & Ihsane (2016) (following Ihsane & Sleeman 2016) distinguish four types of animate nouns in French, based on the strategy used to derive the feminine form of the noun:

Tab. 1: Classification of animate nouns according to Sleeman & Ihsane (2016)

Class A	suppletive forms: stem alternation resulting in two unrelated forms for masculine and feminine	un frère – une sœur 'a brother – a sister' un garçon – une fille 'a boy – a girl'
Class B	alternating forms: masculine and feminine forms derived from the same morphological stem by suffix alternation or affixation	un étudiant – une étudiante 'a student' (affixation) un policier – une policière[4] 'a police officer' (affixation) un directeur – une directrice 'a director' (suffix alternation)
Class C	epicene forms: one stem for female and male referents, triggers either feminine or masculine agreement	un ministre – une ministre 'a minister' un élève – une élève 'a pupil'
Class D	fixed-gender forms: one stem for female and male referents, can only trigger agreement with one fixed gender	un personnage 'a character' une sentinelle 'a guard'

Sleeman & Ihsane's group of class B nouns could be further split into two distinct groups, based on the way the feminine and masculine forms of these nouns are derived: nouns with a feminine form, which derives from the masculine one by adding a suffix (e.g. *étudiant > étudiante*), labelled 'affixation class B', and nouns for which there is a suffix alternation (e.g. *chanteur – chanteuse*), called 'suffix alternation class B'.[5]

According to Sleeman & Ihsane, gender mismatches should not be possible with class A and class D nouns (7-8). Therefore, they did not include these nouns in their study, since class A and class D nouns should always trigger syntactic agreement. With class C nouns (9), on the other hand, gender mismatches in superlative partitives seem to be possible, as the judgements of Sleeman & Ihsane's informants suggest.

---

[4] We leave aside here the question whether the feminine form *policière* derives from the masculine form *policier* by affixation, or, instead, the masculine form derives from the feminine form by a deletion operation.

[5] An anonymous reviewer pointed us towards this distinction, suggesting to investigate if it affects agreement behaviour.

(7) *Le/*La plus jeune des gentils garçons s'appelle Jean-Luc.*
the.M/.F most young of.the kind.M.PL boy.M.PL is.called Jean-Luc
'The youngest of the kind boys is called Jean-Luc.'

(8) *La/*Le plus jeune des nouvelles sentinelles a une longue barbe.*
the.F/.M most young of.the new.F.PL guard.F.PL has a long beard
'The youngest of the new guards has a long beard.'

(9) *La/Le plus jeune des nouveaux ministres est Madame Garnier.*
the.F/.M most young of.the new.M.PL minister.PL is Mrs. Garnier
'The youngest of the new ministers is called Mrs. Garnier.'

With class B nouns, the picture is somewhat more complicated. Some informants accept gender mismatches in superlative partitives with these nouns, whereas others reject them.

(10) *??La/Le plus jeune des nouveaux directeurs s'appelle Mme Héloïse.*
the.F/.M most young of.the new.M.PL director.M.PL is.called Mrs. Héloïse
'The youngest of the new directors is called Mrs. Héloïse.'

Following up on a discussion of some recent theoretical analyses on gender agreement by Kramer (2009) and Atkinson (2015), Ihsane & Sleeman (2016) show that these fail to account for the differences between agreement in partitive constructions, which can display semantic agreement, and agreement in more local environments, such as with attributive adjectives, which only exhibit syntactic agreement. Therefore, they propose an alternative theoretical analysis of gender agreement, which they further develop in Sleeman & Ihsane (2016) and show to account for their observations. In the Minimalist framework (Chomsky 2000, 2001), agreement results from the operation Agree. Agree operates on feature valuation and interpretability and constitutes a relation between a target (i.e. an element that requires a specific feature value) and a controller (i.e. an element bearing a matching feature that saturates the target). In Minimalist terms, the target referred to as the goal is endowed with an unvalued agreement feature that needs to be valued by the probe (i.e., the controller). While feature valuation holds of the licensing of formal syntactic features, these features may have semantic correlates (i.e., they affect interpretation). It is commonly assumed that (un)valued and (un)interpretable features are licensed simultaneously through Agree.

Under standard Minimalist assumptions, however, the fact that the uninterpretable grammatical gender feature is not always accompanied by an interpretable counterpart, as is the case with the class D nouns, would lead the derivation to crash, contrary to facts. Therefore, Sleeman & Ihsane (2016) build on Legate (2002) and Pesetsky & Torrego (2007) in arguing for a view that dissociates Agree from interpretability, which may derive from other (formal) operations. This way a mismatch between feature valuation and feature interpretability does not lead the derivation to crash.

Sleeman & Ihsane's analysis consists of two parts, corresponding to the two parts of a partitive construction: (i) the inner DP, referring to the superset, and (ii) the outer DP, referring to the subset. We will start with the analysis of the inner DP. Sleeman & Ihsane argue that grammatical and semantic gender should be separated. In French, in principle, nouns come with a lexically fixed grammatical gender, which is assumed to be uninterpretable within the current Minimalist framework. Semantic gender, on the other hand, is encoded on a specific functional projection, Gender Phrase (GendP[6]), only present in the structure of animate nouns. Semantic gender is interpretable with class A, class B and class C nouns, but uninterpretable with class D nouns, because with the latter type the referent's biological sex does not always match the noun's grammatical gender.

As Sleeman & Ihsane report, semantic gender agreement seems to be possible with class C and to a lesser extent with class B nouns, but not with class A and class D nouns. They argue that the differences between these noun classes are situated in the lexicon. Class A and class D nouns bear a specific grammatical gender feature in the lexicon. The structures in (11a-b) for the feminine class A noun *fille* 'girl' and the feminine class D noun *sentinelle* 'guard' illustrate this: these nouns bear a feminine-valued uninterpretable feature on the lexical noun, whose value is then transferred from the noun onto the Gend-head.[7]

(11) a. 'a girl'   b. 'a guard'

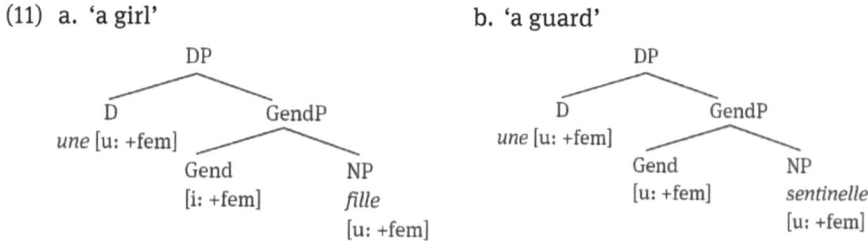

---

[6] Sleeman & Ihsane (2016) abbreviate this functional projection as GenP, but we use the notion GendP instead, to avoid potential confusion with 'Genitive'.

[7] Sleeman & Ihsane (2016) code gender as either [+fem], [-fem] or [_fem], representing feminine, masculine and unspecified gender, respectively, following Kramer (2009) and Atkinson (2015).

Since with class A nouns (11a), the gender feature on Gend is interpretable, it can be interpreted as a biological sex feature and the noun's referent has to be a female, whereas in (11b), with the class D noun *sentinelle*, the gender feature on Gend is uninterpretable and cannot be interpreted as a biological sex feature – the referent of *sentinelle* can either be female or male.

With class C nouns, there is no grammatical gender stored in the lexicon and these nouns enter the derivation unvalued, as the absence of an uninterpretable gender feature on the class C noun *élève* 'pupil' in (12) shows. Gender specification of these nouns takes place through valuation of the semantic gender feature on Gend. In (12), the noun *élève* receives a gender value from the noun's referent in the non-linguistic context.[8] If the referent is a male, the semantic gender feature on Gend is valued as masculine, consequently triggering masculine agreement on the determiner *un*. As the gender feature on Gend is interpretable, it can be interpreted as referring to the biological sex of the noun's referent.

(12)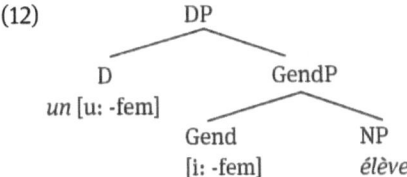

It is also possible that the semantic gender feature on Gend does not receive a gender value, the noun thus being unmarked for gender. Normally, the derivation would crash in such a case. However, Sleeman & Ihsane, following Preminger (2011), argue that this does not happen, because the absence of a gender value results in the spell-out of default gender, which is the masculine form in French. This is what Preminger calls Failed Agree, exemplified in (13).

(13)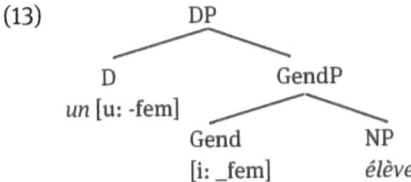

---

8 The assumption that features may also receive their value from the non-linguistic context is defended by studies in multiple domains. With respect to gender, Matushanksy (2013) shows that in Russian, agreement with some animate nouns may not only depend on the noun's grammatical gender, but also on semantic information from the non-linguistic context. Cartographic approaches to syntax also assume valuation from the non-linguistic context (cf. Rizzi 1997).

The interpretable semantic gender feature on the Gend-head in (13) does not receive a value form the non-linguistic context, as marked by the absence of a feature value [i: _fem]. Still, the derivation does not crash, as Failed Agree (Preminger 2011) applies, resulting in default masculine agreement on the determiner *un*. Only in this case, a gender mismatch may occur, as we will see below.

The second part of the analysis concerns the outer DP, referring to the subset. Sleeman & Ihsane, building on Sleeman & Kester (2002), argue for a two-noun analysis of partitives. The noun of the outer DP is a copy of the noun of the inner DP, but remains unpronounced. Importantly, in a superlative partitive – but not in a quantified partitive, as we will see – both DPs are headed by a Gender Phrase. The gender value of the inner DP's Gender Phrase is copied together with the noun into the outer DP and the outer DP's Gender Phrase receives its value from the gender feature on the copy of the noun, as is shown in (14-15).

(14) No mismatch – masculine agreement
 [DP *le* [DegP *plus jeune* [GendP M [FP *juge* [PP *des* [GendP M [NP *juges français*]]]]]]]

(15) No mismatch – feminine agreement
 [DP *la* [DegP *plus jeune* [GendP F [FP *juge* [PP *des* [GendP F [NP *juges françaises*]]]]]]]

However, if Failed Agree has taken place in the inner DP (as in (13)) and no gender value is present on the inner DP's Gender Phrase, there is no gender value to be transferred to the outer DP's Gender Phrase either. In this case, the outer DP's Gender Phrase presents a second opportunity to insert a semantic gender value, as indicated by the arrows in the example in (16).

(16) [DP *la* [DegP *plus jeune* [GendP F [FP *juge* [PP *des* [GendP _ [NP *juges français*]]]]]]]
 ↑ ↑

In (16) there is no gender value on the inner DP's Gender Phrase and Failed Agree has taken place, leading to the spell-out of default masculine gender in the inner DP. The Gender Phrase of the outer DP, in contrast, is valued as feminine, which triggers feminine agreement on the outer DP's determiner *la*.

In quantified partitives, on the other hand, Sleeman & Ihsane assume that the outer DP is not headed by a second Gender Phrase. In this way, they explain why gender mismatches seem not to be possible in quantified partitives, since there is no second opportunity to insert a semantic gender value in the outer DP after Failed Agree has taken place in the inner DP. Instead, the outer DP has to agree with the inner DP's default masculine gender.

(17) [NumP un [FP ~~collègue~~ [PP de [DP mes [GendP _ anciens collègues]]]]]

Until now, we have not addressed class B nouns. As Sleeman & Ihsane's results suggest, some speakers of French seem to accept gender mismatches with class B nouns, whereas others appear not to do so. Sleeman & Ihsane argue that for speakers that accept gender mismatches with class B nouns, these nouns behave like class C nouns and are thus unmarked for grammatical gender in the lexicon. If valuation of the semantic gender feature on the Gend-head through the non-linguistic context does not take place, Failed Agree applies, resulting in default masculine gender in the inner DP and in superlative partitives. Through valuation of the semantic gender feature on Gend in the outer DP, a gender mismatch may arise, as in (18a). In contrast, some speakers do not accept a mismatch with class B nouns, but prefer sentences as the one illustrated by (18b).

(18) a. *La   plus   jeune de mes anciens   étudiants   s'appelle Hélène.*
         the.F most   young of my   former.M.PL   student.M.PL   is.called Hélène
     b. *Le   plus   jeune de mes anciens   étudiants   s'appelle Hélène.*
         the.M most   young of my   former.M.PL   student.M.PL   is.called Hélène
     'The youngest of my former students is called Hélène.'

Sleeman & Ihsane do not present an analysis for speakers that do not accept a mismatch with class B nouns. Ihsane & Sleeman (2016), in turn, propose a lexical analysis to explain speaker differences: for speakers that do not accept a gender mismatch, class B (and class C) nouns bear a grammatical gender feature in the lexicon, which values the feature on the Gend-head too, leaving no room for valuation from the non-linguistic context. For speakers that accept a mismatch, class B (and class C) nouns are unmarked for grammatical gender. Thus, in (18b), the class B noun *étudiant* 'student' is stored as a masculine noun in the lexicon. The masculine gender of the group noun *étudiants* in the inner DP is transferred onto the outer DP and triggers masculine agreement. Feminine agreement in the outer DP, which would give rise to a gender mismatch between inner and outer DP, is not accepted by these speakers. Variation between individual speakers could thus be related to differences in the way nouns are stored in a speaker's mental lexicon.

As Sleeman & Ihsane (2016) report, with class B nouns most of their informants prefer the use of a feminine plural group noun if the subset is a female, as in (19), instead of a sentence potentially presenting a gender mismatch between the inner and the outer DP (18a).

(19) La   plus   jeune de mes anciennes étudiantes s'appelle Hélène.
     the.F most young of my   former.F.PL student.F.PL is.called Hélène
     'The youngest of my former students is called Hélène.'

As opposed to (18a), in (19) no gender mismatch can arise, since both the inner and the outer DP display feminine gender. However, in (19) the feminine plural group noun *étudiantes* only refers to a group of female students, not to a mixed group of female and male students. In (18a/b), on the other hand, the (default) masculine group noun *étudiants* refers to a group of females and males.

3 Research questions and methodology

Sleeman & Ihsane's study involved only 10 (Swiss) French participants and it is not clear to what extent the results and analysis can be generalised to speakers of French in general. Due to the limited number of participants, the authors could not report any statistics. In addition, the participants were only exposed to a small set of sentences which did not include all possible agreement conditions. For instance, their test sentences did not include contexts with syntactic agreement and the investigated sentences did not involve many different nouns for each of the noun classes. The present study aims at further exploring the phenomenon of gender agreement in French partitive constructions, taking into account the limitations of Sleeman & Ihsane's approach. Building on Sleeman & Ihsane's study, we start from the following questions: (i) Do superlative and quantified partitives significantly differ with respect to the acceptance of semantic agreement, as Sleeman & Ihsane's results suggest? (ii) Do class B, class C and class D nouns significantly differ with respect to the acceptance of semantic agreement in superlative partitives? Since we collected grammaticality judgements from a larger number of speakers, we have the possibility to perform statistical analyses on our data. Based on the informants' judgements reported by Sleeman & Ihsane, we formulate the following hypotheses that need to be tested: (a) In superlative partitives, semantic agreement is judged to be significantly more acceptable than in quantified partitives. (b) In superlative partitives, the acceptance of semantic agreement depends on the type of animate noun: semantic agreement is judged significantly more acceptable with class C and then with class B nouns, whereas syntactic agreement is judged significantly more acceptable with class D nouns. We discuss our results in relation to these hypotheses in section 5.

The classification of animate nouns over four classes – of which we include three in our experiment – may prove to be too general, as differences between nouns may not only depend on morphological properties, but also on semantic or frequency-related factors. Therefore, we want to check for differences between individual nouns of all three noun classes under scrutiny too. This translates into our third question, for which we cannot formulate any hypotheses yet: (iii) Is there a significant difference in the acceptability of semantic agreement between individual nouns? Finally, as we already mentioned in the Introduction, we wonder whether the age and/or sex of a participant might influence the acceptability of semantic agreement. Sleeman & Ihsane (2016) could not investigate these factors due to their limited number of participants. These points motivate our final question: (iv) Is there a significant difference in the acceptance of semantic agreement between younger and older and between female and male participants?

In order to investigate which factors determine a speaker's choice between syntactic and semantic agreement in partitive constructions, we carried out a grammaticality judgement task, created in Google Forms, which was spread online, via a linguistic mailing list in France. Participants were not paid for their participation. In addition to the grammaticality judgement task on gender agreement in partitive constructions, the questionnaire we submitted to our participants consisted of two other parts, one on the feminisation of profession nouns and one on inclusive writing, of which the results are not discussed in this paper. Before submitting the final questionnaire, we first carried out a pilot study.

The questionnaire was filled in by 80 people, of which we excluded 18, who either were non-native speakers of French, were not living in France at the moment of testing, or had not completed the tasks. The remaining 62 participants were living in France at the moment of testing and were born and/or raised there too. All participants were asked to fill in a background questionnaire with questions on age, sex, language background, profession, where they were born and raised, where they had lived, as well as some additional questions on different topics to check their attitude towards changes in language and society.[9] In the analysis of our results, however, we will only consider the variables sex and age. Table 2 presents information on our participants concerning these variables. Please note that the imbalanced age and sex groups are partly due to online testing and that we did not specifically target specific age groups.

---

[9] The test was approved by the Ethical Committee of the University of Amsterdam and all participants consented to take part.

Tab. 2: Participant information

Age	< 30	30–40	40–50	50–60	> 60	
	9	5	10	11	27	62
Sex	male	female				
	20	42				62

The Grammaticality Judgement Task consisted of 80 sentences containing a partitive construction. The participants had to judge each sentence on a 5-point scale, 5 indicating a fully acceptable and 1 a fully unacceptable sentence. In the instructions we indicated that the participants should follow their own intuitions and should not reflect too long on each sentence. The participants first saw an example before starting the task.

The test sentences contained 13 different nouns, representing the different noun classes established by Sleeman & Ihsane and listed below in Table 3. The nouns were selected based on the results of a dictionary search (Westveer, Sleeman & Aboh 2018), in which we investigated the inclusion of feminine forms of profession nouns throughout time in different editions of the French monolingual *Petit Robert* dictionary. The selection of nouns was based on the feminisation strategy used to derive the feminine form of the profession noun and on the societal status of the profession referred to. We did not include class A nouns in the test, because these never give rise to a gender mismatch: syntactic and semantic agreement always match with these nouns. As we noted previously, Sleeman & Ihsane's group of class B nouns could be further split into two distinct groups, based on the way the feminine and masculine forms of these nouns are derived: the affixation class B nouns (e.g. *étudiant > étudiante*) and the suffix alternation class B nouns (e.g. *chanteur – chanteuse*). Therefore, for class B, we included nouns of both types: *étudiant* and *policier* as examples of affixation class B and *chanteur* and *recteur* as examples of suffix alternation class B.

Tab. 3: Nouns included in the task

Class B	chanteur	singer
	étudiant	student
	policier	police officer
	recteur	rector
Class C	collègue	colleague
	guide	guide
	ministre	minister
	professeur	teacher
Class D	personne (fem.)	person
	sentinelle (fem.)	guard
	victime (fem.)	victim
	génie (masc.)	genius
	personnage (masc.)	character

As noun class internal differences might be influenced by the relative frequency of the different nouns, we checked the lemma frequency of our 13 test nouns in the online *Lexique* corpus (New & Pallier 2019).[10] The lemma frequencies of our test nouns in the *Lexique* corpus are listed in Table 4.[11]

Tab. 4: Lemma frequency test nouns

Class B nouns	Frequency	Class C nouns	Frequency	Class D nouns	Frequency
chanteur	41.24	collègue	71.02	génie	82.08
étudiant	76.25	guide	40.36	personnage	70.45
policier	55.77	ministre	122.56	personne	336.90
recteur	3.72	professeur	162.47	sentinelle	10.55
				victime	94.92

Next to noun class, the test includes two more predictors: (i) partitive type (quantified or superlative) and (ii) agreement type (syntactic or semantic). Thus, all nouns figured at least in four sentences throughout the task: two times in a quan-

---

10 We thank an anonymous reviewer for pointing us out the importance of investigating the lemma frequency of our test nouns in a corpus.
11 For the class B nouns, the lemma frequencies indicated in Table 4 include both masculine and feminine forms of the nouns.

tified and two times in a superlative partitive. For each noun in each partitive type, we included a sentence with syntactic and one with semantic agreement, as exemplified for the noun *étudiant* in a superlative partitive in (20): in example (20a) the inner DP *de mes anciens étudiants* is default masculine and so is the outer DP *le plus intelligent*, even if the intended referent is female: (20a) presents a case of syntactic agreement. In (20b), the inner DP is default masculine, but the outer DP's gender matches with its referent's biological sex and therefore takes the feminine form, exhibiting semantic agreement.

(20) a. *Le   plus intelligent   de mes anciens   étudiants   s'appelle*
the.M most intelligent.M of my former.M.PL student.M.PL is.called
Françoise.
Françoise
b. *La   plus intelligente   de mes anciens   étudiants   s'appelle*
the.F most intelligent.F of my former.M.PL student.M.PL is.called
Françoise.
Françoise
'The most intelligent of my former students is called Françoise.'

Within the total number of 80 test sentences, 4 x 13 = 52 sentences were constructed in this way. The remaining 28 sentences were control sentences in which no gender mismatch was possible, thus not showing any competition between syntactic and semantic agreement. One of the control sentences was in the masculine form (21a) and one in the feminine form (21b):

(21) a. *Le   plus intelligent   de mes anciens   étudiants   s'appelle*
the.M most intelligent.M of my former.M.PL student.M.PL is.called
Henri.
Henri
'The most intelligent of my former students is called Henri.'
b. *La   plus intelligente   de mes anciennes   étudiantes   s'appelle*
the.F most intelligent.F of my former.F.PL student.F.PL is.called
Françoise.
Françoise
'The most intelligent of my former students is called Françoise.'

These control sentences were included for part of the 13 nouns tested. Table 5 indicates the distribution of our test nouns over the different conditions, as well as the distribution of control sentences.

Tab. 5: Distribution of nouns in the task

Partitive type	Noun class	Noun	Grammatical agreement (sentence number in task)	Semantic agreement (sentence number in task)	Control sentence (sentence number in task)	Feminine control sentence (sentence number in task)	Total number of sentences
Quantified	B	chanteur	34	17	44	59	4
		étudiant	19	26	75	32	4
		policier	65	11	x	x	2
		recteur	1	9	x	x	2
	C	collègue	29	63	x	x	2
		guide	74	53	60	22	4
		ministre	79	13	50	55	4
		professeur	70	5	x	x	2
	D	génie (M)	15	71	47	n/a	3
		personnage (M)	64	48	43	n/a	3
		personne (F)	68	37	3	n/a	3
		sentinelle (F)	24	73	56	n/a	3
		victime (F)	51	78	66	n/a	3
Total No.			13	13	9	4	39
Superlative	B	chanteur	54	49	2	62	4
		étudiant	67	35	4	40	4
		policier	52	18	x	x	2
		recteur	25	38	x	x	2
	C	collègue	57	12	x	x	2
		guide	41	69	46	6	4
		ministre	21	72	28	45	4
		professeur	77	31	36	14	4
	D	génie (M)	20	8	61	n/a	3
		personnage (M)	10	33	58	n/a	3
		personne (F)	30	42	76	n/a	3
		sentinelle (F)	39	80	16	n/a	3
		victime (F)	23	27	7	n/a	3
Total No.			13	13	10	5	41
							80

The test sentences were presented to the participants in a randomised order (identical for all participants), assuring that a noun never reappeared in the next sentence. At this point, a caveat is in order. We decided not to include any fillers, because adding these to our 80 test sentences would have made the task too long. We were aware that this might be a drawback. Apart from assuring that a participant uses all points on the judgement scale, fillers are meant to distract the participant from the actual object of study. In this case, we judged that the different partitive types, the different sentence types, including the controls, the noun types and the various contexts were distinct enough to hide our object of study away from our participants.

All test results were collected in a spreadsheet. The results were statistically analysed in multiple ways. First, we computed a mixed-effects model, because a mixed-effects model provides us with a more profound insight into possible influences of our predictors partitive type, agreement type and noun class on the participants' acceptability rates on the test sentences. We computed a linear mixed-effects model, using the lmer function from the lmerTest package (Kuznetsova et al. 2017) in the R environment (R Development Core Team 2018). Our dependent variable was the acceptability rate of each test sentence, measured on a five-point scale. Agreement type (syntactic or semantic), partitive type (quantified or partitive) and noun class (class B, C or D) were our fixed factors, as well as possible interactions between these factors. For the ternary factor noun class, we specified orthogonal sum-to-zero contrasts: (i) class D nouns (coded as -2/3) were compared to class B and C nouns (both coded as +1/3) and (ii) class B nouns (coded as -1/2) opposed to class C nouns (coded as +1/2). We specified participant as a random factor. Second, we carried out Two Related Samples T-Tests in SPSS to check for each noun class and for each individual noun in both partitive constructions whether the difference between the sentence with syntactic and the one with semantic agreement was significant. In a next step, we also carried out correlation tests between the test noun's lemma frequency and the acceptability scores to control for the influence of noun frequency on the results.

4 Results

In the following sections, the results of the grammaticality judgement task will be reported. First, we present the results that answer research questions (i-ii), investigating the influence of partitive type and noun class on the acceptability of semantic agreement in partitives. We will show that these results are compatible with those of Sleeman & Ihsane's study and confirm our hypotheses listed above.

In a next step, we take a closer look at the individual nouns of the different noun classes investigated, including a possible relation of their frequency on the results, addressing research question (iii). Finally, we discuss the influence of the metalinguistic variables sex and age on the acceptance of semantic agreement in partitives, answering research question (iv).

4.1 The influence of partitive type and noun class

First, we investigate whether the type of partitive constructions (quantified or superlative partitive) influences the acceptability of semantic agreement. Figure 1 visualises the average judgements for the test sentences with grammatical and semantic agreement for both partitive types.[12]

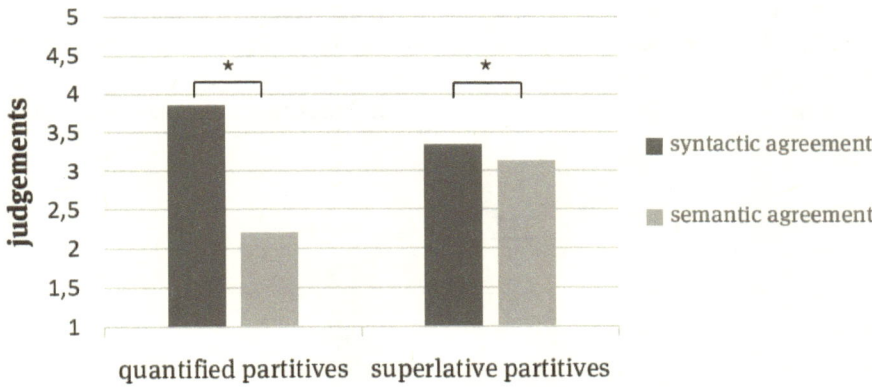

Fig. 1: Partitive types

Figure 1 shows that our participants judge syntactic agreement to be significantly more acceptable than semantic agreement in quantified partitives ($p < 0.001$). For superlative partitives, semantic agreement receives a significantly higher acceptability score than syntactic agreement too ($p = 0.013$), even though the difference is considerably smaller than for the quantified partitives. If we compare both partitive types, we observe that grammatical agreement is judged significantly better in quantified than in superlative partitives ($p < 0.001$), whereas semantic agreement receives a significantly higher acceptability score in superlative than in

---

[12] Significant differences ($p < 0.05$) are marked in the Figures by means of the * sign.

quantified partitives (p < 0.001). This latter point is confirmed by the results of our mixed-effects model, which show that there is a significant effect of partitive type on the acceptability of semantic agreement (estimated difference in judgement = 1.44; 95% confidence interval = 1.17 ... 1.71; p < 0.001), indicating that native speakers of French judge semantic agreement to be significantly more acceptable in superlative than in quantified partitives. This answers research question (i). As we will see in what follows, however, noun class differences play an important role in the acceptance of semantic agreement in superlative partitives.

Next, we look at the influence of noun class on the acceptability of semantic agreement, addressing research question (ii). Figures 2 and 3 show the average acceptability rates of the different noun classes in quantified and in superlative partitives in sentences with either syntactic or semantic agreement (class B = suffix alternation, affixation, e.g. *un chanteur – une chanteuse*; class C = one stem that can trigger both feminine and masculine agreement, e.g. *un/une ministre*; class D = fixed-gender nouns, e.g. *une sentinelle*). In the figures below significant differences are marked with an *, as computed using Two Related Samples T-Tests in SPSS. The figures do not include the judgements on the control sentences.

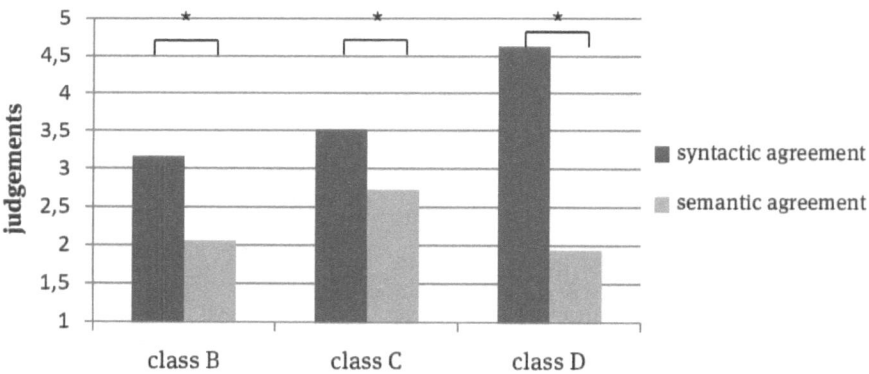

Fig. 2: Quantified partitives noun classes

With quantified partitives, sentences with syntactic agreement are judged to be considerably more acceptable than sentences with semantic agreement for all three noun classes. The differences in average judgement of syntactic versus semantic agreement are all significant (p < 0.001 for all noun classes), but the difference looks more pronounced for class D nouns. According to our participants, quantified partitives with syntactic agreement are highly acceptable with class D nouns. With class B and class C nouns, on the other hand, the overall judgement for the sentences with syntactic agreement is considerably lower than for class D nouns, although the sentences with syntactic agreement are significantly preferred over those with semantic agreement.

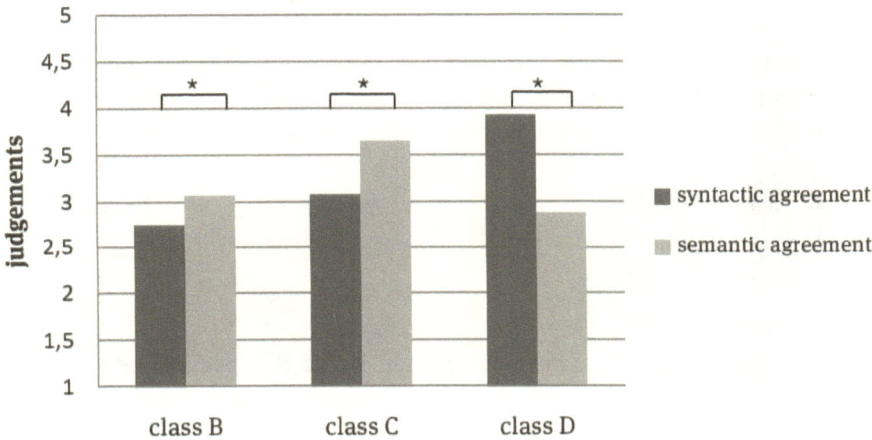

Fig. 3: Superlative partitives noun classes

In superlative partitives, semantic agreement is judged more acceptable than syntactic agreement with class B ($p = 0.020$) and class C nouns ($p < 0.001$), whereas the class D nouns show the opposite pattern (class D, $p < 0.001$). However, the difference in judgement of the sentences with either syntactic or semantic agreement is smaller with class B nouns than with class C nouns. This indicates a stronger competition between syntactic and semantic agreement for class B nouns.

The results of the mixed-effects model, comparing noun classes B and C to noun class D, show that there is a significant effect of noun class on the acceptability of semantic agreement between class B and C nouns on the one hand and class D nouns on the other hand (estimated difference in judgement = 1.78; 95% confidence interval = 1.52 ... 2.04; $p < 0.001$), showing that native speakers of French judge semantic agreement to be significantly more acceptable with class B and C nouns than with class D nouns. If we only look at class B and class C nouns, we observe a significant effect of noun class on the acceptability of semantic agreement too (estimated difference in judgement = 0.27; 95% confidence interval = 0.04 ... 0.50; p = 0.018), indicating that native speakers of French judge semantic agreement to be significantly more acceptable with class C nouns than with class B nouns.

Interestingly, our participants judge sentences with class C nouns in which the subset is a female and the set is referred to by a default masculine plural noun, as more acceptable than similar sentences with class B nouns for both partitive types. The examples with a superlative partitive below illustrate this for the class C noun *ministre* (22) and for the class B noun *chanteur* (24). Still, these sentences with semantic agreement are preferred over those with syntactic agreement, as shown in (23) for *ministre* and (25) for *chanteur*, respectively. The numbers between square brackets indicate the participants' average judgements.

(22) *La   plus   intelligente   des   nouveaux   ministres   est Madame*
the.F most intelligent.F of.the   new.M.PL   minister.PL is   Mrs.
Ranquière.
Ranquière
'The most intelligent of the new ministers is Mrs. Ranquière.' [3,99]

(23) *Le   plus   intelligent   des   nouveaux   ministres   est Madame*
the.M most intelligent.M of.the   new.M.PL   minister.PL is   Mrs.
Ranquière.
Ranquière
'The most intelligent of the new ministers is Mrs. Ranquière.' [3,29]

(24) *La   plus   jeune   des   chanteurs   présents   est Françoise Hardy.*
the.F most young of.the singer.M.PL   present.M.PL is Françoise Hardy
'The youngest of the singers present is Françoise Hardy.' [2,63]

(25) *Le   plus   jeune   des   chanteurs   présents   est Françoise Hardy.*
the.M most young of.the singer.M.PL   present.M.PL is Françoise Hardy
'The youngest of the singers present is Françoise Hardy.' [2,33]

As we can conclude from the contrasts in judgements between the examples involving the class C noun *ministre* (22-23) on the one hand, and the examples with the class B noun *chanteur* (24-25), on the other hand, the sentences with the class

C noun turn out to have higher acceptability scores than those involving the class B noun.

In fact, with class B nouns, the participants prefer the presence of a feminine set noun if the subset is a female, as suggested by the results on the control sentences. The example in (26) below shows the control sentence with the feminine set noun *chanteuses*, which can be compared to the examples above involving semantic (24) and syntactic agreement (25).

(26) La   plus jeune   des   chanteuses présentes   est   Françoise Hardy.
     the.F most young   of.the singer.F.PL present.F.PL is   Françoise Hardy
     'The youngest of the singers present is Françoise Hardy.' [4,97]

Whereas sentence (26), with the feminine set noun *chanteuses*, is unsurprisingly judged as fully acceptable by nearly all participants, the sentences (24-25), with the default masculine set noun *chanteurs*, are judged to be far less acceptable, both with syntactic (25) and semantic agreement (24). Both differences (i.e. (25 vs. 26) and (24 vs. 26)) are significant ($p < 0{,}001$).

Class C nouns generally show the same pattern: the control sentences with a feminine set noun, as exemplified in (27) for the noun *ministre*, receive higher judgements than the mismatch sentences with semantic (22) or syntactic agreement (23).

(27) La   plus intelligente   des   nouvelles ministres   est   Madame
     the.F most intelligent.F   of.the new.F.PL minister.F.PL is   Mrs.
     Ranquière.
     Ranquière
     'The most intelligent of the new ministers is Mrs. Ranquière.' [4,71]

As we can observe, the difference in judgement for the class C noun *ministre* between the sentence with the feminine set phrase *nouvelles ministres* in (27) and the sentences in (22-23) is smaller than for the class B noun *chanteur*. Still, both differences are significant for *ministre* too ($p < 0.001$ for (23 vs. 27), $p = 0.001$ for (22 vs. 27)).

Surprisingly, however, with the class C noun *professeur* 'teacher' this pattern does not hold, as the examples (28-30) show.

(28) Le   plus intelligent   des   nouveaux professeurs est   Madame
     the.M most intelligent.M of.the new.M.PL teacher.PL is   Mrs.
     Arbelette.
     Arbelette
     'The most intelligent of the new teachers is Mrs. Arbelette.' [3,59]

(29) La   plus intelligente   des   nouveaux professeurs est   Madame
     the.F most intelligent.F   of.the new.M.PL teacher.PL is   Mrs.
     Arbelette.
     Arbelette
     'The most intelligent of the new teachers is Mrs. Arbelette.' [3,87]

(30) La   plus intelligente   des   nouvelles professeurs est   Madame
     the.F most intelligent.F   of.the new.F.PL   teacher.F.PL is Mrs.
     Arbelette.
     Arbelette
     'The most intelligent of the new teachers is Mrs. Arbelette.' [2,89]

As the judgements indicate, the feminine control sentence (30) is judged to be less acceptable than the sentences with and without a gender mismatch (28-29), whereas in general the control sentences are judged more acceptable than the actual test sentences. The difference between (29) and (30) is significant ($p = 0.001$), as well as the difference between (28) and (30) ($p = 0.049$), but than in the other direction, the sentence with syntactic agreement and a masculine group noun (28) or with a gender mismatch (29) being significantly preferred over the control sentences with a feminine group noun (30). Why would this be the case? We will return to this point in the discussion.

4.2 Further insight

Apart from research questions (i-ii), aiming at checking the findings of Sleeman & Ihsane's study, we raised two additional research questions, asking about differences between individual nouns (iii) and about the influence of the participants' sex and age on the acceptability rates (iv). The results related to these questions are presented in this section. First, we will take a closer look at the judgements on the individual nouns of each noun class, answering research question (iii). We start with the class B nouns. Figure 4 reports the results of quantified partitives, while Figure 5 represents superlative partitives.

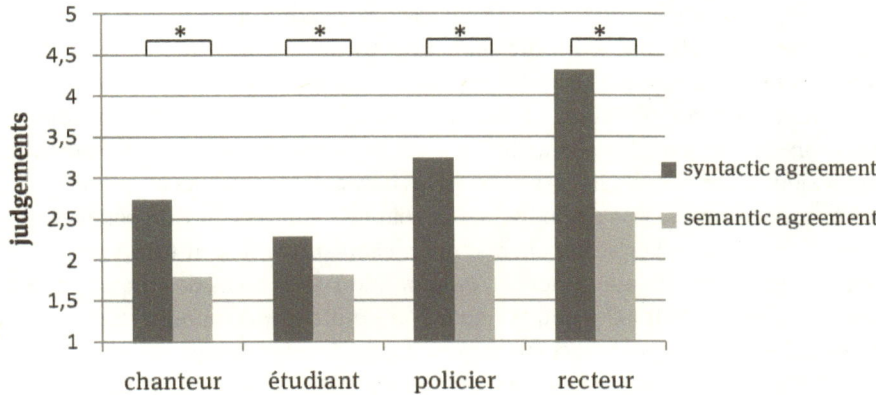

Fig. 4: Quantified partitives individual class B nouns

As Figure 4 shows, the sentences with syntactic agreement are judged significantly better than those with semantic agreement for all class B nouns in quantified partitives. However, we can observe some differences in that the overall judgements for the nouns *chanteur, étudiant* and *policier* are lower than for the noun *recteur*. In contrast, when comparing both suffix change class B nouns *chanteur* and *recteur* to the affixation nouns *étudiant* and *policier*, we cannot observe a clear difference between these two types. Rather, the suffix change noun *chanteur* seems to pattern with both affixation nouns *étudiant* and *policier*, whereas the other suffix change noun *recteur* behaves somewhat differently.

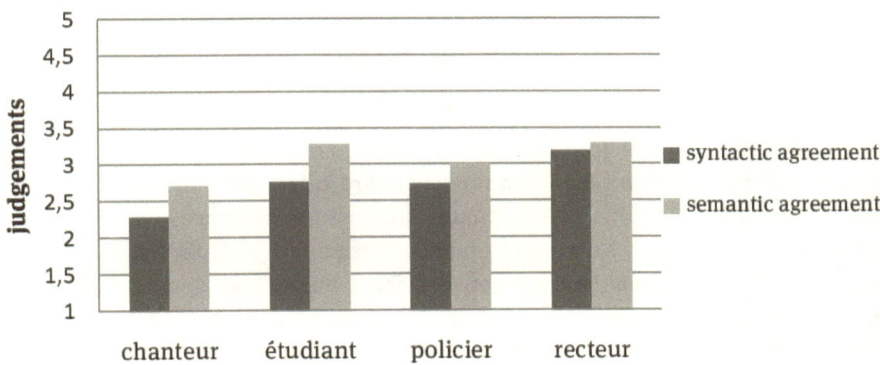

Fig. 5: Superlative partitives individual class B nouns

As for superlative partitives, Figure 5 shows that semantic agreement is judged to be more acceptable than syntactic agreement with the nouns *étudiant* and *chanteur* and to a lesser extent also with *policier*, although the differences are not significant. For the noun *recteur*, on the other hand, there is only a very small difference in judgement between the sentences with syntactic and semantic agreement. Again, we do not see differences between the suffix change and affixation class B nouns. It is again the suffix change noun *recteur* that behaves differently from the other suffix change noun *chanteur*, which in turn appears to pattern with both affixation nouns *étudiant* and *policier*. Besides, note that the overall judgements for the noun *chanteur* are quite low compared to the other three class B nouns. We will come back to this in the discussion.

The results for the individual class C nouns are visualised in Figure 6 for the quantified and in Figure 7 for the superlative partitives.

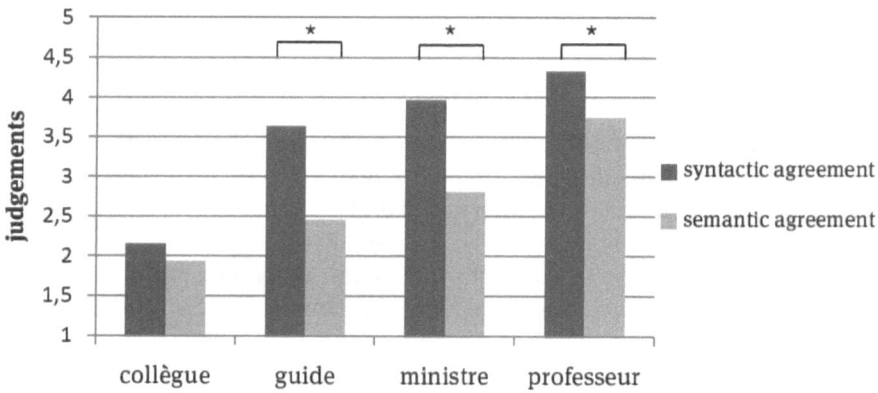

Fig. 6: Quantified partitives individual class C nouns

As we can see from this graph, the noun *collègue* falls apart, since both the sentences with syntactic and semantic agreement are judged to be rather unacceptable, whereas for the other class C nouns, at least the sentences with syntactic agreement are accepted by our participants. This pattern is confirmed by the fact that the differences in judgement between the sentences with syntactic and semantic agreement are significant with the nouns *professeur* (p = 0.020), *guide* (p < 0.001) and *ministre* (p < 0.001), but not with the noun *collègue* (p = 0.368). Furthermore, for the noun *professeur*, the sentence with semantic agreement is judged to be quite acceptable too; to a lesser extent this also holds for the noun *ministre*.

Competing genders: French partitive constructions — 75

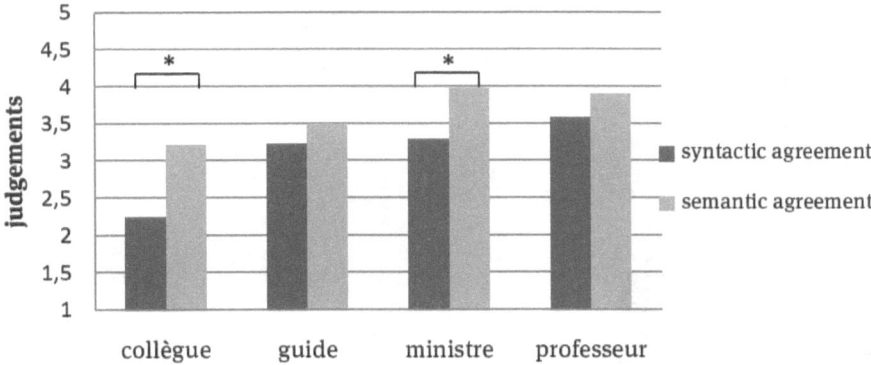

Fig. 7: Superlative partitives individual class C nouns

For all class C nouns semantic agreement is judged to be more acceptable than syntactic agreement in superlative partitives, although the differences are only significant with the nouns *ministre* (p = 0.013) and *collègue* (p = 0.001), but not with the nouns *professeur* (p = 0.126) and *guide* (p = 0.303). Again, the noun *collègue* behaves differently, since for this noun the sentence with syntactic agreement is judged to be rather unacceptable, whereas this is not the case with the other class C nouns.

Finally, the results for the class D nouns are presented in Figure 8 for quantified partitives and in Figure 9 for superlative partitives.

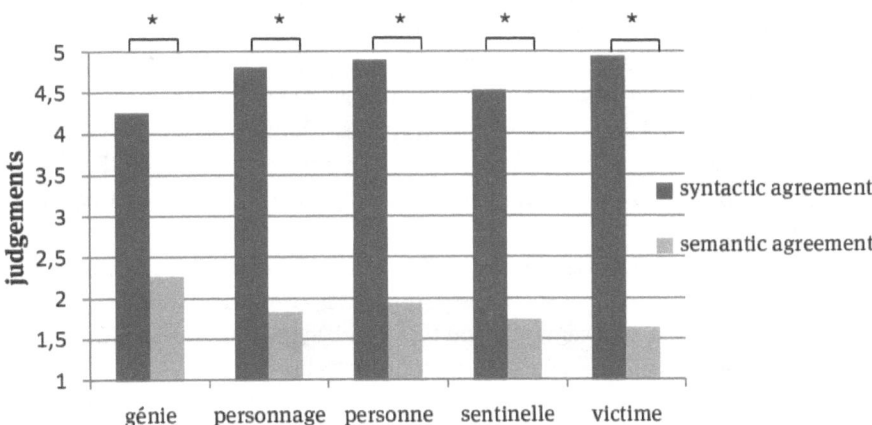

Fig. 8: Quantified partitives individual class D nouns

In quantified partitives, with class D nouns the sentences with syntactic agreement are judged to be significantly more acceptable than the sentences with semantic agreement (p < 0.001 for all nouns).

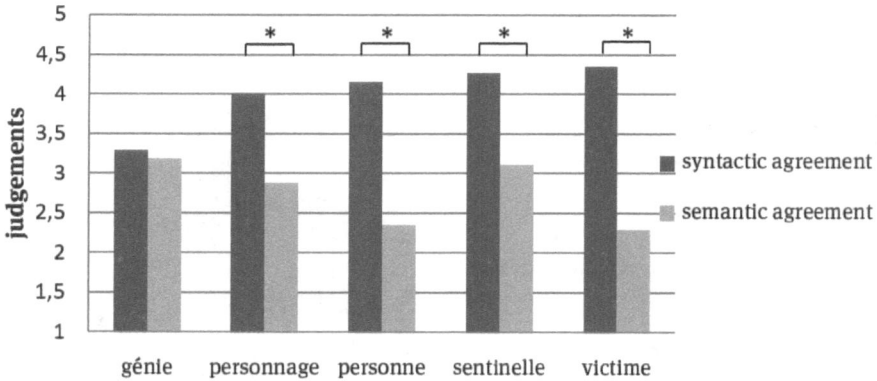

Fig. 9: Superlative partitives individual class D nouns

With all class D nouns, syntactic agreement is judged to be more acceptable than semantic agreement in superlative partitives. However, for the noun *génie* the difference between the sentences with semantic and those with syntactic agreement is not significant (p = 0.653). This contrasts with the nouns *personne* (p < 0.001), *victime* (p < 0.001), *sentinelle* (p = 0.002) and *personnage* (p = 0.001). The overall judgement of the sentences with the noun *génie* is lower too. For *sentinelle*, as opposed to both other feminine class D nouns *personne* and *victime*, the sentence with semantic agreement appears to be more acceptable, which is comparable to the judgements on the masculine class D nouns *génie* and *personnage*.

As we mentioned earlier, the noun class internal differences may depend on the relative frequency of the different nouns. Therefore, we checked the lemma frequency of our 13 test nouns in the online *Lexique* corpus (New & Pallier 2019) (see Table 3).

In a next step, we carried out separate correlation tests for each noun class between the lemma frequencies in the corpus and our participants' judgements on the test sentences with semantic and those with syntactic agreement. The correlation coefficients and p-values are reported in Table 6.

Tab. 6: Correlation coefficients

Noun class	Class B		Class C		Class D	
	semantic agreement	syntactic agreement	semantic agreement	syntactic agreement	semantic agreement	syntactic agreement
Correlation coefficient	-0.092*	-0.253*	0.238*	0.233*	-0.061	0.060
p-value	0.042	< 0.001	< 0.001	< 0.001	0.131	0.134

As we can observe form the correlation coefficients, there are only weak – though significant – correlations for classes B and C. For class D, the correlations are very weak, but not significant. This suggests that the lemma frequency of a noun does not significantly influence our participants' judgements on the test sentences with either semantic or syntactic agreement. However, it should be noted that we only investigated a limited number of nouns for each noun class, which were all carefully selected based on a dictionary search (see section 3).

A final point to mention is the variation across participants that follows from our results. Whereas some participants judge partitive constructions in general to be unacceptable, either with syntactic or semantic agreement, other participants almost always consider these constructions to be acceptable, irrespective of semantic or syntactic agreement. Likewise, some participants judge sentences with semantic agreement acceptable with some nouns of a noun class, whilst others accept them with all nouns of the same class. We included two metalinguistic factors, sex and age, to investigate whether these factors influence the acceptability rates of individual participants. Using an Independent Samples T-Test in SPSS, we established that there are no significant differences between males and females on the one hand (p = 0.726), and between our five age groups (see Table 2) of participants on the other hand (p = 0.696). We therefore conclude that sex and age do not seem to influence the acceptability rates, answering research question (iv). We will discuss an alternative explanation for the participant variation in section 5.3.

5 Discussion

The goal of the present study was to further explore gender agreement in partitive constructions in French, building on Sleeman & Ihsane (2016), who investigated this phenomenon and proposed a theoretical analysis of gender agreement, based on a limited number of informants' judgements and sentences. We carried out a Grammaticality Judgement Task with native speakers of French to answer the following questions: (i) Do superlative and quantified partitives differ significantly with respect to the acceptance of semantic agreement, as Sleeman & Ihsane's results suggest? (ii) Do class B, class C and class D nouns differ significantly with respect to the acceptance of semantic agreement in superlative partitives? (iii) Is there a significant difference in the acceptability of semantic agreement between individual nouns? (iv) Is there a significant difference in the acceptance of semantic agreement between younger and older and between female and male participants? Based on Sleeman & Ihsane's study, in section 3 we formulated hypotheses for the first two research questions: (a) In superlative partitives, semantic agreement is judged to be significantly more acceptable than in quantified partitives. (b) In superlative partitives, the acceptance of semantic agreement depends on the type of animate noun: semantic agreement is judged significantly more acceptable with class C and then with class B nouns, whereas syntactic agreement is judged significantly more acceptable with class D nouns. In the next section, we will address research questions (i–ii) and compare our results with Sleeman & Ihsane's findings to check whether our hypotheses are borne out. Subsequently, we will further discuss our results and return to research questions (iii–iv) as well.

5.1 Comparing our results to Sleeman & Ihsane's findings

The results of both studies, separated for the different conditions (partitive type, noun class and agreement type), are summarised in Table 7.

Tab. 7: Comparison of results

Partitive type	Noun class	Agreement type	Sleeman & Ihsane (2016)	Present study
Quantified partitives	class B	syntactic	not tested	accepted
		semantic	not accepted	not accepted
	class C	syntactic	not tested	accepted
		semantic	not accepted	not accepted
	class D	syntactic	not tested	accepted
		semantic	not tested	not accepted
Superlative partitives	class B	syntactic	not tested	in general accepted
		semantic	in general accepted (participant variation)	accepted (but less than with class C)
	class C	syntactic	not tested	in general accepted
		semantic	accepted	accepted
	class D	syntactic	not tested	accepted
		semantic	not tested	not accepted

Sleeman & Ihsane did not investigate the acceptability of syntactic agreement in partitives. They also did not test sentences with class D nouns, because they expected gender mismatches not to occur with these nouns. Our results confirm this assumption, since the participants in our study judged the sentences with syntactic agreement to be more acceptable than those with semantic agreement for class D nouns.

With respect to research questions (i–ii), aiming at verifying the results of Sleeman & Ihsane's study based on a larger sample of speakers, we can conclude the following: Indeed, quantified partitives readily allow syntactic agreement, which is judged to be significantly more acceptable than semantic agreement. As our results show, the acceptance of semantic agreement in superlative partitives depends on the class of the animate nouns. Whereas with class C nouns, the sentences with semantic agreement are judged to be significantly more acceptable than those with syntactic agreement, the class D nouns show the opposite pattern. With class B nouns, superlative partitives seem to be more acceptable with semantic than with syntactic agreement, but this difference is not significant, indicating that our participants judge semantic agreement to be more acceptable with class C nouns than with class B nouns. We can conclude that our hypotheses on the first two research questions are borne out. The results of our study are largely compatible with those of Sleeman & Ihsane, but they also give further insights into gender agreement in partitives.

Considering the theoretical analysis of gender agreement in partitives, we can conclude that our findings do not invalidate Sleeman & Ihsane's analysis. The difference in acceptability of semantic agreement in quantified and superlative partitives could be explained if we adopt their claim that these partitive types are structurally different, in that the structure of superlative partitives contains a second Gender Phrase in the outer DP, allowing for later insertion of semantic gender, contrary to quantified partitives, whose structure only contains a Gender Phrase in the inner DP. Next, we could also adopt their analysis to account for the differences between the noun classes: Whereas grammatical gender is marked in the mental lexicon on class D nouns, it is unmarked for class C nouns, in the latter case giving the opportunity to let semantic gender play a role. If a speaker accepts semantic agreement with a class B noun, this noun is unmarked for grammatical gender in the speaker's mental lexicon, as is the case for class C nouns; if, on the contrary, a speaker does not accept semantic agreement with a class B or a class C noun, this noun is marked for grammatical gender, just like class D nouns. It should be noted, however, that other accounts of gender agreement may also explain our observations in a convincing manner, just as Sleeman & Ihsane's account adopted here. A thorough discussion of such alternative accounts exceeds the scope of this paper and will be left for future work.

5.2 Class B versus class C nouns

Although we cannot conclude from our results that there is a significant difference in acceptability of semantic agreement between class B and class C nouns, we observe differences between these noun classes in terms of the participants' overall judgements. As Figures 2 and 3 show, the sentences with class B nouns are judged to be slightly less acceptable than the sentences with class C nouns in both quantified and superlative partitives. The class C noun *collègue* constitutes an exception to this pattern, because the sentences with this noun are judged less acceptable overall than the other class C nouns. We do not have an explanation for this unexpected result yet, although it might be the case that the participants rejected the sentences with *collègue* for other reasons than agreement issues.

If we look at the control sentences for the class B and class C nouns, we cannot observe the difference reported above. This indicates that the lower overall acceptability of sentences with a class B noun is not due to the use of these nouns in a partitive construction, but rather seems to be related to the presence of a default masculine group noun in combination with a female subset. The participants seem to judge a sentence containing a default masculine group noun and a female subset to be less acceptable with class B nouns than with class C nouns, as a comparison of examples (22) and (24) shows. A possible explanation for this observation might be the fact that for class B nouns, there exist two distinct forms for the feminine and the masculine (e.g. *la rectrice* 'the rector.F' – *le recteur* 'the rector.M'), whereas this is not the case for class C nouns (e.g. *la/le ministre* 'the.F/.M minister'). Thus, there seems to be a blocking effect: If two distinct forms exist, participants seem to prefer the use of the feminine form for female and of the masculine form for male referents. The preference for the use of a feminine group noun when referring to a female in the subset is already reported by Sleeman & Ihsane.

The differences between class B and class C nouns could thus be related to morphology, as for the class B nouns, two distinct forms exist, whereas for class C nouns, there is only one form for both masculine and feminine. The existence of a distinct feminine form might influence a speaker's acceptance of semantic agreement. But how? Recall that according to Sleeman & Ihsane's analysis, the noun of the outer DP is a copy of the noun of the inner DP. In (31), we have a partitive construction with the class B set noun *étudiants* in the default masculine plural form – the result of Failed Agree due to the absence of a semantic gender value in the inner DP's Gender Phrase. A copy of this noun is then transferred onto the outer DP, but remains unpronounced. This unpronounced copy *étudiant* is also in the default masculine (singular) form.

(31) [DP *la/le* [DEGP *plus jeune* [GendP _ [FP *étudiant* [PP *des* [GendP _ [NP *anciens étudiants*]]]]]]]

The outer DP's Gender Phrase is not valued yet, so we can add a semantic gender value to it. If the outer DP refers to a female subset, we could value the gender feature as feminine, resulting in feminine agreement on the determiner *la* in the outer DP and in a gender mismatch between the inner DP (default masculine) and the outer DP (feminine), as in (32).

(32) [DP *la* [DEGP *plus jeune* [GendP F [FP *étudiant* [PP *des* [GendP _ [NP *anciens étudiants*]]]]]]]

However, in the outer DP we still have the unpronounced copy of the noun in the masculine default form *étudiant* and not in the feminine form *étudiante*. With a class C noun such as *ministre*, on the other hand, there would not be such a difference, since both masculine and feminine genders correspond to a single morphological form (*ministre*), with the only element visibly indicating gender being the determiner – although underlying grammatical gender is present, of course. So, with a class C noun, there would not be an overt clash in the outer DP between the unpronounced copy of the noun in the masculine default form and the inserted feminine semantic gender value. In this way we can explain why gender mismatches are less acceptable with class B nouns than with class C nouns: with class B nouns the existence of a distinct feminine form causes the participants to prefer the presence of this feminine form when the sentence refers to a female, as the judgements on the feminine control sentences show, even if this feminine form remains unpronounced in the outer DP. With class C nouns, on the other hand, there are no distinct forms, so no blocking effect can occur.

A related issue to discuss concerns the low acceptability rate of the feminine control sentence with the class C noun *professeur*, as opposed to the judgements for the other feminine control sentences, as we already pointed out in section 4.1. A possible explanation for this low judgement might be that our participants do not consider the noun *professeur* to be a class C noun, as we did, but rather classify this noun as a class B noun. As a class B noun, the feminine form of *professeur* would not be *la professeur*, but *la professeure*. In that case, the feminine control sentence would not be (30), as included in the test, but rather (33).

(33) *La   plus intelligente   des   nouvelles professeures est   Madame*
     the.F most intelligent.F of.the new.F.PL   teacher.F.PL is   Mrs.
     Arbelette.
     Arbelette
     'The most intelligent of the new teachers is Mrs. Arbelette.'

On the other hand, the overall judgements of the noun *professeur* are more consistent with the overall judgements of class C nouns than with the overall judgements of class B nouns, as we can take from the comparison of Figures 4–7. This supports our choice for classing the noun *professeur* as a class C noun. Since it is this default masculine plural form that is present in our task, this would not make a difference. The only visible difference would concern the feminine control sentence. Still, when repeating the test in future, it would be interesting to include both possible control sentences (30) and (33), in order to investigate which version is preferred.

5.3 Variation

Compared to Sleeman & Ihsane's study, our test involved more different nouns for each of the noun classes and was filled in by a larger number of participants. Accordingly, we observed a lot of variation in our results. First, the results show variation with regards to the different noun classes tested, not only across, but also within the different noun classes. It is, however, worth noting that our data contain no nouns that seem to display a completely distinct agreement pattern than all other nouns within the same noun class. Second, there is variation between individual participants. We will come back to the latter type of variation later on, but let us focus on the most intriguing cases of noun class internal variation first, addressing research question (iii). Although we do not observe contradictory patterns with one noun class, there are still slight differences between nouns in the same class. We investigated the lemma frequency of our test nouns in the online *Lexique* corpus (New & Pallier 2019) and checked for correlations between a test noun's lemma frequency in the corpus and the acceptability rates on the test sentences with either semantic or syntactic agreement containing this noun. The correlation tests revealed only (very) weak correlations between noun frequency and acceptability rate for class B, class C and class D nouns, suggesting that a noun's lemma frequency did not significantly influence our participants' judgements. However, our results show inter group differences, which we will briefly discuss below.

In the group of class D nouns, the masculine noun *génie* shows slightly different acceptability rates in superlative partitives as opposed to the other nouns. Whereas the sentences with syntactic agreement are generally judged to be more acceptable than those with semantic agreement, with the noun *génie* the difference in judgement between the superlative partitives with syntactic and semantic agreement is smaller than for the other class D nouns. This indicates a greater likelihood of semantic agreement, possibly due to the fact that *génie*, traditionally a masculine fixed-gender noun, could become an epicene noun in the future, allowing for both a masculine and a feminine use, following processes that have affected traditionally masculine animate nouns such as *le ministre* 'the.M minister', of which the feminine form *la ministre* 'the.F minister' has become common over the last decades. The possibility of such a change is supported by the comparable, originally masculine fixed-gender noun *témoin* 'witness', of which the feminine form *la témoin* 'the.F witness' is indicated in a recent version (2016) of the French *Le Petit Robert* dictionary (Rey-Debove & Rey 2016).

Within the group of class B nouns, we did not observe any clear differences between the suffix alternation (i.e. *chanteur* and *recteur*) and the affixation (*étudiant* and *policier*) nouns. For the class B noun *recteur*, the results of the superlative partitives show only a very small difference in judgement between the sentence with semantic and the one with syntactic agreement, whereas for all the other class B (and class C) nouns, the differences in judgement between the sentences with semantic and syntactic agreement are more prominent. Probably, the title of *recteur* is seen as generally attributed to men, in which case the use of the default masculine would be more suitable than with a noun like *chanteur*, for which it is more likely to have an equal number of *chanteuses* 'female singers' and *chanteurs* 'male singers'. Accordingly, the masculine form *recteur* would thus be more frequent than the feminine form *rectrice*, which could also be related to the number of female rectors.

With respect to research question (iv), we did not observe an influence of the participant's age and/or sex on the acceptance of semantic agreement. Age and sex thus not seem to explain the variation present in our results. We think that the variation could be partially related to the way in which a specific noun is stored and classified in a person's mental lexicon, an explanation also suggested by Ihsane & Sleeman (2016), to account for the observation that gender mismatches with class B nouns are not accepted by all their informants. For one speaker, a specific noun could be marked with feminine grammatical gender in the mental lexicon, whereas for another speaker, this same noun might be unmarked for grammatical gender, thus resulting in different agreement situations: for the first speaker, the entire sentence would have to show agreement with the noun's feminine grammatical gender; for the second speaker, in the absence of a grammatical gender value on the noun, semantic gender can play a role in agreement. Further exploring this intriguing variation between participants goes beyond the scope of the present study, but we hope to return to this issue in future work.

5.4 Final remarks

With regard to methodology, the present study involves some potential drawbacks which we mentioned in the methodology section: the absence of filler sentences in the grammaticality judgement task, the length and monotonicity of the task and the online distribution of the questionnaire. Another improvement would be to check the lemma frequency of the test items in advance, rather than after having submitted the questionnaire to the participants. It might also be worthwhile to think about a different type of test, that does not only address passive knowledge, as did our grammaticality judgement task, but would also test actual language use, although the constructions investigated are quite rarely used.

In addition, the investigation of gender agreement in partitive constructions in other languages than French might also help to shed more light on native speakers' intuitions. In future work, we at least plan to investigate gender agreement in partitive constructions in a Germanic language, German. Compared to French, German presents an interesting case to investigate gender agreement, since German has three different genders – masculine, feminine and neuter – instead of two, but gender agreement in partitive constructions presents the same challenges as in French. A comparison of both languages might therefore provide us with additional insights into the mechanisms at stake.

6 Conclusion

The goal of this paper was to provide a more thorough investigation of gender agreement in partitive constructions in French, building on an explorative study by Sleeman & Ihsane (2016). Sleeman & Ihsane concluded that the acceptability of semantic gender agreement in French depends on the type of partitive construction and on the type of noun. In quantified partitives, semantic agreement is not accepted. In superlative partitives, semantic agreement is accepted with class B and even more with class C nouns, but not with class D nouns. By means of a grammaticality judgement task, the results of the present study, while generally compatible with the patterns reported by Sleeman & Ihsane, displayed a lot of variation on different levels. We observed variation between individual nouns within the same noun class and across participants. We suggested that both types of variation could be accounted for by assuming differences in the encoding of grammatical gender on specific nouns in the mental lexicon of a language user. However, more research is needed to further explore potential sources of the variation, which may provide more insights into the mechanisms behind gender agreement in situations that present a competition between syntactic and semantic agreement.

Acknowledgement: We thank two anonymous reviewers for valuable comments and suggestions. All remaining errors are our own. Furthermore, we thank Tabea Ihsane for valuable comments on an earlier version of this paper.

7 References

Atkinson, Emily. 2015. Gender features on *n* & the root: An account of gender in French. In Jason Smith & Tabea Ihsane (eds.), *Romance linguistics 2012: Selected papers from the 42nd Linguistics Symposium on Romance Languages (LSRL)*, 229–244. Amsterdam: John Benjamins.

Audring, Jenny. 2013. A pronominal view of gender agreement. *Language Sciences* 35. 32–46.

Chomsky, Noam. 2000. Minimalist inquiries: the framework. In Roger Martin, David Michaels & Juan Uriagereka (eds.), *Step by step: Essays on minimalist syntax in honor of Howard Lasnik*, 89–155. Cambridge MA: MIT Press.

Chomsky, Noam. 2001. Derivation by phase. In Michael Kenstowicz (ed.), *Ken Hale: A life in language*, 1–52. Cambridge MA: MIT Press.

Compernolle, Rémi Adam van. 2009. What do women want? Linguistic equality and the feminization of job titles in contemporary France. *Gender and Language* 3(1). 33–52.

Corbett, Greville G. 1991. *Gender*. Cambridge: Cambridge University Press.

Corbett, Greville G. 2006. *Agreement*. Cambridge: Cambridge University Press.

Haspelmath, Martin & Andrea D. Sims. 2010. *Understanding morphology*, 2nd edn. New York: Routledge.

Ihsane, Tabea & Petra Sleeman. 2016. Gender agreement with animate nouns in French. In Christina Tortora, Marcel den Dikken, Ignacio Montoya & Teresa O'Neill (eds.), *Selected Papers of the 43rd Linguistic Symposium on Romance Languages*, New York, 17–19 April 2013, 159–175. Amsterdam/Philadelphia: John Benjamins.

Kramer, Ruth. 2009. *Definite markers, phi-features and agreement: A morphosyntactic investigation of the Amharic DP*. Santa Cruz, CA: UC Santa Cruz Ph.D. dissertation.

Kučerová, Ivona. 2018. Φ-features at the syntax-semantics interface: Evidence from nominal inflection. *Linguistic Inquiry* 49(4). 813–845.

Kuznetsova, Alexandra, Per Bruun Brockhoff & Rune Haubo Bojesen Christensen. 2017. lmerTest package: Tests in linear mixed effects models. *Journal of Statistical Software* 82(13). 1–26.

Labbé Grunberg, Hernán. 2020. *Storage and processing of Dutch morphological information. Early electrophysiological responses to lexical, morphological and syntactic information.* Amsterdam: LOT.

Legate, Julie Anne. 2002. Phases in 'beyond explanatory adequacy'. Manuscript. MIT.

Lyster, Roy. 2006. Predictability in French gender attribution: A corpus analysis. *French Language Studies* 16. 69–92.

Matushansky, Ora. 2013. Gender confusion. In Lisa Lai-Shen Cheng & Norbert Corver (eds.), *Diagnosing syntax*, 271–294. Oxford: Oxford University Press.

New, Boris & Christophe Pallier. 2019. *Lexique*. Retrieved from: www.lexique.org (12 September, 2019).

Pesetsky, David & Esther Torrego. 2007. The syntax of valuation and the interpretability of features. In Simin Karimi, Vida Samiian & Wendy Wilkins (eds.), *Phrasal and clausal architecture*, 262–294. Amsterdam/Philadelphia: John Benjamins.

Preminger, Omer. 2011. *Agreement as a fallible operation*. Cambridge MA: MIT dissertation.

R Core Team. 2018. R: A language and environment for statistical computing. R Foundation for statistical computing, Vienna. URL: https://www.R-project.org/.

Rey-Debove, Josette & Alain Rey. 2012. *Le Petit Robert*. Paris: Dictionnaires Le Robert.

Rizzi, Luigi. 1997. The fine structure of the left periphery. In Liliane Haegeman (ed.), *Elements of grammar*, 281–337. Dordrecht: Springer.

Sleeman, Petra & Tabea Ihsane. 2016. Gender mismatches in partitive constructions with superlatives in French. *Glossa* 1(1). 1–25.

Sleeman, Petra & Ellen-Petra Kester. 2002. Partitive constructions and antisymmetry. In Claire Beyssade, Reineke Bok-Bennema, Frank Drijkoningen & Paola Monachesi (eds.), *Romance languages and linguistic theory* (Current Issues in Linguistic Theory 232), 271–286. Amsterdam: John Benjamins.

Westveer, Thom, Petra Sleeman & Enoch O. Aboh. 2018. Discriminating dictionaries? Feminine forms of profession nouns in dictionaries of French and German. *International Journal of Lexicography* 31(4). 371–393.

Part 2: **Clitics and Null Subjects**

Antonio Fábregas and Teresa Cabré
Towards a syntactic account of ungrammatical clitic sequences and their repairs

Abstract: The goal of this chapter is to show how a syntactic approach can accommodate in a natural way the main empirical generalisations formulated within morphological theories in their study of impoverished clitic clusters, as well as to show that a syntactic approach accounts for one extra property. We will argue that, when two clitics compete for the same syntactic space, a minimally bigger structure that contains the two clitics is used, if available inside the space of the clitic area.

Keywords: clitics, morphological defaults, movement, clitic combinations, Spanish, Italian

1 Introduction: morphological and syntactic approaches to clitic combinations

One of the main topics in the study of the syntax and morphology of Romance languages is the existence of invalid clitic combinations, such as those in (1).

(1) a. *{Le   lo   /   lo   le}   he   dado.   (Spanish)
       her.DAT it.ACC   it.ACC her.DAT have.1SG   given
       Intended: 'I have given it(masc.) to her.'
    b. *Nel   medioevo, si   si   lavava   raramente   (Italian)
       in.the Middle.ages IMP REFL   washed   seldom
       Intended: 'In the Middle Ages, one washed seldom.'
       (Pescarini 2007)

Antonio Fábregas: University of Tromsø, Office E-1019, HSL-Fakultet, 9037 Tromsø, Norway, antonio.fabregas@uit.no
Teresa Cabré: Universitat Autònoma de Barcelona, Facultat de Lletres Edifici B, Departament de Filologia Catalana, Despatx B9/0046, 08193 Bellaterra (Barcelona), Spain, teresa.cabre@uab.cat

https://doi.org/10.1515/9783110719154-004

c. *{La   li   / Li   la}   he   donat.   (Cent. Catalan)
   it.ACC her.DAT   her.DAT it.ACC have.1SG   given
   Intended: 'I have given it(fem.) to her.'

(1) illustrates three situations where the grammar of different languages or languaguage varieties does not allow that two clitics combine in the same sequence – technically, the clitics cannot be inside the same cluster. In both Spanish and Catalan, a third person dative cannot combine with a third person accusative (1a, 1c). The fact is surprising because in principle each clitic signals a different syntactic function, and when the syntactic function is expressed by other means there is no incompatibility.

(2) (Le)   he   dado   un libro a   María.
    her.DAT   have.1SG given   a   book   to María
    'I have given a book to María.'

In Italian, two clitics *si* cannot combine in the same cluster, again even though they fulfill different syntactic functions: one marks the sentence as impersonal ('one does something'), while the second marks the verb as reflexive.

Descriptively, these ungrammatical sequences are resolved by removing or substituting one of the two clitics in the cluster.

(3) a. Se   lo   he   dado.   (Spanish)
       REFL   it.ACC   have.1SG   given
       Intended: 'I have given it(masc.) to her.'
    b. Nel   medioevo,   ci   si   lavava   raramente.¹   (Italian)
       in.the   Middle.ages   LOC   REFL   washed   seldom
       'In the Middle Ages, one washed seldom.'
       (Pescarini 2007)
    c. L'   hi   he   donat.²   (Cent. Catalan)
       it.ACC LOC   have.1SG   given
       Intended: 'I have given it(fem.) to her.'

---

1 Unless otherwise explicitly stated, 'Italian' here refers to standard Italian. The facts vary considerably in specific varieties; see Manzini & Savoia (2005).
2 Even though orthographically Catalan would represent the combination as *la hi*, oral Catalan pronounces the equivalent of *l'hi*, /li/.

In Spanish, the 3rddative+3rdaccusative combination is resolved by substituting the dative with a reflexive pronoun, also in third person (3a). In Central Catalan, the same ungrammatical sequence is replaced, but this time by a locative clitic (3c). In Italian, the reflexive pronoun marking impersonality is replaced by a locative (3b).

Not all sequences can be repaired by substitution. In Italian a sequence of two pronouns *ci* is repaired by removing one of them (4). In Spanish (5), a sequence of two pronouns *se* is ungrammatical, and removing one of them does not repair the structure. (5b) cannot be interpreted as the reflexive verb *lavarse* 'to wash oneself', but as the non reflexive *lavar* 'to wash'. The meaning that (4b) can have in Italian involves in Spanish the non-clitic pronoun *uno* 'one', with *se* being reflexive.

(4) a. *A Roma ci ci porta Mario.
 to Rome LOC us.ACC brings Mario
 Intended: 'To Rome, Mario takes us there.'
 b. A Roma ci porta Mario.
 to Rome us.ACC brings Mario
 Intended: 'To Rome, Mario takes us.'
 (Pescarini 2007)

(5) a. *En la Edad Media, se se lavaba poco.
 in the Age Middle, IMP REFL washed little
 b. En la Edad Media, se lavaba poco.
 in the Age Middle, IMP washed little
 'In the Middle Ages, one seldom washed (things).'
 c. En la Edad Middle, uno se lavaba poco.
 in the Age Middle, one REFL washed little
 'In the Middle Ages, one seldom washed oneself.'

As can already be seen, ungrammatical clitic clusters and their repairs have two sides: superficial effects –what combination is ungrammatical irrespectively of the syntactic function, and how it is repaired–, and deeper effects related to the interpretation and the syntactic functions involved –because the clitics reflect syntactic objects, and there are meanings that cannot be expressed with them. The existing analyses have mainly concentrated on the surface effects, treating the phenomenon as morphological (cf. Perlmutter 1971, Bonet 1991, 1993, 1995, Grimshaw 1997, Pescarini 2007, Rivero 2008, Nevins 2012, to name just a few).

Even though this perspective is the dominant one, there are syntactic analyses where both the ungrammaticality and the repairs are at least partially conditioned by the syntactic derivation (cf. in particular Kayne 2010, Walcow 2011, Cabré & Fábregas in press).

In this article, we will ask the question of how a syntactic theory should be in order to account for the properties of ungrammatical clitic sequences and their repairs. We will sketch an analysis focused on Spanish where we will argue that a syntactic approach can in principle account for the right generalisations of the morphological account, and additionally explain some additional properties that do not directly follow from a morphological account. We will occasionally refer to Italian as a way to compare with Spanish, even though our conclusions are more speculative with respect to this language.

In the next section, we will present the main claims of the morphological approach, and their right empirical generalisations. §3 argues that the right generalisations of this approach can be restated in syntactic terms as competition for licensing by the same heads, and points out a few facts that the morphological approach cannot explain. Here we will show that the repairs in principle affect to adjacent regions within the area, and that the solution is to use a minimally bigger syntactic structure to accommodate two arguments. §4 details the reasons for the clitic incompatibility, reinterpreting the clash between clitics as syntactic; §5 talks about how the repair happens, and derives the use of less specified clitics from Preminger's (2014) proposal about agreement. §6 provides the preliminary conclusions.

2 The right empirical observations of the morphological approach, and its limits

The dominant morphological approach can be characterised by four properties. First of all, both the nature of the clitic incompatibility and the repair used are surface effects located in a specific morphological component. In Distributed Morphology (cf. Halle & Marantz 1993) morphology is post-syntactic, that is, it is a level where the structure built in syntax is mapped to a morphological representation, at a minimum substituting the syntactic heads (X^o) for positions for morphological exponence (M) where specific vocabulary items are introduced. The second property is that within that morphological surface level, the incompatibility between clitics in the same cluster is stated as a filter that bans sequences of clitics where the two elements are 'too similar' in their feature endowment (thus, they are the effect of a morphological Obligatory Contour Principle leading to general haplology, cf. Nevins 2012). Specifically the ungrammaticality of Spanish *le lo* is codified in Bonet (1991: 155).

(6)   [le]   [lo, la, los, las]

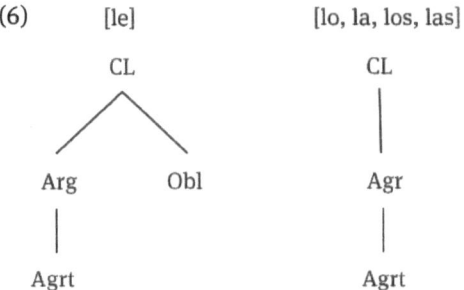

Morphology marks (6) as an invalid sequence, because the features are too similar to each other. Leaving additional details aside, the repair involves removing the feature obl(ique), that differentiates dative from accusative, and the agreement node (agrt), which differentiates masculine / feminine and singular / plural. The result is a configuration with only the features cl(itic) and arg(ument), which in Spanish correspond to the clitic *se*. The clitic se does not differentiate between dative and accusative, masculine or feminine, or singular and plural.

The third and fourth properties follow from this general proposal. Because the infraction and the repair act on a surface morphological component, the operation has no effects on the syntax or semantics of the sequence: in principle, even if the reflexive clitic *se* is used in the sequence, there is nothing reflexive about its syntax and interpretation. Finally, the problem is stated in terms of the surface expression of the clitic, which means that the filter in (6) acts provided that the clitics *le* and *lo* are present in the structure, independently of their syntactic behaviour.

The morphological account makes several right empirical predictions. The first one is that the feature incompatibilities are more likely to occur when the clitics themselves share more properties with each other –the more features shared between them, the more likely it is that they will trigger an OCP violation. For instance, in Spanish the incompatibility affects two 3rd person clitics (1a), but not a combination of a 1st or 2nd person dative and a 3rd person accusative (7).

(7) Me   lo   dio.
    me.DAT it.ACC gave.3SG
    'He gave it to me.'

In Italian, the incompatibility in (1b) affects two reflexives. Another well-studied incompatibility, the *me-lui* effect, involves a crash between datives and 1st or 2nd person accusatives (8). 1st and 2nd person pronouns, like dative pronouns, share in Spanish the property that they do not spell out gender distinctions –they are identical in masculine and feminine– and that they are marked by *a* 'to' when used as pronouns.

(8) *Me   le   presentó.
    me.ACC her.DAT presented.3SG
    Intended: 'He presented me to her.'

Another right prediction is that the repair always involves using a clitic form that has fewer features. In Spanish *le lo*, the repair involves removing a 3rd person clitic that makes a number distinction (*le ~ les*, singular and plural respectively) for a clitic that makes no number distinctions and merely expresses third person, *se*. If 3rd person is in fact absence of person marking (cf. Benveniste 1966), then *se* is the most underspecified clitic in Spanish, lacking gender, number and person marking. In Italian, the *si si* crash is repaired substituting a clitic that intervenes at least in a person opposition (*mi ~ ti ~ si*) for a locative clitic *ci* that as a locative does not even make such distinctions.

Finally, another right prediction is that if the crash involves the clitics that are already the most underspecified within the language, the only chance to repair it is by removing one of the clitics. This is what happens with Italian *ci ci*, and Spanish *se se*, although with different results.

However, the approach fails to predict some important properties. One property that is arbitrary in the morphological account is the generalisation that when the two clitics in a sequence conflict, the one that undergoes the change is the one to the left. Consider Italian *si si* in (3b). From the two clitics, the one that is replaced is the first, producing *ci si* and not *si ci*. Similarly, in Spanish the sequence *le lo* is repaired by replacing the left-one, *se lo* (3a) and not *le se* or anything involving the accusative. In the morphological account, this is an accident that does not follow from any principle.[3]

---

[3] Central Catalan seems to be an exception on the surface, but notice that the resulting sequence –leaving orthography aside– of accusative and locative is identical to one single dative: /li/ in

There are also wrong predictions in the morphological account. One of the claims is that the surface shape of the clitic is what triggers the repair, not the syntactic properties that the clitic reflects. Thus, two *ci* in Italian trigger the repair even though one is locative and the other one is a 1st person accusative (cf. Pescarini 2007). However, this is not always right. For instance, the Spanish me-lui effect is influenced by whether the pronoun is reflexive or not. Contrast the two sequences in (9).

(9) a. ?No   te   me   quieres   lo   suficiente.
        not   you.REFL   me.DAT   love.2SG   the   enough
        'You don't love yourself enough, and that affects me.'
    b. *No   te   me   quieren   lo   suficiente.
        not   you.ACC   me.DAT   love.3PL   the   enough
        Intended: 'They don't love you enough, and that affects me.'

(9a) and (9b) minimally contrast in that the accusative *te* 'you' is a reflexive pronoun in the first, but not in the second. In both cases, the dative *me* is the so-called ethical dative which presents the whole event as affecting the speaker (positively or negatively). (9a) is much more acceptable than (9b); in fact, the imperative *Quiére-te-me* 'Love-yourself-ME.DAT, Love yourself, because it affects me' was the slogan of a famous supermarket chain in Spain during Christmas 2016. The nature of the dative is identical in both sentences in (9), so the only difference is that the first *te* is reflexive and the second is non-reflexive. This implies that the same surface clitic can have different effects, depending on its morphosyntactic nature.

---

both cases. Cabré & Fábregas (in press) argue in detail that Central Catalan datives are in fact combinations of accusative clitics with a locative NP-layer spelled out as /i/. In essence, the repair in Central Catalan involves producing only one 'dative' pronoun that in fact contains the accusative within it. Cabré & Fábregas (in press) argue for a sequence where the Central Catalan locative clitic *hi* /i/ is licensed as a place noun at the lowest position within the locative region, with the accusative clitic being a DP structure built on top of it. The dative is, in essence, an accusative DP structure that contains at its bottom a locative /i/. The clash is due to the accusative and the dative being both accusative clitics competing from the same area, and grammar solves it by licensing the locative part of the dative at the bottom and the accusative at the top, resulting on what seems to be a single dative on the surface. Seen from this perspective, the generalisation is that when two clitics compete for the same heads, the grammar builds a bigger structure to make room for both clitics; in the case of Catalan, that bigger structure is a dative because the dative contains both the accusative and the locative. In the case of Spanish *le lo*, because none of the clitics contains the other, the grammar builds a reflexive structure (bigger than the sequence of dative and accusative) to host both clitics, as we will argue in detail in §3.

Also, Alcaraz (2017) has convincingly argued that the *se* pronoun used to repair the sequence *le lo behaves syntactically as a real reflexive, meaning that the repair also has syntactic effects. Among the different pieces of evidence that Alcaraz offers, we have the interpretations that *se* but not *le* allows in ellipsis contexts. Compare (10a) and (10b).

(10) a. *Juan le echó la culpa a María$_i$, y ella$_i$ también.
        Juan her.DAT threw the blame to María and she too
        Intended: 'Juan blamed María and María blamed herself too.'
    b. Juan se la echó a María$_i$, y ella$_i$ también.
        Juan REFL it.ACC threw to María, and she too
        Intended: 'Juan blamed María, and María blamed herself too.'

The reason for the asymmetry is that *se* acts as a real reflexive in (10b). Being a reflexive, it allows for the reconstruction in (11b) without violating Principle B of Binding Theory (cf. Torrego 1995 for the observation that strong pronouns in Spanish do not violate Principle B if they are cross-referenced by the reflexive *se*). The pronoun *le* in (10a) is not an anaphor, and because of this in (11a) it would trigger an Infraction of Principle B.

(11) a. ...*y María$_i$ le echó la culpa a ella$_i$.
        ...and María her.DAT threw the blame to her
        Intended: '...*and María$_i$ blamed her$_i$.'
                                                Violation of Principle B
    b. ...y María$_i$ se$_i$ la echó a ella$_i$.
        ...and María REFL it.ACC threw to her
        '...and María blamed herself.'

See also Romero (2012), where he argues that the apparent surface substitution of a dative for a feminine accusative in some European Spanish varieties also comes accompanied of syntactic effects and restrictions. All in all, it seems that the morphological account went too far in the claim that the repairs have no syntactic or semantic effects. Combined with the observation that the first clitic tends to be the one repaired, this suggests that a more syntactic account should be attempted. In the next section we will sketch a syntactic theory for Romance clitic combinations.

3 Towards a syntactic reinterpretation: syntactic effects and the plausibility of hierarchical explanations

Our starting point is Sportiche's (1996) proposal that languages with clitic systems, like Romance languages, define between V and T an area to introduce the clitics: that is, clitics are not only phonologically special, but also syntactically special in that they are elements that have to be licensed in a specific area. Starting from this assumption, the question is how many clitics and in which order can be licensed within that area. We assume that Wiltschko (2014) is right in her claim that Universal Grammar defines domains, but is neutral with respect to the conceptual content of those domains or to the specific heads that a language allows within them – linguistic variation involves, among other things, to determine the set of heads that languages define starting from the primitives provided by Universal Grammar.[4]

For Spanish, Kayne (2010) makes the proposal that the clitic sequence in (12) should be reflected in the syntax.

(12) se > me/te/nos/os > le, les > lo, la, los, las

His main argument comes from Halle & Harris (2005) observation that subject agreement in Spanish varieties can follow some of these clitics, but following that hierarchy. If a variety only allows that subject agreement follows one clitic, it is the reflexive (13a). If a variety allows that agreement follows a 1st or 2nd person clitic, then it also allows that it follows the reflexive (13b). If the variety allows (13c), with a dative clitic, then it also allows (13a) and (13b). The less frequent construction is the one where the accusative clitics are followed by agreement (13d), but if a variety allows it, then it allows the previous three as well.

---

[4] We see this as a prerequisite to be able to provide a syntactic account of the clitic combinations. One strength of the morphological approach is the empirical fact that the clitic sequences are subject to considerable variation even within Romance; the ungrammatical sequences and the repairs are also variable, sometimes from one variety to another. If one starts from the assumption that the set of heads and the feature endowment of those heads is invariable in Romance (or universally), then the only option would be to treat variation as a surface effect, which is what the morphological account does. As we will see, we will simply accept that the clitic area in Italian and Spanish is different in terms of the number of heads and how they are ordered, and take these as choices performed inside the space that Universal Grammar defines.

(13) a. Siente-se-n
    sit.IMP-REFL-3PL
    'Sit (yourself) down'
  b. Siente-me-n
    sit.IMP-me-3PL
    'Sit me down'
  c. Diga-le-n
    say.IMP-her.DAT-3PL
    'Tell her'
  d. Diga-lo-n
    say.IMP-it.ACC-3PL
    'Tell it'

Kayne (2010) shows that a morphological account where the ordering between agreement and clitic is derived in morphology overgenerates, and argues that the conclusion should be that these four types of clitics are located in distinct regions within the clitic area (14).[5]

(14) [se   [me/te...   [le/les   [lo/la...   ]]]]
    reflexive person clitics dative clitics accusative clitics

The difference between varieties depends on how low the agreement can be generated: in a variety that only allows (13a), it is generated between the reflexive and the person clitic regions; if (13d) is allowed, agreement is located below the region for accusative clitics, and by transitivity also below the other three classes, thus explaining the implicational hierarchy.

Consider now how this approach in itself will be able to capture the right empirical observations of the dominant morphological analyses.

One first observation within that model is that the ungrammaticality is more likely when the clitics share properties. This, instead of being due to an OCP, could be reinterpreted syntactically: if clitics must be licensed in the right region of (14), the ungrammaticality is produced when two clitics try to be licensed by the same region. If two clitics have the same features, they cannot appear together because the region can license only one of them.

---

5 We assume that the Linear Correspondence Axiom (cf. Kayne 1994) applies, so that linear precedence indicates c-command. This eliminates the option that the same projection hosts two specifiers, and therefore each head can only license one clitic.

In this respect it is interesting that the ungrammatical combinations always involve clitics that either belong to the same region or that are placed inside adjacent regions. A sequence of two *se* pronouns is ungrammatical because both compete for licensing in the reflexive region (15a).[6] A sequence of one dative and one accusative 3rd person clitics is ungrammatical, and they are hosted in adjacent regions (15b); if the dative is a person clitic, it is not incompatible with the third person accusative (15c), and notice that now the regions are not adjacent. A *me-lui* infraction involves a 3rd person dative, and a person clitic, again in adjacent regions (15d), but the infraction is ameliorated if the person clitic is reflexive, and then they are not in adjacent regions again (15e).

(15) a. [ReflCl *se se
     b.   [DatCl *le   [AccCl lo
     c.   [PersonCl me   [DatCL   [AccCl lo...
     d.   [PersonCl *te   [DatCl le
     e. [ReflCl te [PersonCl   [DatCl le

Importantly, the repair also involves moving away from the adjacent region to a higher region. In Spanish, *le lo* is repaired by replacing *le* with *se*. From the perspective of the regions, this involves taking a pronoun that would have been placed in a lower region and introducing it in a higher region.

(16) a. [ReflCl   [PersonCl   [DatCl *le   [AccCl lo
     b. [ReflCl se   [PersonCl   [DatCl   [AccCl lo

In the case of Italian *si si*, the infraction is that two clitics try to be hosted in the reflexive area, and the repair involves substituting the first with a locative. We assume that Standard Italian defines an additional region in its clitic area, for locative clitics –Spanish lacks this region, as there are no locative clitics in the language. As *ci* always precedes *si* in any combination, we conclude that the locative clitic region is defined higher than reflexives.

(17) a. [LocCl   [ReflCl *si si

---

6 The same facts hold for Catalan, and we argue that for the same reason: *A l'Edat Mitjana se's rentava poc* 'At the Ages Middle ES ES washed little'. The clitic *es* is, like Spanish *se*, the leftmost clitic in the sequence. While Central Catalan does have a locative clitic *hi*, this clitic has a different distribution than Italian *ci*: it is located below accusative and dative clitics, which makes it unavailable to avoid the conflict of having two clitics *es* in the same position.

b. [$_{LocCl}$ ci   [$_{ReflCl}$ si

The general shape of the repair is the following: if the head that licenses a reflexive clitic is already occupied, the second clitic that could have been reflexive must be licensed somewhere else. It then has to move in the structure searching for another licensor. Movement, of course, is always to a higher position. This explains that the area used for the repair is always higher than the one that the clitic would have occupied.

Another property of movement is that when two elements share features, the one that moves to a higher position is the one that is closer to that position (Relativised Minimality, cf. Rizzi 1990). For this reason, in (17a), the repair cannot involve the accusative clitic: it is hierarchically lower than the dative clitic, and they share features (responsible for the crash, to start with). The only option is to move the dative.

With the combination of these two well-known properties of movement – 'move to a higher position' and 'move the closest element' – we have derived two generalisations that the morphological approach can at most stipulate. The repair involves always a structure that is bigger than the one that produced the crash, and if two clitics that do not contain each other are in a sequence the one that undergoes repair is the one to the left –in other words, the one that is hierarchically higher.

Moreover, note that the operation takes place in syntax, following the syntactic restrictions on movement. This explains that –contra the morphological approach– the repair has syntactic and semantic effects. The clitic *se* that appears as a repair of *le lo* is not a dative that is pronounced as a reflexive, but a real reflexive clitic.

There are other properties that we have not clarified yet: (i) What exactly produces the crash between the clitics?; (ii) In (16) why cannot the dative move to the person clitic area?; (iii) How is licensed the clitic exactly, in the cases where there is competition? and (iv) Why are there cases in which one clitic can be supressed, and cases where it cannot be supressed? However, before we go into these details, we must say more about the logic with which the heads within the clitic region are ordered.

3.1 The internal logic of the clitic region in Spanish and Italian

We will argue now that the four regions in Spanish are not ordered arbitrarily. Consider the clitics hosted in each one of them, from bottom to top. The lowest ones are accusative third person clitics. They codify three distinctions: (i) gender –their shape reflects masculine and feminine forms–, (ii) number –singular and plural– and (iii) case, differentiating themselves from dative clitics.

(18) a. lo ~ la
    b. lo ~ los, la ~ las
    c. lo ~ le

The dative clitics lack the gender distinction, but still differentiate (i) number and (ii) case.

(19) a. le ~ les
    b. lo ~ le

The person clitics do not make a difference in gender or case. *Me* can be accusative or dative, and can refer to a first person masculine or a feminine. Moreover, the personal pronouns are morphologically invariable in number: the first person plural is not built by combining plural *-s* with *me*, but is specified as the undecomposable form *nos*. This means that *me* must be singular, and *nos* must be plural. The only distinction that they make is, of course, person.

(20) a. me ~ te
    b. nos ~ os

The reflexive pronouns are identical in shape to the person pronouns, with the exception of the third person, which is *se*.

What we see is that, uncontroversially for the first three groups, the pronouns make less distinctions the higher we go on the clitic area: gender is lost in datives, case is lost in person clitics – possibly also number. Interestingly, case is relevant to establish the argument structure of the verb, while person is relevant to anchor the sentence to the two main participants in the speech, the speaker and the hearer. It makes intuitive sense, then, that person is defined higher than accusative and dative pronouns: the person clitic region can be viewed as the point where the properties that related the arguments to the predicate become less relevant, and the clause structure starts defining how these event participants correspond to the speech act participants.

What about the reflexives? Reuland (2011) has argued that anaphors –a subcase of which are reflexive pronouns– should be viewed as matrixes of uninterpretable features. They might exhibit number, gender and person contrasts depending on the language, but these are triggered by agreement with the antecedent that compulsorily must c-command them in the syntactic structure. If we assume this proposal, then we obtain a clean generalisation about the four regions.

Specifically, we propose that each region is defined by a head that licenses through agreement the properties of the clitic. The lowest region contains a head that licenses number and gender (21a). The dative region head licenses number (21b). The person region head introduces person but does not license number (21c). The reflexive region head cannot license any property, leaving the reflexive pronoun subject to checking its features with the antecedent (21d). We assume that additionally each of the heads licenses a [clitic] feature, following Bonet's (1991) proposal that this feature differentiates clitics from other pronominal objects.

(21) a. AccCl^0 [Clitic, Gen, Num]
 b. DatCl^0 [Clitic, Num]
 c. PerCl^0 [Clitic, Person]
 d. ReflCl^0 [Clitic]

The shape we observe on the surface is the spell out of the clitic, placed in the specifier position of the head, with which it enters in a licensing relation.

(22) [$_{PerClP}$ [me] PerCl$^0_{[cl, 1p]}$ [$_{AccClP}$ [lo] AccCl$^0_{[cl, m., sg., acc.]}$ ... [$_{vP}$...]]]

Thus, we propose a what-you-see-is-what-you-get approach to the clitic endowment: if *me* lacks distinctions in gender, number and case, it is because it is licensed by a head that only assigns a person value to it; *lo* has more distinctions because the head that licenses it assigns number and gender to it.

The clitic region in Italian is more complex (cf. Wanner 1977, Manzini & Savoia 2002, 2004, Cardinaletti 2008, Benincà & Tortora 2009, Pescarini 2010, 2011), with different orderings depending on the syntactic function, as illustrated in (23) for the reflexive vs. the impersonal *si*.

(23) a. (Luisa) se lo compra nella libreria.
 Luisa REFL it.ACC buys in.the bookstore
 'Luisa buys it for herself in the bookstore.'

b. Lo   si   compra   nella   libreria.
   it.ACC REFL   buys   in.the   bookstore
   'One buys it in the bookstores.'
   (Wanner 1977: 112)

We will not provide a full analysis of Italian clitic clusters here, and instead concentrate on the claim that the competition between clitics involves a solution that uses syntactically higher layers. Wanner (1977: 114) proposes the surface sequence in (24) for Standard Italian.

(24) mi/ti... > ci > gli > si^{refl} > lo/la... > si^{imp}

The logic in Italian is different from the one in Spanish, in terms of the ordering. The highest layer is the one that introduces person features. The pronoun *ci* can be used both as a 1pl pronoun or as a locative (as in 4). To the extent that it is a locative, it lacks person but –like person pronouns– it contains deixis. The idea is that *ci* is a deictic element (cf. Reisig Ferrazzano 2003) whose interpretation depends on the conceptual domain where deixis is established. Just like the difference in speech between a speaker and a hearer must be differentiated by assigning those values in context, the value of the location denoted by *ci* must be determined in context. Thus, if *ci* does not get a person value, it will be locative, and if it gets it, it will be interpreted as a first person pronoun.

Dative pronouns are higher than accusative pronouns, just like in Spanish. The main difference with Spanish is the reflexive pronoun *si*, which is licensed at very low positions. The impersonal is licensed even lower than the accusative pronouns. We can speculate that this might mean that the impersonal clitic is licensed in a position that is as close as possible to the verbal complex, so that it can still receive the external argument interpretation (25a). The reflexive is licensed a little bit higher, which could mean that from that position it needs to move to a head where accusative or dative case is licensed (25b). However, the details about which position is occupied by the reflexive are orthogonal to our purposes: we are just interested in the generalisation that the areas for reflexives in Italian are very low compared to Spanish.

(25) a.   [$_{xP}$ si x^0 [vP]]
     b. [$_{AccClP/DatClP}$ si AccCl/DatCl ...[$_{xP}$ s̶i̶ x^0 [vP]]]

The details of the Italian clitic area cannot be developed in the boundaries of this chapter. For our purposes, what is crucial is that the Italian reflexive pronouns can be independently diagnosed to occupy a lower position than in Spanish, with the region for *ci* occupying a higher layer than the reflexive.

3.2 The Burning House Principle: movement is always upstairs

At this point, we can tie all the different generalisations in one single package. Some languages, those that have syntactic clitics, define an area between V and T where clitics are placed.

That area is composed of heads that license different properties of the clitic. Different languages, or different language varieties, define differently the heads in that region, and their relative ordering. When there is one single clitic for one head, it is fully licensed, as it is the case in (22). When two clitics compete for licensing by the same head –and we will make explicit the reason for three such cases in the next section–, only one of them is licensed.

The unlicensed clitic will attempt then to be licensed by the following head. As movement is upwards, this will involve one of the higher heads. However, that licensing cannot involve features that the argument did not carry to begin with: specifically, if the argument did not carry person, attempting licensing by the PerCl head will produce a vacuous result, and therefore the relation between that clitic and the PerCl cannot be established. The only possibility, then, would be to attempt licensing with a head that carries a subset of the features of the clitic. Thus, we derive from the notion of feature checking part of the effect that the repairing clitic seems to be less specified in features; the second part of the explanation is provided in §5.

Of course, the clitic region is not unlimited. Each language defines a maximal number of heads within that region, and because movement is always upstairs, if the infraction involves clitics that would attempt licensing within the highest layer, there is no place to go to. A relevant case is *se se* in Spanish. As *se* is a reflexive pronoun, it lacks person, number, gender and case. It cannot be licensed in AccCl, which checks gender, in DatCl, which checks number, or in PerCl, which checks person. The only position compatible is, thus, ReflCl, which in Spanish is the higher head. The unlicensed *se*, then, has no place to go, so there is no way to license it.

(26) a. [ReflCl *se se [PersonCl [DatCl [AccCl
 b. [ReflCl se   [PersonCl [DatCl [AccCl

Italian contrasts with Spanish in two properties. The first one is that there is an additional head for *ci*, which, as we suggested above, spells out deicitic information that is compatible with person deixis (1st person) or with locative deixis. The second one is that reflexive pronouns are generated very low, specifically always below the position where dative clitics are licensed.

This has two consequences. The first one is that Spanish will be able to solve a conflict between 3rd person accusative and 3rd person dative by turning one of the clitics into a reflexive. Standard Italian, in contrast, will not be able to solve any clitic combination with the reflexive because that clitic is produced at a very low position.

Second, because the se clitic is generated very high in Spanish, Spanish will not have any strategy to solve the problem that two *se clitics appear together. However, Italian will. Following the linear evidence, both types of *si*, reflexive and impersonal, are generated below the locative clitic *ci*. If both clitics *si* have to be licensed at some point by the same head –which is presumably the case, given that they are surface-identical[7]–, the second clitic will attempt licensing with the next available head. If the reflexive in order to be interpreted as an anaphor must lack values for gender, number and person, the only available head upstairs will be the one that licenses the locative, which also lacks gender, number and person.

(27) a. [$_{LocCl}$ [$_{xP}$ *si si ...
     b. [$_{LocCl}$ ci [$_{xP}$ si   ...

However, in Italian, a sequence *ci ci* cannot be resolved unless one of the clitics is totally deleted. The reason is that a competition between two *ci* clitics does not find an even higher head that can license the locative.

We call this the Burning House Principle: as in a house on fire, the fire extends from the lower floor to the higher floors. A clitic that fails to be licensed by a head will attempt licensing at the higher layers. If the fire starts in the first floor, higher floors are available to escape the fire, but if it starts in the penthouse there is nowhere to go, and the clitic will be totally consumed in the flames, so to say. In Italian, there is at least one extra available floor above the reflexive area, so

---

[7] But see Vicentino Italian (cf. Pescarini 2011), where *se se* is allowed. Pescarini's proposal is that each one of the two clitics in this variety is licensed in a different area within a clitic sequence. Translated to our terms, the availability of the sequence would derive from each clitic, impersonal and reflexive, being licensed by different heads in this variety: the clitics will be generated in different positions, and if they ever move, they would move to different heads.

the second clitic finds shelter there; in Spanish, reflexives are at the top floor, so an infraction cannot be solved within the clitic area and one of the two clitics dies.

At this point, we have only shown that the clitic sequences can be defined hierarchically, accounting for the linear ordering, that the crash involves always clitics that belong to the same or adjacent areas, and the repair involves clitics that are placed higher. We have not made explicit, though, what the trigger for the incompatibilities are and how the partial licensing that produces the surface effect of impoverishment is produced. In the next two sections we will consider each one of the two aspects.

4 A syntactic reinterpretation of clitic incompatibility

We have focused in several types of incompatibility here, and we have pointed out that the similarity in features between clitics that cannot occur together in the same cluster should be reinterpreted as a clash between the heads that license those features. Let us start with the me-lui constraint in Spanish. What triggers it? There are a lot of different approaches to this type of crash (for instance, restricting ourselves just to the syntactic approaches, cf. Anagnostopoulou 2003, Ormazábal & Romero 2007, Adger & Harbour 2007 for different ways of accounting for the crash). There are two observations that relate a person clitic with a dative clitic in a language like Spanish.

First of all, both person arguments and dative arguments are compulsorily introduced in Spanish with the preposition *a* 'to'. For person arguments, this is irrespective of whether the person argument is a direct object or an indirect object.

(28) a. Le doné el libro a la biblioteca. [dative, no person feature]
      it.DAT donated the book to the library
      'I donated the book to the library.'
   b. Me lo dio a mí. [dative, person feature]
      me.DAT it gave to me
      'He gave it to me.'
   c. Me vio a mí. [accusative, person feature]
      me.ACC saw to me
      'He saw me.'

This suggests that, in a sense, all person-marked pronouns are datives with respect to the marking. This is in fact the position taken by Ormazábal & Romero (2007), that the *a*-marking in Spanish is a manifestation of the same case always. Second, person pronouns must be doubled by the clitic in the standard varieties (29a). In the case of datives, they must be doubled by the clitic if they are interpreted as animate (29b), or if the interpretation stays non-animate, if the entity can be viewed as internally affected by a relation of part-whole with the direct object (29c). In (29c), notice that the group is affected by adding a new member to it.

(29) a. *(Me) vio a mí.
 me.ACC saw to me
 'He saw me.'
 b. Le regaló un libro a la biblioteca.
 it.DAT gave a book to the library
 'He gave a book to the (people that are part of the) library.'
 c. Le añadió un componente al grupo.
 it.DAT added a component to.the group
 'He added a member to the group.'

We follow here Adger & Harbour's (2007) theory for the interpretation of these facts. These authors propose that 1st and 2nd person compulsorily carry an animacy feature that is formally identical to the feature that doubled dative goals carry, which is related to affectedness. A language like Spanish would grammaticalise not animacy, but affectedness, and assign it compulsorily to speakers and hearers by virtue of them being sentient.

We propose that this implies that the affectedness feature is checked in the head that deals with dative clitics. Here is where the crash takes place between a dative and a person marked clitic (30a).[8] The difference between a dative pronoun and a person pronoun is that additionally the second moves to the person head, where it gets person assigned (cf. 30b vs. 30c).

---

8 We restrict ourselves here to varieties where the me-lui constraint applies in its strong version, namely that in the presence of a dative third person clitic there is no place for a person clitic. The weak version that allows sequences of two person-marked pronouns (*te me* 'you me', as in *Te me presentaron* 'they introduced you to me' or 'they introduced me to you', only acceptable for some speakers) minimally differs from the more general variety in that there the first and the second person clitics are licensed by different heads, with the second person head preceding the first person one.

(30) a. *[PerClP me PerCl [DatClP ~~me~~ le DatCl ...
     b. [PerClP me PerCl [DatClP ~~me~~ DatCl ...
     c. [PerClP PerCl [DatClP le DatC ...

With respect to the crash between 3rd person dative and 3rd person accusative in Spanish, notice that there are also independent similarities between the two types of pronoun that differentiate them from both personal pronouns and the reflexives. Uriagereka (1995) –see also Bleam (1999)– notice that both dative *le/les* and accusative *lo/la/los/las* contain the *l-* that marks definiteness in the Spanish article system (31). The morpheme *l-* can be treated as D, while *a/o* is the nominal class marker that is at least indirectly related to gender (Harris 1991). The exponent *-s* spells out plural number. Note that the four accusative clitics are identical to one of these articles.

(31) a. (e)l   m.sg
     b. l-a   f.sg   (cf. la)
     c. l-o-s m.pl   (cf. los)
     d. l-a-s f.pl   (cf. las)
     e. l-o   neuter (cf. lo)

While dative *le/les* also contains the determiner *l-*, it lacks gender features. Our proposal is that the presence of D explains the clash: the *l-* is common to both accusative and dative pronouns, so it is checked in the lower position. Accusatives stay there, while dative must further move to check the affectedness feature to DatClP.

(32) a. *[DatClP le DatCl [AccClP ~~le~~ lo AccCl ...
     b. [DatClP le DatCl [AccClP ~~le~~ AccCl ...
     c. [DatClP DatCl [AccClP lo AccCl ...

For this reason, there is no clash between a person pronoun and a third person accusative. The accusative is checked just in AccClP, while the person pronoun is checked at DatClP –for affectedness– and at PerClP –for person.

(33) [PerClP me PerCl [DatClP ~~me~~ DatCl [AccClP lo AccCl ...

With respect to **si si* in Italian the reason for the clash is less clear. Obviously, both clitics are formally third person reflexives. Both Schäfer (2008) and Koontz-Garboden (2009) have emphasised that reflexive pronouns, cross-linguistically, can be involved in the anticausativisation of verbs and in building impersonal constructions, which suggests that the relation between the two uses of *si* cannot be just purely formal. We can speculate that both *si* must undergo licensing by a low head even if then the non-impersonal one must enter into a licensing relation with a second head. Leaving this unclear aspect of the analysis aside –given that it would force us to discuss the whole range of uses of reflexives, something impossible in a few paragraphs–, the pattern is that ci substitutes one of the *si*. We follow Reisig Ferrazzano (2003) in the proposal that *ci* (and the second plural *vi*, used as a locative clitic in literary Italian) simply express deixis. When used as a locative, they are fully licensed in LocClP. When they express person, they must be assigned person by PerClP, at which point deixis is reinterpreted as the speaker/addressee contrast. (34a) shows the conflicting *si si* and (34b) its repair, which involves licensing the reflexive clitic's absence of reference by deixis. (34c) shows the *ci ci* conflict: even though one of them further moves to PerClP, both had to check deixis in the same position. (34d) shows one single 1pl *ci*, and (34e), one single locative *ci*.

(34) a. *[PerClP   PerCl [LocClP   LocCl [xP si si X ...
     b. [PerClP   PerCl [LocClP ci   LocCl [xP si   X ...
     c. *[PerClP ci   PerCl [LocClP e̶i̶ ci   LocCl [xP   X ...
     d. [PerClP ci   PerCl [LocClP e̶i̶   LocCl [xP   X ...
     e. [PerClP   PerCl [LocClP ci   LocCl [xP   X ...

There is an additional asymmetry between Italian and Spanish with respect to the total deletion of the clitic that cannot be licensed. Specifically, in Italian the deletion of the locative clitic does not trigger ungrammaticality, while in Spanish the deletion of the reflexive triggers it –remember the contrast between (4) and (5). We propose that this is related to the fact that Italian *ci* is deictic, while Spanish *se* is just an anaphor that must receive all its features from a linguistic antecedent. Deixis anchors the clitic to the wider context, which allows that its absence is recoverable by the utterance, while the reflexive pronoun in Spanish cannot be recovered in a context.

5 Non-agreeing objects as a syntactic reinterpretation of 'impoverishment'

Finally, how can the clitic that carries a number of features be licensed by a head that lacks those features? We assume here Preminger's (2014) proposal about agreement as an operation that has to take place when the objects are in the right configuration. Against a 'ticking-bomb' approach to agreement, where agreement is a property of an object that must be satisfied on the course of the derivation, Preminger argues for a view of agreement as the sign that a particular operation has been applied to an object. Nothing ungrammatical emerges, per se, of a situation where an object has failed to agree with another. Ungrammaticality is produced only when the two objects are in the configuration that allows agreement, and agreement is not performed. If the agreeing object is not in the right configuration with a probe, then default features will be assigned to the agreeing categories.

From this perspective, the impoverishment of the clitics in the course of the repair strategy follows naturally. Let us take the case of *le lo, focusing on what the dative clitics undergoes. The corresponding argument is a DP with a particular gender and number. If the argument is singular, the optimal result would be *le*. This would imply checking the D feature in AccClP, and then checking the number feature in DatClP. However, the accusative argument has already checked D with AccCl, which is manifested as *l-* on the surface of the clitic. This forces the clitic to go to ReflClP, where there are simply no features for D or number. At this point, the features of D and number will have to be filled with a default value. This is what triggers *se* on the surface: as we saw, *se* does not exhibit any contrasts, and itself carries the value of the non-person, the third person.

In other words: the result on the surface correctly suggests that a less specified pronoun is used in all cases, as the morphological account proposes. However, this follows naturally from the syntactic competition approach, because the unlicensed features will receive a default value when the clitic fails to agree with the appropriate head. There is no reason to resort to Distributed Morphology impoverishment to account for this property, then.

6 Conclusions

In this paper, we have proposed that the main empirical discoveries of the morphological treatment of ungrammatical clitic sequences and their repairs can be naturally restated in syntactic terms, and that a syntactic treatment has advantages both to explain the syntactic effects of those repairs and to capture the preference to repair the first clitic in the sequence in both Italian and Spanish.

We have argued that if the clitic sequence is seen as a syntactic hierarchy, following Kayne (2010), a few generalisations become apparent. First of all, the infractions affect clitics placed in adjacent heads. The repairs –ceteris paribus– apply to the leftmost clitic, and replace them with clitics that are hierarchically higher: this naturally follows from the standard view of movement as always targeting higher nodes, and Relativised Minimality (cf. Rizzi 1990). Secondly, we have argued that there are plausible syntactic reasons for the ungrammaticality of the sequences: the feature similarity noted in the morphological approach is translated as syntactic competition to have the similar features licensed by the same head –as only one specifier per projection is allowed, if two clitics have the feature [F] and there is a head H that licenses [F], introducing both clitics at once is ungrammatical. Finally, we have proposed that Preminger's (2014) view of agreement –where a default value is introduced for the features that failed to agree– naturally produces the effect that the resulting form of the clitic will be less specific –the features that could not be licensed in the projection occupied by another clitic are simply assigned a less specific value.

An anonymous reviewer points out that our proposal has direct connections to some observations made in the literature on language acquisition. Specifically, Wexler (1998) proposed the Unique Checking Constraint, which proposes that only one feature can be checked and realised at a time during acquisition. This is coherent with our proposal, to the extent that it suggests that at early stages the child is trying to determine the checking domain for each clitic by postulating a sequence of functional heads and trying to identify the property that is realised in each one of them. As Schmitz (2006) notes, French and Italian children avoid combinations of two clitics carrying case, something that is explained if at that early stage children have not postulated separate heads for accusative and dative case clitic realisation in their grammar. Although we have not explored these connections in this article, it opens an interesting avenue to connect the early acquisition grammars and the adult language.

There are of course many phenomena that have been treated by the morphological account, and we want to emphasise that this paper has dealt with a very small subset of the facts. This paper has tried to provide the reader with the general shape of how a syntactic account would work, and why it should be explored. Even if the proposal has dealt with just a few facts, we hope that the general shape is explicit enough to allow others to test it with other languages and phenomena. Moreover, we cannot exclude the possibility that some repairs are purely morphological: we have just shown that there are reasons to consider some of these syntactic, but other combinations might be excluded by other components, perhaps even phonology. In essence, we hope to have at least been able to convince the reader that the syntactic account is worth exploring.

Acknowledgement: We are grateful to the audience of the XXXV Romanistentag (Universität Zurich, October 2017), the editors of the volume and the anonymous reviewers for comments and suggestions to previous versions of this article. Fábregas' research has been partially financed by project FFI2017-87140-C4-1-P, Redes de variación microparamétricas en las lenguas románicas. Cabré's research is partially financed by project FFI2016-76245-C3-1-P, Dominios prosódicos y morfosintácticos: análisis de los fenómenos morfofonológicos en las interfaces. All disclaimers apply.

7 References

Adger, David & Daniel Harbour. 2007. Syntax and syncretisms of the Person Case Constraint. *Syntax* 10(1). 2–37.
Alcaraz, Alejo. 2017. *Spurious vs. dative*. Bilbao: Universidad del País Vasco.
Anagnostopoulou, Elena. 2003. *The syntax of ditransitives. Evidence from clitics*. Berlin: De Gruyter.
Benincà, Paola & Christina Tortora. 2009. Towards a finer-grained theory of Italian participial clausal architecture. *University of Pennsylvania Working Papers in Linguistics* 15. 17–26.
Benveniste, Émile. 1966. *Problèmes de linguistique générale*. Paris: Gallimard.
Bleam, Tonia. 1999. *Leísta Spanish and the syntax of clitic doubling*. Ph.D. dissertation. Delaware: University of Delaware.
Bonet, Eulàlia. 1991. *Morphology after syntax*. Ph.D. dissertation. Cambridge (MA): MIT Press.
Bonet, Eulàlia. 1993. 3rd person pronominal clitics in dialects of Catalan. *Catalan Working Papers in Linguistics* 3(1). 85–111.
Bonet, Eulàlia. 1995. Feature structure of Romance clitics. *Natural Language and Linguistic Theory* 13. 607–647.
Cabré, Teresa & Antonio Fábregas. 2019. 3rd person clitic combinations across Catalan varieties: Consequences of the nature of the dative clitic. *The Linguistic Review* 36. 151–190.
Cardinaletti, Anna. 2008. On different types of clitic clusters. In Cécile De Cat & Katherine Demuth (eds.), *The Bantu-Romance connection*, 41–82. Amsterdam: Benjamins.

Grimshaw, Jane. 1997. The best clitic: constraint interaction in morphosyntax. In Liliane Haegeman (ed.), *Elements of grammar*, 169–196. Dordrecht: Kluwer.
Halle, Morris & James W. Harris. 2005. Unexpected plural inflections in Spanish: reduplication and metathesis. *Linguistic Inquiry* 36. 195–222.
Halle, Morris & Alec Marantz. 1993. Distributed Morphology and the pieces of inflection. In Kenneth Hale & Samuel J. Keyser (eds.), *The view from building* 20, 111–176. Cambridge (MA): MIT Press.
Harris, James W. 1991. The exponence of gender in Spanish. *Linguistic Inquiry* 22. 27–62.
Kayne, Richard S. 1994. *The antisymmetry of syntax*. Cambridge (MA): MIT Press.
Kayne, Richard S. 2010. Toward a syntactic reinterpretation of Harris & Halle 2005. In Brigitte Kampers-Manhe, Reineke Bok-Bennema & Bart Hollebrandse (eds.), *Romance Languages and Linguistic Theory* 2008, 145–170. Amsterdam: Benjamins.
Koontz-Garboden, Andrew. 2009. Anticausativization. *Natural Language and Linguistic Theory* 27. 77–138.
Manzini, Rita & Leonardo M. Savoia. 2002. Clitics: lexicalization patterns of the so-called 3rd person dative. *Catalan Journal of Linguistics* 1. 117–155.
Manzini, Rita & Leonardo M. Savoia. 2004. Clitics: cooccurrence and mutual exclusion patterns. In Luigi Rizzi (ed.), *The structure of CP and IP*, 211–250. Oxford: Oxford University Press.
Manzini, Rita & Leonardo M. Savoia. 2005. *I dialetti italiani e romanci*. Alessandria: dell'Orso.
Nevins, Andrew. 2012. Haplological dissimilation at distinct stages of exponence. In Jochen Trommer (ed.), *The morphology and phonology of exponence*, 84–116. Oxford: Oxford University Press.
Ormazábal, Javier & Juan Romero. 2007. The object agreement constraint. *Natural Language and Linguistic Theory* 25. 315–347.
Perlmutter, David. 1971. *Deep and surface structure constraints in syntax*. Holt: Reinhart and Winston.
Pescarini, Diego. 2007. Types of syncretism in the clitic systems of Romance. *Anuario del Seminario de filología vasca Julio de Urquijo* 41. 285–300.
Pescarini, Diego. 2010. Elsewhere in Romance: evidence from clitic clusters. *Linguistic Inquiry* 41. 427–444.
Pescarini, Diego. 2011. Mapping Romance clitic pronouns. *Quaderni di lavoro ASIt* 12. 1–30.
Preminger, Omer. 2014. *Agreement and its failures*. Cambridge, MA: MIT Press.
Reisig Ferrazzano, Lisa. 2003. The morphology of ci and its 'distal' relative vi. Unpublished manuscript, CUNY Graduate Center.
Reuland, Eric. 2011. *Anaphora and language design*. Cambridge, MA: MIT Press.
Rivero, María Luisa. 2008. Oblique subjects and person restrictions in Spanish. In Susa Fischer, Roberta D'Alessandro & Gunnar Hrafnbjargason (eds.), *Agreement restrictions*, 215–250. Berlin: De Gruyter.
Rizzi, Luigi. 1990. *Relativized minimality*. Cambridge, MA: MIT Press.
Romero, Juan. 2012. Accusative datives in Spanish. In Beatriz Fernández & Ricardo Etxepare (eds.), *Variation in datives: a microcomparative perspective*, 283–300. Oxford: Oxford University Press.
Schäfer, Florian. 2008. *The syntax of (anti-)causatives*. Amsterdam: Benjamins.
Schmitz, Katrin. 2006. *Zweisprachigkeit im Fokus. Der Erwerb der Verben mit zwei Objekten durch bilingual deutsch-französisch und deutsch-italienisch aufwachsende Kinder*. Tübingen: Narr.

Sportiche, Dominique. 1996. Clitic constructions. In Laura Zaring & Johan Rooryck (eds.), *Phrase structure and the lexicon*, 213–276. Dordrecht: Kluwer.
Torrego, Esther. 1995. From argumental to non-argumental pronouns: Spanish doubled reflexives. *Probus* 7. 221–241.
Uriagereka, Juan. 1995. Aspects of the syntax of clitic placement in Western Romance. *Linguistic Inquiry* 26. 79–123.
Walcow, Martin. 2011. Person effects and the representation of third person. An argument from Barceloní Catalan. In Janine Berns, Haike Jacobs & Tobias Scheer (eds.), *Romance Languages and Linguistic Theory* 2009, 343–361. Amsterdam: Benjamins.
Wanner, Dieter. 1977. On the order of clitics in Italian. *Lingua* 43. 101–128.
Wexler, Kenneth. 1998. Very early parameter setting and the Unique Checking Constraint: a new explanation of the optional infinitive stage. *Lingua* 106. 23–79.
Wiltschko, Martina. 2014. *The universal structure of categories*. Cambridge: Cambridge University Press.

Michael Zimmermann
Investigating the setting of the null-subject parameter in Early Classical French

Insights from diaries

Abstract: French from the first half of the 17th c. is commonly considered a non-null-subject language. Yet, subject pronoun omission in formal writing as well as metalinguistic comments on its appropriateness raise the issue of a general availability of null subjects in this stage. The paper addresses this issue by drawing on the written register of the diary, known to allow for a distributionally restricted omission of subject pronouns in prototypical non-null-subject languages. On the basis of a specifically designed corpus of Early Classical French diary writing, the paper essentially uncovers that omitted subject pronouns are governed by the very same distributional restrictions. From this and further insights the paper concludes that, in the first half of the 17th c., French was indeed a non-null-subject language. Also, it is established on principled grounds that the omission of subject pronouns in formal writing from this period, along with corresponding metalinguistic comments, relate to an archaizing style mimicking in particular earlier authors' use of genuine null subjects.

Keywords: subject pronoun, subject omission, null subject, null-subject parameter, diary, French

1 Introduction

In the realm of morpho-syntax, Modern French stands out among the major Romance languages due to the regular occurrence of (prosodically weak) subject pronouns in finite clauses, especially those otherwise lacking an overt, i.e. phonologically realized, subject. On the view widely held ever since Kayne (1975)

Michael Zimmermann: University of Konstanz, Fachbereich Linguistik, Fach 189, 78457 Konstanz, Germany, dr.michael.zimmermann@gmx.de

https://doi.org/10.1515/9783110719154-005

that, at least in the standard, formal variety, these pronouns constitute arguments occupying the canonical subject position, SpecTP, Modern (Standard) French is generally analyzed as a non-null-subject language.[1]

It is commonly assumed that the regular occurrence of subject pronouns in French dates back to the close of the 16th c. (e.g. Meyer-Lübke 1899; Adams 1987; Roberts 1993; de Bakker 1997; Marchello-Nizia 2000), ordinarily considered the very end of the medieval period. In the latter, subject pronouns could be null, i.e. phonologically unrealized, whence the usual analysis of Medieval French as a null-subject language (e.g. Vanelli, Renzi & Benincà 1985; Adams 1987; Roberts 1993; Vance 1997; Mathieu 2006).[2]

The common assumption that, in French, subject pronouns occur regularly from the close of the 16th c. onwards seems underpinned by various works from grammarians as well as critics of language use from the first half of the 17th c. In these, subject pronouns constantly show up in conjugation tables and/or their consistent use is insisted on in metalinguistic comments (e.g. Deimier 1610; Serrier 1623; Oudin 1632; Vaugelas 1647).

Yet, as noted in numerous philological and linguistic studies (e.g. Regnier 1869; List 1881; Haase 1888; Fournier 1998; Spillebout 2007), formal writing from in particular the first half of the 17th c. manifests the omission of subject pronouns in syntactic contexts in which their use is mandatory in the contemporary language.[3] In effect, subject pronouns of any person and number are omitted in Early Classical French formal writing, as exemplified in (1) for first, second, and third person plural subject pronouns.

---

[1] Cf. Zimmermann (2016) for extensive discussion of alternative analyses of prosodically weak subject pronouns in Modern Standard French and, concomitantly, this variety as a null-subject language. Arguing likewise for an alternative analysis of the pronouns at issue, many researchers hold the view that Modern Colloquial French, the present-day informal variety, constitutes a null-subject language (e.g. Roberge 1986; Zribi-Hertz 1994; Auger 1995; Culbertson 2010; Palasis 2015), while others adhere to an analysis along the lines of that generally adopted regarding the standard variety (Meisenburg 2000; De Cat 2005; Zimmermann & Kaiser 2014).

[2] For an alternative analysis of Medieval French, cf. e.g. Zimmermann (2014, 2018); Balon & Larrivée (2016).

[3] This paper focuses on subject pronoun omission other than that encountered in the modern language in the form of residual structures and fixed expressions, on which cf. Zimmermann (2014, 2018); Zimmermann & Kaiser (2014) for extensive discussion.

(1) a. Et **iouyrons** d' un âge ourdy d' or
and enjoy.FUT.1PL part a age covered of gold
'And we will enjoy a golden age' (Racan, *Chanson de bergers* [1630] (Brunot 1891: 383))
b. ce que **fçavez** il y a long-temps
this which know.PRS.2PL it there have.PRS.3SG long.time
'what you have known for a long time' (Guez de Balzac, *Lettre à M. L'Evesque d'Ayre* [1622] (Haase 1888: 10))
c. Non **feront**, Philothee
no make.FUT.3PL Philothee
'They will not, Philothee' (F. de Sales, *Introduction à la vie dévote* [1609] (Fournier 1998: 21))

Several Early Classical French grammars likewise evince subject pronoun omission, either without further ado or as part of a metalinguistic comment, in which appropriate syntactic contexts are designated. A prime example for both cases is Maupas' (1618) comment in (2).

(2) Rarement **advient** que nous obmettions ces
rarely happen.PRS.3SG that we omit.PRS.SBJV.1PL these
pronoms nominatifs [...]. Exceptez és refponfes concefsives [...]
pronouns nominative except the responses concessive
Non **fay**, *Si* **faites**. [...] Item [...] quand la
no make.PRS.1SG yes make.PRS.2PL also when the
conjonction & *et fi*, conjoingnent quelque appendice [...]
conjunction and and thus conjoin.PRS.3PL some appendix
Vous m' avez bien confeillé, & vous
you.PL me have.PRS.2PL well advise.PST.PTCP and you.PL
croiray *une autre fois.* [...] les premiere & feconde
believe.FUT.1SG a other time the first and second
perfonnes plurieres aufsi en fuite de propos, & apres les
person plural also in continuation of words and after the
conjonctions & , *Auffi, Que, Auffique.*[...] *Vous voyez qu'*
conjunctions and also that as.if you.PL see.PRS.2PL that
avons *foin de vous*
have.PRS.1PL care of you.PL
'It rarely happens that we omit these nominative pronouns. Except in concessive responses: *Non fay* 'I shall not do so', *Si faites* 'You shall do so'. Likewise, when the conjunctions & 'and', *et fi* 'and thus' conjoin

some appendix: *Vous m'avez bien conſeillé, & vous croiray une autre fois* 'You gave me good advice, and I will believe you another time'. The first and second person plural subject pronouns also when following an utterance as well as after the conjunctions *et* 'and', *auſſi* 'also', *que* 'that', *auſſique* 'as if': *Vous voyez qu'avons ſoin de vous* 'You see that we take care of you'.' (Maupas 1618: 63, *Grammaire et syntaxe françoise*)

The crucial issue that arises in view of such an apparently conflicting state of affairs is whether Early Classical French constituted a non-null-subject language, as is commonly assumed, or rather a null-subject language. Depending on the analysis adopted, omitted subject pronouns in formal writing from this period would represent either archaisms, as has been generally claimed (e.g. Darmesteter 1897; Fournier 1998; Spillebout 2007; Grevisse & Goosse 2011; Marchello-Nizia 2018), or instances of genuine null subjects.

The paper investigates this issue by essentially drawing on morpho-syntactic insights from diary writing. As a preliminary, a set of criteria is established that relate to the distribution of omitted subject pronouns in such writing and are deemed to allow determining in a straightforward manner the setting of the null-subject parameter in any language (stage) with a diary register (Section 2). Subsequently, the paper expounds on the compilation of a corpus of French diary writing from the first half of the 17th c. (Section 3). This corpus is then inquired in accordance with the previously established set of criteria. It is hereby uncovered that subject pronoun omission in the diary register in Early Classical French is governed by the same distributional restrictions as that in the diary register in prototypical non-null-subject languages. This crucial finding is taken as reflective of the former's status as a non-null-subject language (Section 4). From this as well as other insights the paper eventually concludes that omitted subject pronouns in formal writing from the first half of the 17th c. result from the occasional employment by writers from this period of an archaizing style mimicking in particular earlier authors' use of null subjects (Section 5).

2 Unequivocal criteria for the determination of the setting of the null-subject parameter

The issue of whether the null-subject property held in Early Classical French is anything but trivial. It has generally been claimed that the omission of subject pronouns in formal writing from the first half of the 17th c. follows from the mimicry of a morpho-syntactic possibility whose availability in the language had recently been lost. Yet, it is far from clear whether such omission relates exclusively to the realm of stylistics. In effect, pertinent observations do not represent unequivocal evidence for this general claim.

It has been repeatedly argued that subject pronouns are omitted less frequently in particularly literary writing from the period under investigation than in pre-17th c. literary writing. This claim, however, is based on personal impression, rather than sound evidence, as empirically based analyses of Early Classical French literary writing are virtually lacking.[4]

As noted in Section 1, numerous grammars from the first half of the 17th c. constantly display subject pronouns in conjugation tables and occasionally underscore their mandatory use. Still, as likewise noted, various Early Classical French grammars evince subject pronoun omission and/or indicate syntactic contexts in which such omission is deemed possible.

Several of these contexts are reprimanded and dismissed as "antiquailles [...] ne [...] plus en vſage"[5] (Chiflet 1659: 40) in grammars as well as critical works on language use from the middle and, essentially, the second half of the 17th c. The following comment by Vaugelas (1647: 420-422) proves to be particularly enlightening in this regard:

> pluſieurs abuſent de cette ſuppreſſion, ſur tout ceux qui ont eſcrit il y a vingt ou vingt-cinq ans; car en ce temps là, [...] c'eſtoit vn vice aſſez familier à nos Eſcriuains [...] [qui] tenoi[en]t encore de l'ancien ſtile cette façon d'eſcrire ; car les anciens ſupprimoient ſouuent ce pronom, & les modernes qui ont voulu ſe former ſur vn modelle ſi eſtimé, l'ont ſuiuy meſme aux choses, qui n'eſtoient plus en vſage.[6]

---

4 There are two notable exceptions that actually corroborate the claim at issue, viz. Zimmermann (2014) and Marchello-Nizia (2018), who report a rate of subject pronoun omission of around 1% and 3% in extracts from, respectively, Sorel's *Histoire comique de Francion* (1623) and Descartes' *Discours de la méthode* (1637).
5 My English translation reads: "antiquated language no longer in use."
6 My English translation reads: "several [authors] overindulge in this [= the subject pronoun's] suppression, above all those who have written twenty or twenty-five years ago; for back at that

Already in 1610, the poet Deimier (1610: 447) considers the omission of subject pronouns in one of the syntactic contexts endorsed by e.g. Maupas (1618) (cf. (2) in Section 1) an infraction of common speech, whence his advise to consistently use them in poetry:

> quand on parle communement , on ne dit iamais , *puisqu'il vous plaiſt Monſieur, & qu'auez tant d'affection* [...] ſi l'on obferue cefte reigle au commun langage , à plus forte raifon la doit on employer aux vers [...].[7]

Yet, caution seems to be in order, if one wants to conclude from such remarks that subject pronouns were regularly employed in the French spoken in the first half of the 17th c. A case in point is the expletive subject pronoun *il*. In effect, its occasional omission in writing from various grammarians and critics of language use from the period under investigation strongly conflicts with firm metalinguistic comments and illustrations elsewhere in their writing. This state of affairs seems to be indicative of the involvement of grammar in subject pronoun omission in this period.

Maupas' grammatical treatise is a prime example in this regard. In this work, Maupas (1618: 124r) explicitly notes that "la [...] nature d'imperfonnels, eft de voix active, au moyen de cette particule *il*"[8]. For illustrative purposes, Maupas (1618: 124v) has this note directly followed by an extensive list of impersonal verbs in the present tense indicative that are all appended by the expletive subject pronoun *il*, among which *il advient* 'it happens'. In stark contrast to this, however, he omits this pronoun with *advient* in the introductory clause of his comment on the possibility of subject pronoun omission (cf. (2) in Section 1), in which he moreover fails to address the particular syntactic context in which *il* is omitted.

A similarly instructive case comes from the French poet Malherbe. In his commentaries on Desportes' poetry, Malherbe constantly rebukes the omission of expletive *il*. From this one is inclined to conclude, along with e.g. Le Bidois & Le

---

time, it was a vice quite familiar to our writers, who still adopted from the old style this manner of writing; for the elders often suppressed this pronoun, and the modern writers who wanted to adapt themselves to a model which is so much estimated copied even those things which were no longer used."

7 My English translation reads: "when one commonly speaks, one never says *puisqu'il vous plaiſt Monſieur, & qu'auez tant d'affection* 'since it pleases you, Sir, and since you show so much affection'; if one follows this rule in common speech, one must all the more adhere to it in poetry."

8 My English translation reads: "the nature of the impersonals is in the active voice formed by means of the particle *il*."

Bidois (1935: 179), that "à partir de Malherbe [...] la présence de *il* fut de règle"[9]. Still, such a conclusion is unwarranted, since, in his own literary writing, Malherbe frequently omitted the expletive (e.g. Regnier 1869; Holfeld 1875; Haase 1888; Brunot 1891; Spillebout 2007). Evidently, this starkly contradicts his rebukes of its omission in Desportes' poetry.

Despite a number of observations that, to some extent, suggest an analysis in terms of a non-null-subject language, then, the issue of the actual setting of the null-subject parameter in Early Classical French is not yet settled, awaiting further investigation.

In this regard, an approach along the following lines might be envisaged: (i) compilation of a corpus of literary writing from the first half of the 17th c.; (ii) detection of the syntactic contexts allowing for subject pronoun omission; (iii) comparison of such contexts with those established from pre-17th c. literary writing. Though appealing on the face of it, this endeavor would presumably prove futile, as there is a fair probability that the syntactic contexts from the two periods to be investigated converge. In effect, if it were indeed the case that Early Classical French was a null-subject language, the structural conditions on null subjects would naturally be expected not to significantly differ from those in Medieval French, but rather to coincide largely, if not entirely. If, on the other hand, it were the case that Early Classical French constituted a non-null-subject language, the natural expectation would be that authors from the first half of the 17th c. did not fail to minutely mimic a morpho-syntactic possibility which had been available in the language until recently and which such authors were most likely well acquainted with. By adopting an approach along the lines under discussion, then, one would in all probability be none the wiser.

In an attempt to look more closely into the issue of the setting of the null-subject parameter in Early Classical French, I shall establish a number of morpho-syntactic criteria bearing on a specific written register that allow deciding on this issue in a straightforward manner. In this respect, I shall draw on fundamental insights from Haegeman (1990a,b, 1997, 2000, 2007, 2013, 2017) on subject pronoun omission in diary writing in particular and abbreviated writing in general.[10]

---

[9] My English translation reads: "since Malherbe, the presence of *il* was standard practice."

[10] Aside from diaries, abbreviated writing comprises, albeit less typically so according to Haegeman, postcards, letters, emails, point-form notes, notices on commercial packaging, list type summaries, encyclopedia type entries, stage directions as well as mobile phone text messages. At least as far as French is concerned, subject pronoun omission is furthermore encountered in the following types of abbreviated writing: telegrams, descriptions, and administration reports (Plattner 1907; Sandfeld 1928; Steinmeyer 1979; Togeby 1982; Grevisse & Goosse 2011) as well as newspaper headlines (e.g. *Sarkozy et les enseignants : coupera, coupera pas ?* 'Sarkozy and the

In numerous work, Haegeman has uncovered that, in the two non-null-subject languages considered prototypical in generative theorizing, Modern English and Modern (Standard) French, subject pronouns of any person and number, including expletives, can be omitted in the diary register.[11] Fundamentally, though, such omission is grammatically governed, in that it is not generally possible, unlike in prototypical null-subject languages such as Spanish. In effect, the omission of subject pronouns in the register of the diary in Modern English and Modern (Standard) French is distributionally restricted:[12] while possible in some syntactic contexts, it is, essentially, impossible in others.[13] Specifically, omitted

---

teachers: Will he cut down or won't he cut down?' (http://www.liberation.fr/france/2014/10/16/sarkozy-et-les-enseignants-coupera-coupera-pas_1122930)), advertisements relating to housing and employment (e.g. *Recherchons un barman ou une barmaid* (https://www.cornerjob.com/fr/i/recherchons-barman-une-barmaid-pour-notre-nouvelle-enseigne-personne-disponible-wVrd-Ftu1r6/), and information displays in public transport (e.g. *Ne prend pas de voyageurs* 'It does not admit any passengers' (https://farm5.static.flickr.com/4169/34422187446_9bf73c6202_b.jpg)). Cf. Stark (2013), Stark & Robert-Tissot (2017), Robert-Tissot (2020) as well as Stark & Meier (2017) for extensive discussion on subject pronoun omission in, respectively, mobile phone and WhatsApp text messages in Swiss French.

11 Note that, in this register, omission is typically encountered with first and third person subject pronouns. Rather than from principled morpho-syntactic reasons, the general absence of omitted second person subject pronouns is arguably "due to the non-interactive nature of diary-writing" (Haegeman 2000: 133) and, thus, the usual lack of second person subjects in such writing.

12 The omission of the referential set of subject pronouns is moreover pragmatically governed, as Haegeman (1990b: 165f.) underscores: "[T]he omission of the [referential] subject in the register discussed is dependent on a general contextual condition of interpretation. The referent of the understood subject must be 'accessible' in the context in which the utterance is processed. The first person subject interpretation is readily available in this register: the global topic of the diary is the writer. Similarly, first person plural subjects will be closely associated with the writer, hence accessible. Third person subjects will only be non-overt when their referent has explicitly been referred to in the preceding context and can be unambiguously identified. [...] The accessibility of the referent is [...] a matter of pragmatics: the interpretation of the sentence in a context." Note, incidentally, in this regard that pragmatically governed subject pronoun omission is a hallmark of "[a] good number of languages which are otherwise typologically and genetically distinct (Chinese, Japanese, Korean, Thai, Vietnamese and others)" (Robert & Holmberg 2010).

13 In view of these distributional restrictions, Haegeman vehemently rejects an analysis of such elements in terms of null subjects, i.e. *pro*. Cf. Haegeman (1990a,b, 1997, 2000, 2007, 2013, 2017) for various alternative analyses. Whatever their eventual analysis, it is crucial to note in this regard that these elements are represented at the level of syntax. This fundamental insight is evinced by their syntactic interaction with other sentential elements in the form of e.g. person and number agreement of the finite verb, gender and number agreement of past participles, and

subject pronouns in diary writing in non-null-subject languages such as Modern (Standard) French are, according to Haegeman, not possible in any of the following syntactic contexts: (i) all types of finite subordinate clauses (3a); (ii) finite declarative root clauses with a fronted argument (3b); (iii) finite interrogative root clauses with a fronted *wh*-expression, be it argumental or not (3c); (iv) finite *yes/no*-interrogative root clauses involving subject-verb-inversion (3d); (v) finite exclamative root clauses with a fronted *wh*-expression (3e).

(3) a. *Il$_i$ voyait   Jean$_j$ quand   Ø$_{i/j/k}$ quittait   la   fête.
       he   see.IPFV.3SG   John   when   leave.IPFV.3SG   the   party
       'He was seeing John, when he/she was leaving the party.'
       (adapted from Haegeman 1990a: 169)
    b. *[Ce   livre]$_i$,   Ø   l$_i$'   aime.
       this   book   it   like.PRS.3SG
       'This book he/she likes.'
       (adapted from Haegeman 1990a: 169)
    c. *Quand Ø   me   reverra   Ø ?[14]
       when   me   see.FUT.3SG
       'When will he/she see me again?'
       (adapted from Haegeman 1990a: 169)
    d. *Me   reverra   Ø ?
       me   see.FUT.3SG
       'Will he/she see me again?'
       (adapted from Haegeman 1990a: 169)

---

the binding of reflexives, as (i) illustrates. Here, as in other examples in the paper, 'Ø' is employed for and indicates the position of an omitted subject pronoun. Note, essentially, with regard to the latter that its determination in the modern diary register is straightforward, as it coincides with the position in which an overt subject pronoun occurs.

(i) Jamais   Ø^i_i ne   s$_i$'   serait^i attendue^i à   cela.
     never   not   REFL   be.COND.3SG   wait.PST.PTCP.F.SG   to   this
     'Never would she have expected this.'
     (Léautaud, *Journal particulier* (adapted from Haegeman 2013: 91))

14 The double employment of 'Ø' in (3c) takes account of Haegeman's (2000: 162, n. 15) appraisal that, while overt subject pronouns can appear in both pre- and postverbal position in finite interrogative root clauses with a fronted *wh*-expression, omitted subject pronouns are not possible in either position in this type of clause.

e. *Quelle belle surprise Ø avait pour nous !
   which nice surprise   have.IPFV.3SG for us
   'What a nice surprise he/she had for us!'
   (adapted from Haegeman 2000: 140)

Fundamentally, I shall consider these contexts crucial for the determination of the setting of the null-subject parameter in Early Classical French – and, by extension, any language (stage) with a diary register. Following pertinent implications by Haegeman, I shall in fact regard the possibility of subject pronoun omission in the five syntactic contexts in diary writing of a given language (stage) inextricably linked with the setting of the null-subject parameter in this language (stage). Particularly, I shall assume that a language (stage) whose diary writing allows omitted subject pronouns in the syntactic contexts in (3) constitutes/constituted a null-subject language, while a language (stage) in whose diary register the omission of subject pronouns is impossible in such contexts represents/represented a non-null-subject language.

Having thus put forth a set of criteria to determine in a straightforward manner the setting of the null-subject parameter in a given language (stage) with a diary register, I shall next turn to the compilation of a corpus of Early Classical French diary writing. The following section will lay out the pertinent details of the established corpus, which is to provide the basis for the subsequent inquiry into the issue of the possibility of subject pronoun omission in any of the syntactic contexts given in (3) above.

3 A corpus of Early Classical French diary writing

To determine the setting of the null-subject parameter in the French language from the first half of the 17th c. based on the set of morpho-syntactic criteria just expounded, a corpus consisting of diary writing from this period by native speakers of French needs to be set up. What is essential in this regard is that only diaries from writers with relatively little education be taken into consideration. The reason behind this is the endeavor to minimize the likelihood of diary writers' acquaintance with stylistics in general and the employment of an archaizing style in particular that, among other things, possibly mimicked earlier authors' use of null subjects.

As it happens, an edited volume of autobiographic writing has recently been published that comes in particularly useful: Ernst & Wolf's (2005) *Textes français privés des XVIIe et XVIIIe siècles*. This volume, which faithfully transcribes the manuscripts in the relevant respects, is a compilation of "private texts from less educated persons of the 17th and 18th century"[15] (Ernst & Wolf 2005: 1) who "n'avaient pas d'ambitions littéraires"[16] (Ernst & Wolf 2005: 5). Among these texts, the four listed in Table 1 prove of special interest, in that they constitute diaries written in the first half of the 17th c. (as well as beyond) by native speakers of French "d'une condition sociale plutôt basse et d'une formation scolaire peu profonde"[17] (Ernst and Wolf 2005: 1588).

Tab. 1: Particulars on relevant writings from Ernst & Wolf's (2005) *Textes français privés des XVIIe et XVIIIe siècles*[18]

title	time period	information on (major) writer(s)				
		last name	year of birth	origin/residence	sex	occupation
Journal	1607–1662	Valuche	1597	Candé (west)	male	unknown (lower middle class)
Journal	1610–1624	Durand	unknown	Lons-le-Saunier/ Poligny (east)	male	modest country doctor
Journal	1610–1644	Le Trividic	unknown	Guingamp (north-west)	male	legal and/or administrative profession
Mémoires/ Journal	1611–1780	Goyard	unknown	Bert-en-Bourbonnais (center)	male	farmer, *procureur d'office*

Meeting all of the above-mentioned requirements, (parts of) these four writings, neither of which had in fact been destined for a large readership (Ernst & Wolf 2005: 1128; 1424; 1587), have been selected as a textual basis for subsequent morpho-syntactic analysis. The Durand and the Le Trividic diaries, both written in the first half of the 17th c., have been selected in their entirety. The Durand diary encompasses a total of 113 manuscript pages, authored by Guillaume Durand

---

15 My translation. The original reads: "private[...] Texte[...] wenig gebildeter Personen des 17. und 18. Jahrhunderts."
16 My English translation reads: "did not have literary ambitions."
17 My English translation reads: "with a fairly low social rank and little education."
18 Apart from that provided in Table (1), no further information on the writers is available (cf. Ernst & Wolf 2005: 1126; 1424; 1523; 1587–1588).

with the exception of the last nine pages, which were composed by his son Lionel Durand. The Le Trividic diary, as given by Ernst & Wolf (2005),[19] amounts to a total of 100 manuscript pages, all written by Yves Le Trividic. Regarding the Valuche and the Goyard diaries, which exceed the period under investigation, only the parts that predate 1650 have been taken into account. The one from the Valuche diary comprises 132 manuscript pages, which were composed by Jacques Valuche, except for the last seven pages, "écrites par [...] un membre de la famille, peut-être l'un des fils de Valuche"[20] (Ernst & Wolf 2005: 1127). The pertinent part from the Goyard diary encompasses 63 manuscript pages, of which all but two were authored by Blaise Goyard and the remaining ones by his son Philibert Goyard.

Having presented the particulars on the compilation of a corpus of Early Classical French diary writing comprising altogether 408 manuscript pages, I shall proceed with its analysis, in particular the inquiry into the syntactic contexts (dis-)allowing subject pronoun omission.

4 The distribution of omitted subject pronouns in Early Classical French diary writing

The approach to be presently adopted to determine the setting of the null-subject parameter in Early Classical French consists in exploring the syntactic contexts of subject pronoun omission in contemporaneous diary writing. Of particular relevance in this regard is the exploration of convergence of (a subset of) these contexts with those identified by Haegeman as strictly excluding such omission in the diary register in non-null-subject languages. Should convergence obtain, Early Classical French would be considered a null-subject language. In the case of consistent non-convergence, it would on the contrary be taken as a non-null-subject language.

To determine the syntactic contexts of subject pronoun omission as well as to assess impressionistically the extent of such omission, all instances of a finite

---

19 For principled reasons, Ernst & Wolf's (2005) volume disregards a number of manuscript pages from the Le Trividic diary, viz. those solely containing a register of births and deaths, which often lack names and dates.
20 My English translation reads: "written by a member of the family, conceivably one of Valuche's sons."

clause with either an omitted subject pronoun of the relevant sort or an overt subject pronoun were extracted from the established corpus. They were subsequently manually analyzed using Microsoft Excel.

As shown in Figure 1, subject pronouns are omitted to varying degrees in the four diaries selected. Typically, subject pronoun omission is found in finite declarative root clauses without a fronted argument (483/507 or 95.3% of all pertinent instances).

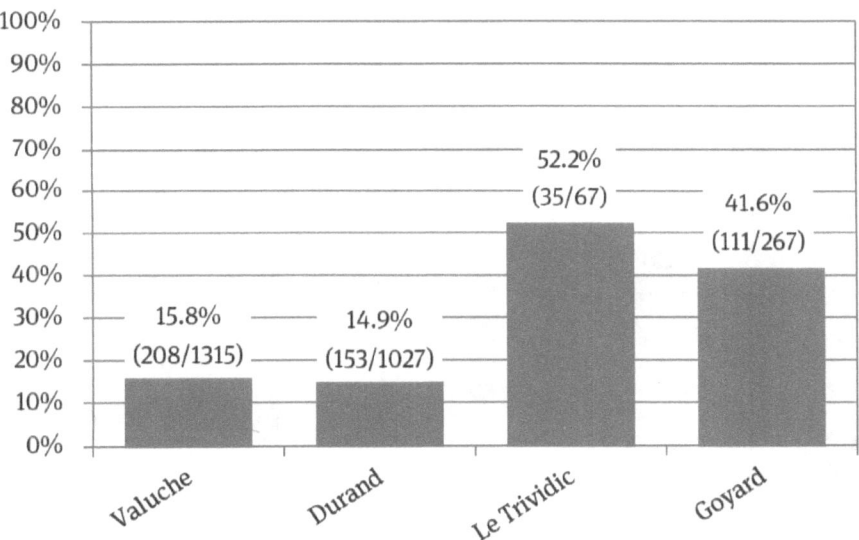

Fig. 1: Frequency as well as total number of instances of a finite clause with an omitted subject pronoun

Regarding the five syntactic contexts considered crucial in the determination of the setting of the null-subject parameter, only one proves to abound: finite subordinate clauses. While finite exclamative root clauses with a fronted wh-expression are absent, finite interrogative root clauses with a fronted wh-expression as well as finite yes/no-interrogative root clauses involving subject-verb-inversion are each encountered once and finite declarative root clauses with a fronted argument are detected five times.

All instances of the latter three syntactic contexts display an overt subject pronoun. This finding is reflective of what obtains in non-null-subject languages such as Modern (Standard) French and, thus, suggestive of the analysis of Early Classical French as a non-null-subject language.

Proceeding with the single abundantly occurring and, therefore, empirically most sound syntactic context, Figure 2 shows that, in finite subordinate clauses, subject pronoun omission is encountered in three of the four diaries selected.[21]

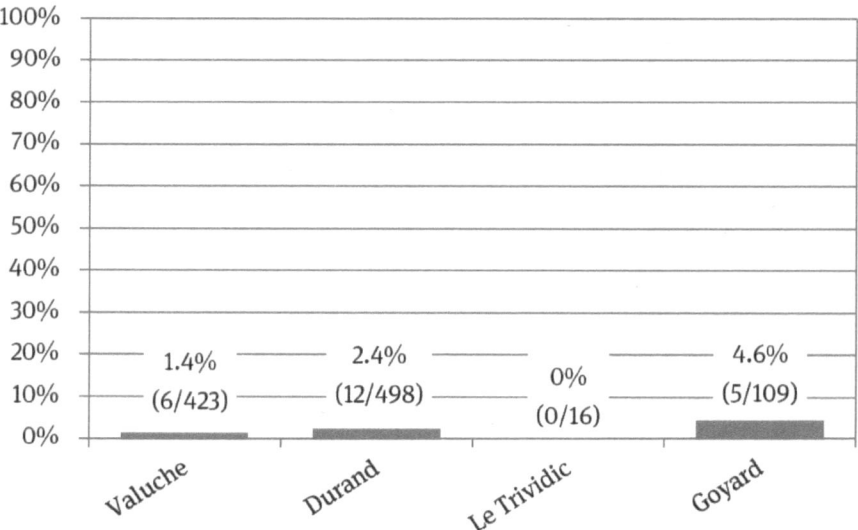

Fig. 2: Frequency as well as total number of instances of a finite subordinate clause with an omitted subject pronoun

From this state of affairs one is inclined to conclude that, contrary to what the finding from root clauses, based on a small number of relevant instances only, has suggested, Early Classical French was a null-subject language. As the following discussion will, however, demonstrate, such a conclusion is misguided.

Note, first of all, that, in the Le Trividic diary, all instances of a finite subordinate clause have an overt subject pronoun, as established for Modern (Stand-

---

21 Possibly, the divergence in the rates of subject pronoun omission in the four diaries selected follows from differences relating to individual style and/or level of education (of which almost nothing is known, cf. footnote 18). Corroboration for this surmise comes from the findings, expounded farther on, that all established instances of subject pronoun omission essentially involve the recourse to either conventionalized structures or an archaizing style pertaining to non-abbreviated written registers.

ard) French, a non-null-subject language. Abstracting away from the small number of these instances, one is thus led to assume that, in the language of its writer, the null-subject property did not hold.

More crucially, a comparison of the rates of subject pronoun omission in finite subordinate clauses (cf. Figure 2) with those in declarative root clauses without a fronted argument, given in Figure 3, reveals that such omission represents an altogether scarce phenomenon in the former clauses (0% to 4.6%), unlike in the latter ones (22.6% to 67.1%).

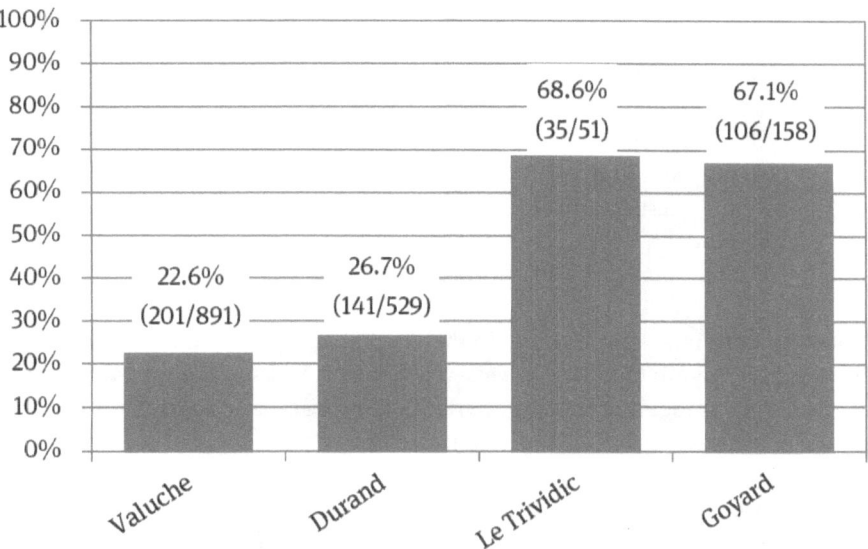

Fig. 3: Frequency as well as total number of instances of a finite declarative root clause lacking a fronted argument with an omitted subject pronoun

Fundamentally, when looked at closely, instances of a finite subordinate clause with an omitted subject pronoun prove to be even scarcer (cf. Figure 4). Specifically, in two out of the three relevant diaries, several such instances coincide with (at times slightly modified versions of) fixed expressions in the contemporary language and must therefore be left out of consideration:[22] four instances in the ex-

---

[22] Cf. footnote 3.

tract from the Valuche diary – out of which three represent the construction highlighted in (4a) and one the construction highlighted in (4b), both of which form part of the present-day language – and one instance in the Durand diary (4c), which constitutes a marginally altered incident of contemporary *comme suit* 'as follows'.

(4) a. si **bon** **leur** **semble**
    if good them seem.PRS.3SG
    'if it pleases them'
    (Valuche, *Journal*, f.4r)
   b. dequoy **bien luy** **en** **prins**
    of.which well him of.it take.PST.3SG
    'luckily enough for him'
    (Valuche, *Journal*, f.23r)
   c. **comme** **sensuit**
    as REFL.follow.PRS.3SG
    'as follows'
    (Durand, *Journal*, f.27v)

Moreover, four relevant instances in the Durand and Goyard diaries involve the construction highlighted in (5). This construction lacks a counterpart with an overt subject pronoun in the four diaries analyzed and relates to the contemporary fixed expression *soit dit en passant* 'incidentally'.

(5) ieusques aultremen **soit** **dict**
    until otherwise be.PRS.SBJV.3SG say.PST.PTCP
    'until further notice' (Durand, *Journal*, f.30v)

Eventually, in the Valuche diary, one pertinent instance, highlighted in (6), is evidently due to a misconstrual and, therefore, must also be left out of account. Specifically, unlike what the writing along with the verbal agreement morphology seems to suggest, *ce* does not represent a demonstrative third person singular pronoun in canonical subject position and, thus, the subject of the subordinate clause in question. Rather, as the context clearly indicates, the subject must necessarily be *il* 'they', referring back to the Recollects. To all appearances, *ce* is a misspelling of *se*, the third person reflexive pronoun. This misspelling is recurrently encountered in the Valuche diary and had arguably induced the writer in the present case to spuriously conceive of it as a subject and, hence, to employ the singular verb form *nourisse* instead of the plural verb form *nourissent*.

(6) des   recoller   [...] rendoint   les rantes   [...] et
    ART.INDF.PL Recollect   return.IPFV.3PL the ground.rents   and
    vivoint   daulmonnes / les habitans   leur ont
    live.IPFV.3PL   from.alms   the inhabitants   them have.PRS.3PL
    dit   **que ce nourisse   de leur   ranttes**
    say.PST.PTCP   that CE nourish.PRS.SBJV.3SG of their ground.rents
    sil   voulloint   et quil   ne leur   donneroint
    if.they.M   want.IPFV.3PL and that.they.M   not them   give.COND.3PL
    poinct   lausmonne
    not   the.alms

'the Recollects returned their ground rents and lived from alms. The inhabitants told them that they could live from their ground rents, if they wanted to, and that they would not give them any alms, since they were well off.' (Durand, *Journal*, f.30v)

From the preceding discussion it results that, on closer inspection, the overall small number of relevant instances of a finite subordinate clause with an omitted subject pronoun reduces considerably, viz. from 23 to 13.

As Figure 4 shows, this number contrasts starkly with that of instances of a finite subordinate clause with an overt subject pronoun, amounting to a total of 1,023.

134 — Michael Zimmermann

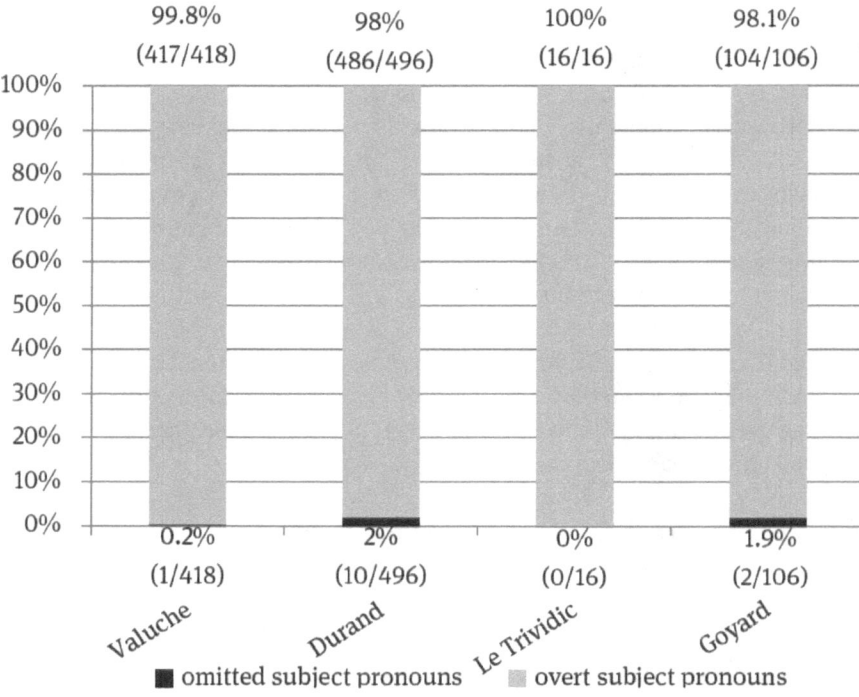

Fig. 4: Frequency as well as total number of instances of a finite subordinate clause with, respectively, an omitted and an overt subject pronoun (revised)

Subject pronoun omission in finite subordinate clauses thus appears to be extremely rare in Early Classical French diary writing. Occurring at a rate of 98% to 100%, subject pronouns are regularly overt in finite subordinate clauses in such writing, contrary to finite declarative root clauses without a fronted argument and unlike in prototypical null-subject languages. As (7) illustrates, this also holds when the subject of a finite matrix clause which is coreferential with that of a finite subordinate clause is omitted.

(7) Ø$_i$ sont   alle   loger   au   lion   dangers   ou
     be.PRS.3PL go.PST.PTCP stay.INF to.the lion of.Angers where
     jl$_i$ ont   faict   de   grande   despensce de
     they.M have.PRS.3PL make.PST.PTCP PART great   expense   of
     plus   de   trois   mille   livres
     more   PART   three   thousand   pounds

'They went to stay in Lion d'Angers, where they went to a great expense of more than three thousand pounds.' (Valuche, *Journal*, f.54r)

Crucially, along with the results from root clauses (interrogatives and declaratives with a fronted argument), those from subordinate clauses are unexpected under an analysis in terms of a null-subject language. On the contrary, the present results are fairly consistent with Haegeman's insights into diary writing from prototypical non-null-subject languages. From such, respectively, divergence and convergence I shall eventually conclude that Early Classical French was a non-null-subject language, hereby concurring on principled grounds with what has commonly been assumed in the literature.

In the remainder of this section, I shall dwell on the scarce instances of a finite subordinate clause with an omitted subject pronoun that seem to conflict with this conclusion. In this regard, I shall abstain from reinterpreting as a strong tendency, rather than a strict rule, Haegeman's original observation that, in this – and, by extension, – any of the other pertinent syntactic contexts, subject pronoun omission is excluded in the diary register of non-null-subject languages. Instead, I shall argue that the altogether 13 instances at issue should not be considered counterexamples at all, as they can conclusively be shown to pertain to written registers different from diary/abbreviated writing.

As explained in Section 3, the writers of the four diaries selected all lacked education to a certain degree. This, however, does not preclude that, in the context of whatever little education they had had, they had been initiated to stylistics and/or literary writing from earlier periods, in which null subjects were prevalent. It might thus well have been the case that, for whatever reasons, these writers made use in their diary writing of constructions that they had come about in contemporaneous and/or pre-17th c non-abbreviated written registers.

That this seems indeed to have been the case is first of all strongly suggested by the observation that 11/13 relevant instances conform to a syntactic context in which subject pronoun omission was, according to several 17th c. grammarians and critics of language use, possible in what appears to have been formal writing from the first half of the 17th c. (cf. Sections 1–2): finite subordinate clauses with a first or second person plural subject pronoun. In effect, all omitted subject pronouns in these 11 instances are second person plural, as can be gathered from the illustrations in (8).

(8) a. comme verres
    as   see.FUT.2PL
    'as you will see' (Durand, *Journal*, f.5r;13r;16v;47v)

  b. que verres
    which see.FUT.2PL
    'which you will see' (Durand, *Journal*, f.20r;48v)
  c. que scavez la pesanteur dun escu
    which know.PRS.2PL the heaviness of.a écu
    'of which you know the heaviness of an écu' (Goyard, *Journal*, f.61)

In the Durand diary, all ten seemingly conflicting instances are actually of this type and, in eight of these, the finite verb form employed is *verres* 'see.PRS.2PL' (cf. 8a–b). This state of affairs is suggestive of a fair degree of conventionalization.

As for the remaining two of the 13 apparently conflicting instances, given in (9), these evince, along with subject pronoun omission, a syntax that is likewise strongly reminiscent of the medieval stage of the language: verb-second configurations, in which the finite verb (*ont* and *fust*, respectively) directly follows a single clause-initial non-subject constituent (*lesdits huissiers*, a direct object, and *enlannee 1617*, a prepositional adjunct, respectively).[23]

(9) a. quant lesdits huissiers ont   veu
    when the.said bailiffs   have.PRS.3PL see.PST.PTCP
    'when they saw the aforementioned bailiffs' (Valuche, *Journal*, f.40v.)
  b. qu' enlannee 1617 ne fust   aulcungtz fruitz ny gland
    that in.the.year 1617 not be.IPFV.3SG not.any fruits nor acorn
    'that, in the year 1617, there were not any fruits nor acorns'
    (Goyard, *Journal*, f.2)

That the syntax of these subordinate clauses is indeed medieval in nature can be straightforwardly established with regard to (9a). Unlike what obtains in the modern language as well as generally in diary writing from the first half of the 17th c., the fronted direct object *lesdits huissiers* is not left-dislocated, i.e. resumed by a (preverbal) direct object pronoun (*les*) in the clause proper, but topicalized, as is usually the case in Medieval French.

Fundamentally, verb-second configurations as in (9) are considered the prototypical syntactic context for null subjects in the medieval stage of the language

---

[23] Note that preverbal negative *ne* 'not', as in (9b), is commonly considered a syntactic clitic in any stage and variety of French and, thus, is not relevant for the calculus. Cf. Zimmermann & Kaiser (2010) for extensive discussion regarding Medieval French.

(e.g. Vanelli, Renzi & Benincà 1985; Adams 1987; Roberts 1993; Vance 1997; Zimmermann 2014).[24] It thus appears that the two instances of subject pronoun omission in (9) are due to the mimicry of the use of null subjects as encountered with earlier writers and, more generally, the employment of an archaizing style pertaining to non-abbreviated written registers.

From the present discussion I shall thus conclude that the scarce instances of a finite subordinate clause with an omitted subject pronoun that seemingly conflict with the suggested analysis of Early Classical French as a non-null-subject language all fall into the domain of stylistics pertaining to written registers different from diary/abbreviated writing. Consequently, they do not constitute evidence against the proposed analysis.

On a more general basis, then, the findings in this section lend further support to the soundness of Haegeman's insights into the morpho-syntax of the diary register in non-null-subject languages. Based on the outcome of this section, I shall eventually embark on the issue of subject pronoun omission in formal writing from the first half of the 17th c.

5 Subject pronoun omission in Early Classical French formal writing revisited

The discussion in the preceding section has provided straightforward results with respect to a number of syntactic contexts in which the omission of subject pronouns was not possible in Early Classical French diary writing. Crucially, these contexts regularly coincide with those established in work by Haegeman as strictly excluding such omission in the diary register in prototypical non-null-subject languages, whence the suggested analysis of Early Classical French as a non-null-subject language.

This analysis actually falls in with illustrations of as well as metalinguistic comments on the mandatory use of overt subject pronouns in various grammars

---

24 Note that, unlike in null-subject languages such as Spanish, the possibility of null subjects in Medieval French was dependent on the fulfillment of specific structural conditions. Particularly, ever since at least Foulet (1928), it has been standardly assumed in this regard that null subjects are strictly limited to the position directly following the finite verb. In generative approaches, this has been conceived of in terms of the licensing and identification of SpecTP by the governing finite verb moved to the C-level.

and related works from the period under investigation (cf. Section 1). Furthermore, such an analysis, which in fact essentially implies that null subjects were generally no longer available,[25] neatly explains the apparent urge felt by some grammarians from this period to indicate specific syntactic contexts in which subject pronouns could be omitted in what appears to have been formal writing. Moreover, the suggested analysis conclusively accounts for the relative scarcity of omitted subject pronouns in literary writing from this period.[26] Eventually and fundamentally, this analysis is in line with rebukes as well as dismissals of subject pronoun omission as archaisms in works from grammarians and critics of language use later on in the century (cf. Section 2) that actually seem to bear witness to the fact that such omission came to be increasingly rejected in the course of the 17th c. (cf. also Fournier 1998). It thus appears that, rather than genuine null subjects, omitted subject pronouns in Early Classical French literary writing in particular and formal writing in general constitute an archaizing stylistic device occasionally employed by authors from this period when mimicking, arguably for reasons of prestige,[27] the language use of authors from earlier periods.

Further corroboration for this view comes from a comparison of the syntactic contexts of subject pronoun omission in formal writing from the first half of the 17th c. with those indicated in contemporaneous grammars. Specifically, when comparing the syntactic contexts of altogether 85 instances of such omission as listed in a number of philological and linguistic studies[28] with those adduced by Maupas (1618) (cf. (2) in Section 1) and rebuked later on in the century, one finds that, in 78/85 or 91.8% of these instances, convergence obtains. Abstracting away from the seven remaining instances, whose syntactic contexts actually coincide with several of those in which null subjects are typically encountered in the medieval stage of the language,[29] it is intriguing to note that, in Early Classical French formal writing, subject pronouns are omitted in an altogether small set of

---

[25] As noted in footnote 3, null subjects may still occur in the modern language in residual structures and fixed expressions.

[26] Cf. footnote 4 as well as the introductory clause of Maupas' (1618) note on subject pronoun omission in (2) in Section 1, according to which such omission constitutes an altogether 'rare' phenomenon.

[27] Cf. the quote from Vaugelas (1647) in Section 2.

[28] The studies are the following: Regnier (1869); Nordström (1870); Holfeld (1875); Benoist (1877); List (1881); Lahmeyer (1886); Haase (1888, 1889); Brunot (1891); Arnould (1896); Quillacq (1903); Guillaume (1927); Roberts (1993); Fournier (1998); Spillebout (2007). Space considerations prevent me from listing instances other than those put forth in (1) in Section 1.

[29] Cf. Zimmermann (2014) for extensive discussion.

well-defined syntactic contexts. Fundamentally, this general restriction to a limited subset of the syntactic contexts in which subject pronoun omission was possible in Medieval French strongly argues against the analysis of Early Classical French as a null-subject language, while underpinning the suggested analysis in terms of a non-null-subject language.

In light of the present discussion, I shall thus concur with pertinent claims in the literature. Specifically, I shall conclude from the insights hitherto gained that the availability of the morpho-syntactic possibility of null subjects in the French language had recently been lost in the wake of the resetting of the null-subject parameter and that subject pronoun omission in formal writing from the first half of the 17th c. is due to the occasional employment of an archaizing style mimicking in particular earlier authors' use of null subjects.

6 References

Adams, Marianne. 1987. *Old French, null subjects, and verb second phenomena*. Los Angeles, CA: University of California dissertation.
Arnould, Louis. 1896. *Racan (1589–1670). Histoire anecdotique et critique de sa vie et de ses œuvres*. Paris: Colin.
Auger, Julie. 1995. Les clitiques pronominaux en français parlé informel: Une approche morphologique. *Revue québécoise de linguistique* 24. 21–60.
Balon, Laurent & Pierre Larrivée. 2016. L'ancien français n'est déjà plus une langue à sujet nul – nouveau témoignage des textes légaux. *Journal of French Language Studies* 26. 221–237.
Benoist, Antoine. 1877. *De la syntaxe française entre Palsgrave et Vaugelas*. Paris: Thorin.
Brunot, Ferdinand. 1891. *La doctrine de Malherbe d'après son commentaire sur Desportes*. Paris: Masson.
Chiflet, Laurent. 1659. *Essay d'une parfaite grammaire de la langue françoise*. Anvers: van Meurs.
Culbertson, Jennifer. 2010. Convergent evidence for categorial change in French: From subject clitic to agreement marker. *Language* 86. 85–132.
Darmesteter, Arsène. 1897. *Cours de grammaire historique de la langue française. Quatrième partie: Syntaxe*. Paris: Delagrave.
Bakker, Cecile de. 1997. *Germanic and Romance inversion in French. A diachronic study*. The Hague: Holland Academic Graphics.
De Cat, Cécile. 2005. French subject clitics are not agreement markers. *Lingua* 115. 1195–1219.
Deimier, Pierre de. 1610. *L'academie de l'art poëtique*. Paris: Bordeaulx.
Ernst, Gerhard & Barbara Wolf. 2005. *Textes français privés des XVIIe et XVIIIe siècles*, 3 CD-ROM. Tübingen: Niemeyer.
Foulet, Lucien. 1928. *Petite syntaxe de l'ancien français*, 3rd edn. Paris: Champion.
Fournier, Nathalie. 1998. *Grammaire du français classique*. Paris: Belin.

Grevisse, Maurice & André Goosse. 2011. *Le bon usage. Grammaire française*, 15th edn. Bruxelles: De Boeck.
Guillaume, Gaston. 1927. *J.L. Guez de Balzac et la prose française*. Paris: Picard.
Haase, Alfred. 1888. *Französische Syntax des XVII. Jahrhunderts*. Jena: Gronau.
Haase, Alfred. 1889. Ergänzende Bemerkungen zur Syntax des XVII. Jahrhunderts. *Zeitschrift für französische Sprache und Literatur* 11. 203–237.
Haegeman, Liliane. 1990a. Non-overt subjects in diary contexts. In Joan Mascaró & Marina Nespor (eds.), *Grammar in progress. Glow essays for Henk van Riemsdijk*, 167–174. Dordrecht: Foris.
Haegeman, Liliane. 1990b. Understood subjects in English diaries. On the relevance of theoretical syntax for the study of register variation. *Multilingua* 9(2). 157–199.
Haegeman, Liliane. 1997. Register variation, truncation, and subject omission in English and in French. *English Language and Linguistics* 1(2). 233–270.
Haegeman, Liliane. 2000. Adult null subjects in non pro-drop languages. In Marc-Ariel Friedemann & Luigi Rizzi (eds.), *The acquisition of syntax: Studies in comparative developmental linguistics*, 129–169. London: Longman.
Haegeman, Liliane. 2007. Subject omission in present-day written English. On the theoretical relevance of peripheral data. *Rivista di Grammatica Generativa* 32. 91–124.
Haegeman, Liliane. 2013. The syntax of registers: Diary subject omission and the privilege of the root. *Lingua* 130. 88–110.
Haegeman, Liliane. 2017. Unspeakable sentences. Subject omission in written registers: A cartographic analysis. *Linguistic Variation* 17(2). 229–250.
Holfeld, Hermann. 1875. *Ueber die Sprache des François de Malherbe*. Posen: Decker.
Kayne, Richard S. 1975. *French syntax. The transformational cycle*. Cambridge, MA: The MIT Press.
Lahmeyer, Carl. 1886. *Das Pronomen in der französischen Sprache des 16ten und 17ten Jahrhunderts*. Göttingen: Huth.
Le Bidois, Georges & Robert Le Bidois. 1935. *Syntaxe du français moderne. Ses fondements historiques et psychologiques. Tome II*. Paris: Picard.
List, Willy. 1881. Syntaktische Studien über Voiture. *Französische Studien* 1. 1–40.
Marchello-Nizia, Christiane. 2000. Le décumul du 'thème' dans l'évolution du français. *Le Français Moderne* 68. 31–40.
Marchello-Nizia, Christiane. 2018. De SO à SV: Vers le sujet obligatoire et antéposé en français, les dernières phases d'un changement. *Journal of French Language Studies* 28. 1–19.
Mathieu, Éric. 2006. Stylistic fronting in Old French. *Probus* 18. 219–266.
Maupas, Charles. 1618. *Grammaire et syntaxe françoise*. Orléans: Boynard et Nyon.
Meisenburg, Trudel. 2000. Vom Wort zum Flexiv? Zu den französischen Pronominalklitika. *Zeitschrift für französische Sprache und Literatur* 110. 223–237.
Meyer-Lübke, Wilhelm. 1899. *Grammatik der romanischen Sprachen. Dritter Band: Syntax*. Leipzig: Reisland.
Nordström, Thor. 1870. *Observations sur la langue et la versification de Mathurin Regnier*. Lund: Berling.
Oudin, Anthoine. 1632. *Grammaire françoise, rapportée au langage du temps*. Paris: Billaine.
Palasis, Katerina. 2015. Subject clitics and preverbal negation in European French: Variation, acquisition, diatopy and diachrony. *Lingua* 161. 125–143.

Plattner, Philipp. 1907. *Ausführliche Grammatik der französischen Sprache. III. Teil: Ergänzungen. Zweites Heft: Das Pronomen und die Zahlwörter*. Freiburg: Bielefeld.
Quillacq, J.-A. 1903. *La langue et la syntaxe de Bossuet*. Tours: Cattier.
Regnier, Adolphe. 1869. *Lexique de la langue de Malherbe. Avec une introduction grammaticale*. Paris: Hachette.
Roberge, Yves. 1986. Subject doubling, free inversion, and null argument languages. *Canadian Journal of Linguistics/Revue Canadienne De Linguistique* 31(1). 55–80.
Robert-Tissot, Aurélia. 2020. Le statut variationnel du sujet clitique dans deux corpus de la Suisse romande. Une comparaison entre *sms4science.ch* et OFROM. *Revue Romane* 55(1). 34–69.
Roberts, Ian. 1993. *Verbs and diachronic syntax. A comparative history of English and French*. Dordrecht: Kluwer.
Roberts, Ian & Anders Holmberg. 2010. Introduction: Parameters in minimalist theory. In Theresa Biberauer, Anders Holmberg, Ian Roberts & Michelle Sheehan (eds.), *Parametric variation: Null subjects in minimalist theory*, 1–57. Cambridge: Cambridge University Press.
Sandfeld, Kristian. 1928. *Syntaxe du français contemporain I*. Les pronoms. Paris: Champion.
Serrier, Jean (Serreius, Joannes). 1623. *Grammatica Gallica nova*. Strasbourg: Zeznerus.
Spillebout, Gabriel. 2007. *Grammaire de la langue française du XVIIe siècle*, new edn. Paris: Eurédit.
Stark, Elisabeth. 2013. Clitic subjects in French text messages. Does technical change provoke and/or reveal linguistic change? In Kirsten Jeppesen Kragh & Jan Lindschouw (eds.), *Deixis and pronouns in Romance languages*, 147–169. Amsterdam: Benjamins.
Stark, Elisabeth & Petra Meier. 2017. Argument drop in Swiss WhatsApp messages. A pilot study on French and (Swiss) German. *Zeitschrift für französische Sprache und Literatur* 127(3). 224–252.
Stark, Elisabeth & Aurélia Robert-Tissot. 2017. Subject drop in Swiss French text messages. *Linguistic Variation* 17(2). 251–271.
Steinmeyer, Georg. 1979. *Historische Aspekte des français avancé*. Geneva: Droz.
Togeby, Knud. 1982. *Grammaire française. Volume I: Le Nom*. Copenhagen: Akademisk.
Vance, Barbara. 1997. *Syntactic change in Medieval French. Verb-second and null subjects*. Dordrecht: Kluwer.
Vanelli, Laura, Lorenzo Renzi & Paola Benincá. 1985. Typologie des pronoms sujets dans les langues romanes. In *Actes du XVIIe Congrès International de Linguistique et Philologie Romanes. Volume 3: Linguistique descriptive, phonétique, morphologique et lexique*, 163–176. Aix-en-Provence: Service des Publications de l'Université de Provence.
Vaugelas, Claude F. de. 1647. *Remarques sur la langue françoise. Utiles à ceux qui veulent bien parler et bien escrire*. Paris: Camusat et Le Petit.
Zimmermann, Michael. 2014. *Expletive and referential subject pronouns in Medieval French*. Berlin: De Gruyter.
Zimmermann, Michael. 2016. The status of subject pronouns in Modern Standard French revisited. In Ernestina Carrilho, Alexandra Fiéis, Maria Lobo & Sandra Pereira (eds.), *Romance Languages and Linguistic Theory 10. Selected papers from 'Going Romance' 28, Lisbon*, 305–324. Amsterdam: Benjamins.
Zimmermann, Michael. 2018. Null subjects, expletives, and the status of Medieval French. In Federica Cognola & Jan Casalicchio (eds.), *Null subjects in generative grammar. A synchronic and diachronic perspective*, 70–93. Oxford: Oxford University Press.

Zimmermann, Michael & Georg A. Kaiser. 2010. Much ado about nothing? On the categorial status of *et* and *ne* in Medieval French. *Corpus* 9. 265–290.
Zimmermann, Michael & Georg A. Kaiser. 2014. On expletive subject pronoun drop in Colloquial French. *Journal of French Language Studies* 24. 107–126.
Zribi-Hertz, Anne. 1994. La syntaxe des clitiques nominatifs en français standard et en français avancé. *Travaux de Linguistique et de Philologie* 32. 131–147.

Part 3: **Functional Categories and the Verb**

Silvio Cruschina and Andrea Calabrese
Fifty shades of morphosyntactic microvariation

Motion verb constructions in southern Italian dialects

Abstract: In this paper, we analyse Motion Verb Constructions (MVCs) in southern Italian dialects, especially in Sicily and Apulia, which provide an ideal illustration of morphosyntactic microvariation. Depending on the grammatical status of the motion verb, we can distinguish between MVCs in which a lexical verb selects a purpose clause and those that involve a restructuring configuration where the motion verb behaves as a functional verb. We focus on the latter configuration and show that in these MVCs, the second verb can occur either as an infinitive or as a verb inflected for the same features as the motion verb. Following the most recent developments in Distributed Morphology, we then offer an analysis of the morphosyntactic and word-internal structure that surfaces as periphrastic morphology, and propose that the difference between the infinitival restructuring and double inflection is due to the nature of the agreement node within the verbal complex. Within this account, double inflection is simply viewed as a case of agreement within the extended vP which arises independently from restructuring. Finally, the defective paradigm of some MVCs and the configurations in which the motion verb has become a prefixal element are discussed and analysed as the result of specific word-internal morphological operations.

Keywords: motion verbs, southern Italian dialects, Sicilian, restructuring, agreement, double inflection, impoverishment, affixation

---

Silvio Cruschina: Department of Languages, University of Helsinki, Finland, silvio.cruschina@helsinki.fi
Andrea Calabrese: Department of Linguistics, University of Connecticut, United States, andrea.calabrese@uconn.edu

https://doi.org/10.1515/9783110719154-006

1 Introduction: Motion verb constructions and morphosyntactic variation

Crosslinguistically, motion verbs such as *go* or *come* are commonly found in complex constructions that display a variety of morphosyntactic patterns. For the purpose of this paper, and in reference to southern Italian dialects, we define *Motion Verb Constructions* (MVCs) as those constructions that are composed of a motion verb (*go, come, pass (by)*, etc.) and a main lexical verb. We will refer to the former as V1 and to the latter as V2, as illustrated in (1). V1 and V2 are often linked by a preposition or pseudo-coordination (P); however, this not obligatory and is in fact absent in some dialects:

(1) V1+ (P) + V2

The V1 in MVCs can in principle be a lexical verb, but in this paper, we will concentrate on those cases in which V1 has grammaticalized into an aspectual marker. The development of a future tense from a construction with the verb GO, where the latter has been 'bleached' of its original movement meaning, is a crosslinguistically common grammaticalization path (see Bybee et al. 1994). Crucially, there is no southern Italian dialect in which GO has developed the temporal function that it has in many other Romance varieties, such as Spanish, Portuguese, and French, where in MVCs V1 functions as a future auxiliary (see, e.g., Squartini 1998, among many others).

An examination of the syntactic and morphological properties of V1 in southern Italian MVCs reveals different types of morphosyntactic structures (Cardinaletti & Giusti 2001, 2003, Manzini & Savoia 2005, Cruschina 2013, Di Caro 2015, 2018, 2019, Ledgeway 2016, Andriani 2017). When it heads a main clause followed by an infinitival clause of purpose, V1 clearly behaves as a lexical verb. This is exemplified in (2):

(2) Ci   jivu   pi ci   purtari na littira.   (Mussomeli, Sicily)
    there go.PST.1SG to him.DAT bring   a letter
    'I went there to bring him a letter.'

This sentence is uncontroversially an instance of a biclausal MVC where the preposition *pi* functions as a subordinating conjunction that introduces the purpose clause. In this paper, however, we concentrate on monoclausal MVCs, which we investigate using tools and insights from formal approaches to syntactic and morphological variation.

Further 'shades' of morphosyntactic microvariation may be identified with respect to other elements of the MVC, including the absence of P between V1 and V2, the presence of connecting elements other than P (e.g. *cu* in Salentino, *mi* in Messinese), and clitic placement in restructuring contexts (e.g. before V2 in some Salentino dialects). For reasons of space, however, we will not discuss these aspects here and leave them for future research. For a comparative overview, see Di Caro (2019).

2 Restructuring: An integrated approach

In most Western Romance varieties, when verbs such as GO and COME feature in MVCs they are typically followed by an infinitive. We will refer to this construction as the *Infinitival MVC*. Here is an example from the Apulian dialect spoken in Bari:

(3) Mə vògg'   a 'ccattà   u   cappìddə névə.   (Bari, Apulia)
    me go.PRS.1SG to buy.INF the hat   new
    'I go buy a new hat.'
    (Andriani 2017: 231)

The Infinitival MVC in southern Italy is not the only option for speakers: a number of different combinations of a motion V1 followed by a finite V2 are available. The two verbs in the constructions can be connected by different connecting elements, most commonly by the linker a.[1] Following Cruschina (2013), we use the name Doubly Inflected Construction (DIC) for this kind of MVC, where the two

---

[1] For the sake of simplicity, we have glossed the connecting element a as if it corresponded to the homophonous preposition a 'to' in the same varieties. Since Ascoli (1886, 1901), however, a long tradition of scholars have considered this element as the continuation of the Latin coordinating conjunction AC used in spoken and late Latin (see also Rohlfs 1969: §710, §761, Leone 1973, Sornicola 1976, Cardinaletti & Giusti 2001, Ledgeway 2016, Di Caro 2019). Indeed, in some cognate Calabrian dialects the connective element is the same as the coordinating conjunction e from Latin ET (see Rohlfs 1969: §759). For this reason, the construction is treated as an instance of pseudo-coordination in several studies (see, e.g., Ledgeway 2016, Di Caro 2018, 2019). In any case, as argued in Cruschina (2013: 271), the origin of the connecting element is not relevant to the synchronic analysis of DIC, given that it is now desemanticized and contributes no meaning to the construction.

verbs act as a single predicate and share the very same inflectional features. Example of DIC are provided below, where both V1 and V2 are in the 1st person singular (4), in the 3rd person singular (5), and in the 3rd person plural (6) of the present indicative:[2]

(4) Vaju   a   pigghiu   u   pani.   (Marsala, Sicily)
    go.PRS.1SG to   take.PRS.1SG the bread
    'I go to fetch the bread.'
    (Cardinaletti & Giusti 2001: 373)

(5) U   veni   a   piglia   dopu.   (Mussomeli, Sicily)
    him   come.PRS.3SG to   collect.PR.3SG later
    'He is coming to pick him up later.'
    (Cruschina 2013: 266)

(6) 'vonə   (a) m'maɲdʒənə.   (Martina Franca, Apulia)
    go.PRS.3PL to   eat.PRS.3PL
    'They're going to eat.'
    (Ledgeway 2016: 159)

In their analysis, Cardinaletti & Giusti (2001) compare DIC with the Infinitival MVC and, on the basis of a number of syntactic and semantic tests, convincingly show that DIC (the inflected construction, in their terminology) is monoclausal. At the same time, they argue that the motion verbs involved as V1 in DIC are "lexical categories merged as functional heads" in the extended projection of the V2. More specifically, they define these verbs as "semi-lexical verbs" because, while it is true that they lack or have lost their canonical lexical properties, they still retain their motion semantics.[3]

It is important to observe, however, that even in Infinitival MVCs in Sicilian dialects, two different structures may be involved: a) a lexical verb governing a purpose clause; and b) a restructuring configuration of the functional type, in

---

[2] The motion verbs that most typically appear in DIC are the local equivalents of *go*, *come*, *come by*/*pass* and *send*. Other verbs may enter the construction as V1 is some dialects. See Di Caro (2018, 2019) for a review of the additional motion verbs that can occur in DIC in different Sicilian varieties. On the special properties of *send* as V1, which involves both a motion and a causative semantics, see Todaro & Del Prete (2018) and Del Prete & Todaro (2020).

[3] See Cardinaletti & Giusti (2019) for a refinement of this analysis, according to which V1 is merged in *t*, a head immediately above T. See Del Prete & Todaro (2019) for a different semantic analysis of the single event interpretation.

which V1 behaves as a functional head (see Rizzi 1976, 1978, Cinque 2001, 2006; on the distinction between lexical and functional restructuring, see Wurmbrand 2001, 2004). Assuming that restructuring involves clitic climbing, the contrasts in (7) and (8) show the existence of these two MVC constructions. They are distinguished by V1's (in)ability in a restructuring configuration to select either for the arguments or for the adjuncts that are typical of motion verbs. While V1 can select for the directional argument *agghiri a casa* ('towards home'), which separates V1 from V2 in the sentence in (7a), the same argument cannot be selected by V1, in (7b), which is characterized by clitic climbing, independently of its position within the sentence. The same difference can be observed in the presence of an adjunct to the lexical motion V1 in (8a), such as the instrumental *cu a machina* ('by car'), which cannot be combined with the functional V1 of (8b) because it has lost its lexical and selectional properties. In fact, a verb merged as a functional head cannot project its arguments and cannot combine with adjuncts that typically modify lexical (motion) VPs. We can conclude that the infinitival complement in (7a) and (8a) is truly a purpose clause, whereas that in (7b) and (8b) is part of a restructuring construction where V1 is a functional head.

(7) a. Va   agghiri a casa   a mangiari.   (Marsala, Sicily)
       go.3SG towards to home to eat.INF
       'He goes towards home to eat.'
       (Cardinaletti & Giusti 2001: 377)
    b. La va   (*agghiri a casa) a mangiari (*agghiri a casa).
       it go.3SG towards to home   to eat.3SG   towards to home

(8) a. Peppe va   a mangiari c'a   machina.   (Marsala, Sicily)
       Peppe go.3SG to eat.INF with-the car
       'Peppe goes to eat by car.'
       (Cardinaletti & Giusti 2001: 379)
    b. Peppe la va   a mangiari (*c'a   machina).
       Peppe it go.3SG to eat.3SG   with-the car

The same properties displayed by the restructured Infinitival MVC in (7) and (8) are characteristic of the DIC, as shown in (9) and (10):

(9) Va   (*agghiri a casa a mangia (*agghiri a casa).   (Marsala, Sicily)
    go.3SG towards to home to eat.3SG towards to home
    (Cardinaletti & Giusti 2001: 377)

(10) *Peppe   va   a   mangia c'a   machina.
     Peppe   go.3SG   to   eat.3SG with-the car
     (Cardinaletti & Giusti 2001: 379)

The conclusion is that DICs are in fact restructuring configurations in which V1 behaves as a functional head. This can account for the different properties of DIC with respect to the Infinitival MVC first examined in Cardinaletti & Giusti (2001), including obligatory clitic climbing, single event interpretation, indivisibility, and incompatibility with the arguments and adjuncts typically associated with motion verbs (see Cardinaletti & Giusti 2001, 2003, Manzini & Savoia 2005, Cruschina 2013, and Di Caro 2019 for more details).

An underlying problem with the structural distinction between Infinitival MVC and DIC is their interpretation. From a semantic viewpoint, the distinction between the two structures is not particularly clear, leading Cardinaletti & Giusti (2001) to claim that V1 retains the semantics of a motion verb and should therefore not be assimilated to an auxiliary proper. Here, we would like to suggest that in DIC and in the Infinitival MVC with restructuring, but not in the structure where the infinitival V2 is part of a purpose clause, the motion verb V1 is a functional verb heading Cinque's (1999) *andative* aspect projection. This aspect signals that a distance away from the speaker must be covered for the action to be realized or executed, thus matching the directional properties of the verb GO. In the case of COME as V1, a *venitive* aspect is encoded, signalling that the distance to be covered is towards the speaker.[4]

In other words, the V1 in DIC and in the Infinitival MVC with restructuring is semantically bleached so as to provide specific aspectual information about the event structure, under a single event interpretation.[5] Under this analysis, the motion meaning is retained to a certain extent, in line with native speakers' intuitions, but as a functional aspect rather than as a lexical semantic property.

DIC differs from the usual Italo-Romance functional restructuring cases, however, in that it presents double inflection as its hallmark. In this respect, we propose that double inflection arises independently of restructuring, and that it can be analysed as a case of agreement within the extended vP which takes place

---

[4] We assume that the venitive aspect is encoded in an independent functional head. In this paper, however, we will focus on MVCs involving the andative functional head and will not further discuss the venitive aspect.

[5] Cardinaletti & Giusti (2001: § 3.7.2) convincingly show that DIC, unlike Infinitival MVC, expresses a single event.

via concord, through a mechanism resembling adjectival agreement (Baker 2010). We will return to this point in Sections 3 and 4.[6]

In some contexts, DIC has completely lost its motion meaning and instead expresses an element of surprise about a past event (Sornicola 1976, Cruschina 2013):[7]

(11) Cuannu u vitti ca sunava nna banna,
when him see.PST.1SG that play.IMRF.PST.3SG in-the band,
vaju a pruvu na gioia!
go.PRS.1SG to feel.PRS.1SG a joy
'When I saw him play in the band, I felt such a joy!'

(12) Ogellannu va a capita ca ci vinni
last-year go.3SG to happen.3SG that to-him come.PST.3SG
a frevi tri boti!
the fever three times
'Last year it happened that he had a fever three times!'

(13) Nun va a mmori propriu oi?
not go.3SG to die.3SG right today
'He just had to go and die today...'

Generally, stative and unaccusative predicates are not compatible with MVCs as V2s. The examples above, however, show that with a desemanticized V1, stative and unaccusative V2 may occur in DIC.[8]

DICs show a great deal of morphosyntactic microvariation. A type of radical impoverishment is found in western and central Sicily, leading to an uninflected V1 in the whole paradigm (Cardinaletti & Giusti 2001, 2003, 2019, Cruschina 2013):

---

[6] See Cardinaletti & Giusti (2019) for an alternative analysis, according to which the features of V1 are parasitically copied on to the features of V2.
[7] The examples in (11) and (12) are from the dialects of Mussomeli (Cruschina 2013: 279), while the example in (13) is from Delia (Di Caro 2019: 132).
[8] We refer to Cruschina (in press) and Cruschina & Bianchi (in press) for an account of the development of the surprise meaning out of a motion verb. See also Cruschina (2018) for another monoclausal MVC characterized by the possibility of expressing surprise and unexpectedness.

(14) 1SG   vaju   a pigghiu / **va**   a pigghiu
     2SG   vai   a pigghi   / **va**   a pigghi
     3SG   va   a pigghia / **va**   a pigghia
     3PL   vannu a pigghianu / **va**   a pigghianu
     IMPER. 2SG   va   pigghia   / **va**   pigghia

It is important to note that the impoverished forms in these Sicilian dialects are not limited to the verb GO, but are also found with other motion verbs (Cardinaletti & Giusti 2019), and that the DIC version with invariant *va* as V1 (cf. (14)) coexists with the version in which GO displays regular endings.

In some areas of eastern Sicily (e.g. Marina di Ragusa, Acireale) the grammaticalization of V1 appears to have reached the final stage of affix (cf. (15)). Native speakers of these dialects are not always aware of this affix, which is realized at the beginning of the finite V2, and of its origins from the verb GO. The data in (15) and (16), from Di Caro (2015: 62–68), illustrate this advanced stage of grammaticalization (see also Di Caro 2019):

(15) a. **Vo**ppigghju   u   pani.   (Marina di Ragusa, Sicily)
        go+fetch.1SG   the   bread   1SG
    b. **Vo**ppigghi   u   pani.   2SG   [full paradigm] ...
    c. **Vo**pigghja   u   pani.   3SG
    d. **Vo**ppigghjamu   u   pani.   1PL
    e. **Vo**ppigghjati   u   pani.   2PL
    f. **Vo**ppigghjanu   u   pani.   3PL

(16) a. **O**ccattu   u   giunnali.   (Acireale, Sicily)
        go+buy.1SG   the   newspaper   1SG
    b. **O**ccatti   u   giunnali.   2SG
      Occattunu   u   giunnali.   3PL
      ... [full paradigm] ...

In this paper, we propose an account for the morphosyntactic differences between the Infinitival MVC with restructuring and DIC. Assuming the existence of an andative functional node, we will then address the variation in its morphosyntactic realization. It can be treated analytically as an independent verbal form (V1), but also synthetically as a prefixal element as in the cases in (15) and (16). What is the nature of these analytic and synthetic morphological treatments of this functional head? It should be noted that Cinque's (1999) cartographic approach to the functional skeleton of the verb, which we adopt here, is ill-equipped to deal with word-internal and word-external correlations such as those under investigation here: Cinque's approach relies on a lexicalist-word based view of syntax which can only adequately deal with word-external (analytic) distributional patterns but not with word-internal ones. It relates only to how sentences and phrases are constructed and not to how words are constructed. We will try to correct this problem by integrating Cinque's model into Distributed Morphology, a syntactic model of word construction.

We assume Cinque's complex functional structure (see (20) below) including the functional andative functional node. A fundamental issue that we will address is that of how this functional skeleton is mapped into surface PF forms. The key operation in mapping is head movement (head raising in our case) which moves the functional heads upwards cyclically and generates X^0 complexes (i.e. morphological words). As a result, verbal forms' construction follows, accordingly, the hierarchial functional structure (cf. the mirror principle). Three additional operations are needed to derive the verbal surface structure of Romance verbal forms. Two of them insert ornamental morphological pieces such as AGR (Halle & Marantz 1993, Bobaljik 2000) and Thematic Vowels (Oltra-Massuet & Arregi 2005). The third prunes nodes with non-overt exponents. This latter operation accounts for why Romance forms do not always have an agglutinative structure, that is, a cumulation of morphological nodes but also a fusional one in which more functional heads are represented by a single exponent. Instead of assuming Halle & Marantz's (1993) fusion to account for the merging of these nodes, Calabrese (2019) proposes cyclic pruning of nodes with non-overt exponence followed by upward docking of the features that consequently become floating. This pruning operation radically simplifies the phonological realization of morphosyntactic structures, and accounts for the convergence of possibly complex morphosyntactic structures and their possibly simpler PF surface shape. It also eliminates fusion and its problematic look ahead relation with vocabulary items, and also removes the problem of exponential zero in surface representations.

We will also assume that periphrastic forms arise from the blocking of head movement along the lines of Bjorkman (2011), Calabrese (2019), Fenger (2020), Embick (2000) and Pietraszko (2018). A simple way of implementing this, without taking a stand with respect with above mentioned theories, is to propose that head movement from one head position in the extended functional verb projection to the one directly higher up may be subject to parametrization along a parameter that either allows or does not allow movement from this position. As a consequence, also periphrastic structures, and the subsequent formation of auxiliaries, follow the hierarchical functional structure. We show that, in this way, we can capture the syntactic and morphological properties and processes that determine the different shades of microvariation in southern Italian MVCs.

3 A morphosyntactic analysis of lexical and functional restructuring

The theory of Distributed Morphology proposes a piece-based view of word formation, in which the syntax/morphology interface is made as transparent as possible by incorporating hierarchical structure into morphology; essentially, it assumes the input to morphology to be syntactic structure where morphosyntactic and semantic features (or feature bundles) are distributed over nodes forming morphemes (see Halle & Marantz 1993). Morphology manipulates these syntactic structures and eventually converts them into linear sequences of phonological representations:

(17) The Grammar

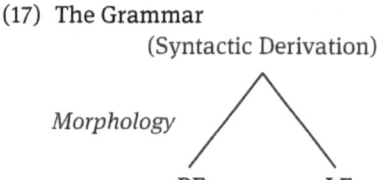

The derivation of all morphological forms then takes place in accordance with the architecture given in (17). Roots and other morphemes are combined into larger syntactic objects, which are moved when necessary (Merge, Move).

In Distributed Morphology, the phonological exponents of the different morphemes are listed in the Vocabulary as part of the *vocabulary items*, where each vocabulary item includes a phonological exponent and an associated set of features that governs its insertion into the terminal nodes of the morphosyntax. The (abstract) morphosyntactic representation is the input to phonological spell out where phonological realizations are assigned to the terminal nodes. In the simplest case, this component linearizes the hierarchical structure by adding phonological material to the abstract morphemes via a process called *Vocabulary Insertion*. During Vocabulary Insertion, individual *Vocabulary Items (VI)* — rules that pair a phonological *exponent* with a morphosyntactic context—are consulted, and the most specific VI that can apply to an abstract morpheme is inserted (in the so-called Elsewhere (Subset, Paninian) ordering).

Vocabulary Items are essentially instructions that insert phonological material into a terminal node given certain specific feature configurations in the terminal node and its adjacent environment. Abstract morphemes are thus said to be *spelled out* during Vocabulary Insertion. As shown by Bobaljik (2000) (see also Embick 2010), Vocabulary Insertion applies cyclically from the inside out, where cyclicity indicates step-by-step VI application to each terminal node:

(18) Vocabulary Insertion proceeds cyclically from the inside out.

We also assume Cinque's (1999) complex verbal functional structure in (19) and (20) (possibly reflecting the way our cognition analyses the world), in which restructuring verbs are auxiliary-like functional heads:

(19) [$_{IP}$ ... Modal field... Tense field... Aspectual field... [v ... Root]]

(20) [Mod$_{EPISTEMIC/ OBLIGATION/ABILITY}$ ... [MOD$_{VOLITION}$... [TENSE$_{PAST/FUTURE}$ ... [ASP$_{HABITUAL}$ ...
     [ASP$_{PREDISPOSITIONAL}$ ... [ASP$_{REPETITIVE}$ ... [ASP$_{TERMINATIVE/CONTINUATIVE}$... [ASP$_{DURATIVE/PROGRESSIVE}$ ...
     [ASP$_{FRUSTRATIVE}$ ... [ASP$_{INCEPTIVE}$ ... [ASP $_{ANDATIVE}$ ... [ASP$_{COMPLETIVE}$ ... [v ...

Cinque's original functional structure contains many different nodes dominating privative features. Following a more traditional approach in Generative Phonology, and subsequently in Distributed Morphology, we will use binary instead of privative features here. This will allow a simplification of Cinque's original functional skeleton, where different functional contrasts can be realized by combining feature specifications under the same node, as in (21). In addition we postulate that the nodes v, Voice and Asp are always syntactically active due to their syntactico-semantic roles in defining the basic inner and outer aspectual structure of the event and its argumental structure role; the other nodes may be optionally present. (For the sake of simplicity, only examples of the nodes present in Cinque's full model are mentioned here. The optional nodes are those in parentheses; they will be mentioned in later syntactic representations only when relevant in the analyses.)

(21)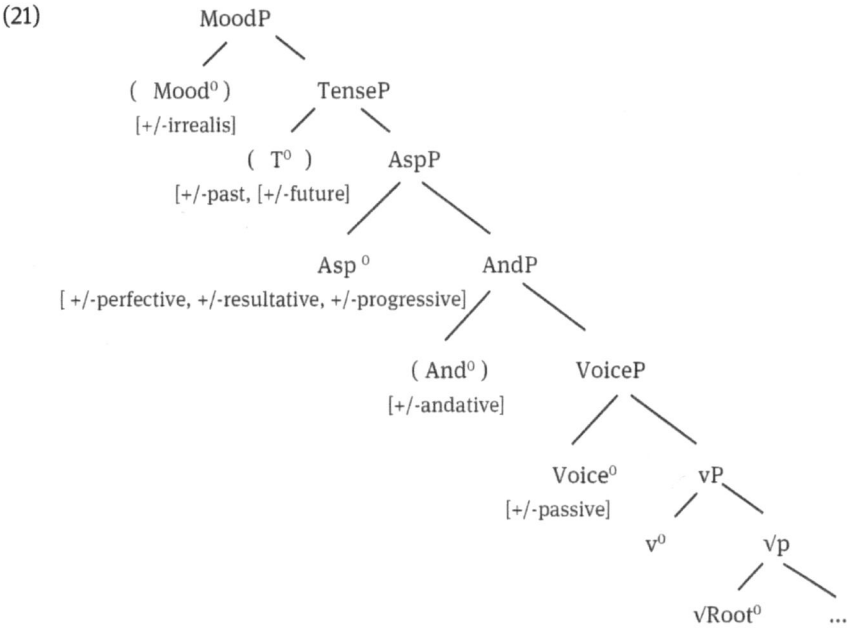

Assuming a universal hierarchical structure like that in (20) raises the question of how it is mapped onto surface morphological forms. If we look at the progressive as an example, we find that in analytic languages, it is, as expected, morphologically realized as an independent particle (see (22), from Cinque 2017: 558–559):

(22) a. dia   sedang   makan   (Indonesian)
       3SG   PROG   eat
      'He/she is eating.'
      (Pustet et al. 2006: § 3.4)
  b. sow   kəmɓuŋ di: roək   nhiəm   (Stieng, Mon-Khmer)
     dog   PROG   look   master
     'The dog is looking for its master.'
     (Bon 2014: 392)

In synthetic languages, it can be expressed periphrastically ('be at', 'be with', 'be in the middle/midst of', 'do', 'be in the course of', 'be on the way', 'now', 'hold', 'engaged/busy in', 'during', etc.), or through morphological affixation or other morphophonological means such as reduplication (examples from Cinque 2017: 559):

(23) Affixation
 a. sawi   ni-ʔafe-a-ʔa   (Tauya, Madang)
    banana   eat-PROG-3SG.-IND
    'He's eating bananas.'
    (MacDonald 1985: 355)
 b. n-iu   ang   me   i-golang   (Western Pantar, Alor-Pantar)
    1SG.POSS-mother   market   LOC   PROG-return
    'My mother is returning from the market.'
    (Holton 2014: § 7.2.2)
 c. pəʃu   lhamo   tənge   ki   na-tʂop-w   (rGyalrong, Sino-Tibetan)
    yesterday lHa.mo   clothes IDEF   PST-PROG-sew-3SG
    'Yesterday lHa-mo was sewing a piece of clothing.'
    (Prins 2011: 402)

(24) Reduplication
 a. i. wadek 'to read'   wadwadek 'to be reading'   (Mokilese)
    ii. piload 'to pick breadfruit' pilpiload 'to be picking breadfruit'
    (Harrison 1976: 220)

 b. i. Daniel nùŋ gúfu-gūfú   (Kom, Niger-Congo)
       Daniel pres drive-drive
       'Daniel is driving.'
    ii. Daniel nùŋ gúf-à
        Daniel pres drive
        'Daniel drives.'
    (Chia 1976: 112ff)

Italo-Romance displays both a periphrastic and an affixal realization of the progressive. Thus, a few southern Italian varieties, e.g. the Salentino dialect spoken by one of the authors of this paper, display a synthetic form of the progressive. In this case the progressive is realized prefixally. Note the realization of subject AGR at the end of the verbal form. Below we contrast the Salentino synthetic progressive forms with those of Italian:[9]

---

[9] There is no difference in meaning between the Italian and the Salentino progressive forms (*pace* Ledgeway 2016; see Calabrese 2019 for discussion).

(25)   Italian   Salentino

PRESENT

Italian		Salentino		
sto	*perdendo*	*sta*	*p'pɛrdu*	'I am losing'
stay.1SG	lose.GER	stay.1SG	lose.1SG	
stai	*perdendo*	*sta*	*p'pɛrdi*	'you are losing'
stay.2SG	lose.GER	stay.2SG	lose.2SG	
sta	*perdendo*	*sta*	*p'pɛrdɛ*	's/he's losing'
stay.3SG	lose.GER	stay.3SG	lose.3SG	
stiamo	*perdendo*	*sta*	*ppɛr'dimu*	'we're losing'
stay.1PL	lose.GER	stay	lose.1PL	
state	*perdendo*	*sta*	*p'pɛr'diti*	'you are losing'
stay.2PL	lose.GER	stay	lose.2PL	
stanno	*perdendo*	*sta*	*p'pɛrdunu*	'they are losing'
stay.3PL	lose.GER	stay	lose.3PL	

IMPERFECT (PAST)

stavo	*perdendo*	*sta*	*ppɛr'dia*	'I was losing'
stay.1SG.IMP	lose.GER	stay	lose.1SG.IMP	
stavi	*perdendo*	*sta*	*ppɛr'dia*	'you were losing'
stay.2SG-IMP	lose.GER	stay	lose.2SG.IMP	
stava	*perdendo*	*sta*	*ppɛr'dia*	's/he was losing'
stay.3SG.IMP	lose.GER	stay	lose.3SG.IMP	
stavamo	*perdendo*	*sta*	*ppɛr'diamu*	'we were losing'
stay.1PL.IMP	lose.GER	stay	lose.1PL.IMP	
stavate	*perdendo*	*sta*	*ppɛr'diuvu*	'you were losing'
stay.2PL.IMP	lose.GER	stay	lose.2PL.IMP	
stavano	*perdendo*	*sta*	*ppɛr'dianu*	'they were losing'
stay.3PL.IMP	lose.GER	stay	lose.3PL.IMP	

The /*sta-*/ in the right column is an integral part of the verbal word. This is shown by the fact that it cannot be separated from the other verbal constituent. For example, consider focal movement of V2, which is possible in southern Italian varieties in the case of *sta*-Infl + V-*ndo*, but not in the form *sta*+V-Infl. At the same time, an adverb may occur between *sta*-Infl and V-*ndo* but not between *sta* and V-Infl:

(26) a. Perdendo, lo stanno.
      lose.GER   it=stay
      'They are losing it.'

b. Lo stanno sempre controllando.
   it=stay always check.GER
   'They are always checking on it.'

(27) a. *Perdunu, lu sta.
         lose.3PL it=stay
     b. *Lu sta sempre controllanu.
         it=stay always check.3PL

As mentioned above, a fundamental issue for Cinque's lexicalist theory is how to account for the surface morphological realization of the functional structure in (21). Calabrese (2019) proposes a model that does account for this mapping of functional structure into surface verbal forms. This model also accounts for when periphrastic morphology occurs. Here we introduce this model by first illustrating the derivation of simple forms such as Italian *mangiava* 'eat.IMP.3SG' or *mangia* 'eat.PRES.3SG' and we will then go on with the issue of progressive aspect and consider the variation observed in this case between periphrasis and affixation.

3.1 The functional structure of periphrastic morphology

In Calabrese (2019), it is proposed that the affixal properties of functional heads follow from the the morphological requirement in (28):[10]

(28) *Synthetic morphology principle*:
    A functional head Y^0 must be adjoined to a root or to X^0 complex including a root.

In this system, syntactic representations in violation of (28) are repaired by m-word formation through the operation in (29), from Harizanov & Gribanova (2019) (for the sake of simplicity, the alternative operation of head lowering is not covered in this paper since it is not directly relevant to the analysis developed here; see Calabrese 2019 for discussion):[11]

---

[10] If we assume that category-defining X^0 nodes are functional elements, we can also account for why they must be adjoined to roots.
[11] In this approach, a single mechanism—the synthetic morphology principle (28) — with head raising (and head lowering) as the associated repair implements word formation. Such an approach is simpler, and more parsimonious, than other approaches such as that of Bjorkman

(29) A syntactic complementation relation [X⁰ [YP ... Y⁰ [ZP ...]]] may be realized in the morphology as a complex head by:

Head Raising:
[XP ... X⁰ ... [YP ... Y⁰ [ZP ...]]] → [XP ... [X0 Y⁰ X⁰] [YP ... [ZP ...]]]

(where Y⁰ and X⁰ are heads, X⁰ c-commands Y⁰, and there is no head Z⁰ that c-commands Y⁰ and is c-commanded by X⁰)

Given the syntactic structure in (30), head raising generates the structure in (31):

(30)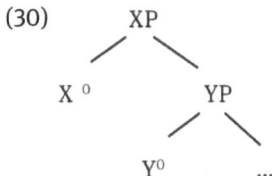

(31) A word-generated by head raising:

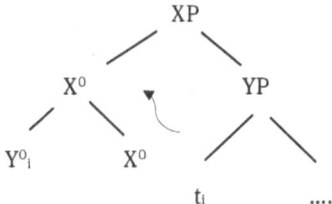

Therefore, given the structure in (21), head raising to satisfy (28) will create the structure in (32) by moving constituents upwards cyclically:[12]

(2011) where m-word formation (head movement in her theory) is associated with infl-agreement, or Pietraszko (2017) where word formation can be implemented by the mechanism of c-selection with m-word formation (head movement in her theory) as an additional strategy. It is closer to what has been proposed by Arregi & Pietraszko (2018) with a single operation (Generalized Head raising) including both head raising and lowering.

12 The positioning of the exponent of the head as a suffix/prefix is due to information associated with the exponent and not a morphosyntactic property (see below).

(32)
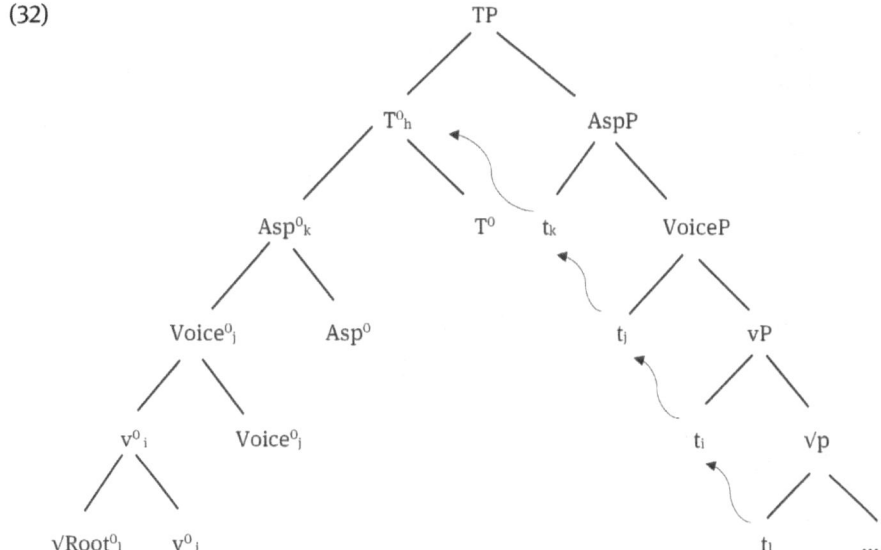

Three important operations are needed to derive the verbal surface structure of Romance verbal forms. Two of them insert ornamental[13] morphological pieces such as AGR (Halle & Marantz 1993, Bobaljik 2000) and Thematic Vowels (Oltra-Massuet & Arregi 2005). The third prunes nodes with non-overt exponents.

As proposed in Calabrese (2019), the rule in (33) inserts AGR. The two rules in (34a) and (34b) insert Thematic Vowels (TV) in Italo-Romance verbal forms. One further rule adjoins a TV to $v°$ (see (34a)). It applies early in the derivation before VI (and the subsequent pruning operations discussed below). Another rule of TV insertion applies after VI and pruning operations and adjoins a TV only to overt functional heads (34b):

---

13 As pointed out by Embick & Noyer (2007: 305), "while all morphemes and interpretable features are present at PF, not all morphemes that are found at PF are necessarily present in the syntactic derivation. Specifically, depending on language-specific well-formedness requirements, certain morphemes are added at PF. Such morphemes are never essential to semantic interpretation, since the derivation diverges onto PF and LF branches prior to the insertion of these morphemes. Thus, we speak of the reflexes of any morphemes inserted at PF as being 'ornamental': they merely introduce syntactico-semantically unmotivated structure and features which 'ornament' the syntactic representation." In other words, ornamental means that they do not have syntactico-semantic functions or content.

(33) AGR-insertion:
Given a Complex X^0 not including inherent phi-features, adjoin AGR_V to its highest X^0 (to be revised later).

(34) TV-insertion:

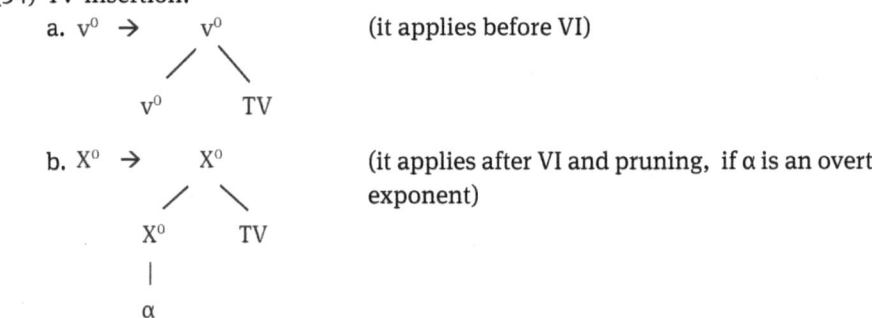

a. $v^0 \rightarrow$ [v^0 [v^0 TV]]   (it applies before VI)

b. $X^0 \rightarrow$ [X^0 [X^0 — α] TV]   (it applies after VI and pruning, if α is an overt exponent)

So before VI, (33) and (34a) apply in the case of complex head structure in (32):

(35)

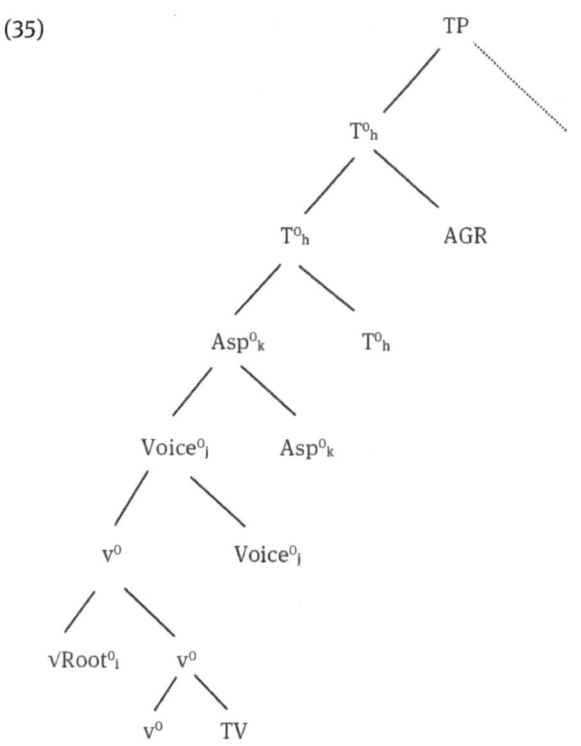

The complex head in (35) is the basic verbal structure of Italian generated by head movement before VI-insertion. It is an agglutinative structure, i.e., a cumulation of morphological nodes. However, in Italian, functional categories such as aspect, tense and mood are no longer represented as independent morphological pieces as in Latin (cf. *laud-a-vi-s-se-mus* 'praise.PLUPRF.SBJV.1PL'). On the contrary, a single morpheme appears for the string Mood+T+Past. Instead of assuming Halle & Marantz's (1993) fusion to account for the merging of these nodes, Calabrese (2019) proposes cyclic pruning of nodes with non-overt exponence followed by upward docking of the features that consequently become floating, as discussed below.[14,15] The rule is given in (36):

(36) 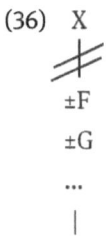   if X is a terminal node containing the features [±F, ±G, ...] and α is phonologically null exponent.

After pruning, the category X is not deleted; it becomes floating and is merged with an adjacent higher terminal node, if there is one.[16] This results in the fusion of the two terminal nodes where terminal node fusion is always triggered by this pruning operation. This operation applies cyclically right after the insertion of a null exponent during cyclic vocabulary insertion in phonological spell out. The delinked floating category can then attach only to the higher adjacent terminal node since the lower adjacent node has already undergone VI, and therefore can no longer be assigned morphological features. This is shown in (37), where Φ_1 and Φ_2 are exponents, and Φ_2 is phonologically empty:[17]

---

14 Pruning was originally proposed by Embick (2010) only for non-overt category defining nodes. Following Christopolous & Petrosino (2017) and Christopoulos (2018), Calabrese (2019) extended it to all types of non-overt category nodes and reformulated it as in (36).
15 It does not follow that all non-overt exponents are automatically pruned. There could be exceptions (see Calabrese 2019).
16 Another possibility is to assume that after pruning, it is not the category that becomes floating but actually its features, which eventually dock onto the adjacent terminal node.
17 Unattached floating features are eventually deleted but only at the end of phonological spell out, so they can play a role in triggering morpho-phonological rules such as ablaut processes.

(37) a. b.

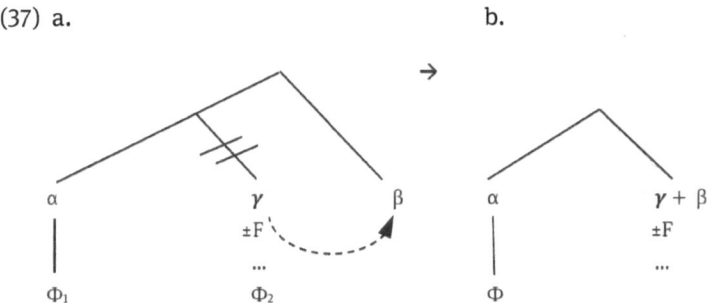

The pruning operation in (36) radically simplifies the phonological realization of morphosyntactic structures, and accounts for the convergence of possibly complex morphosyntactic structures and their possibly simpler PF surface shape. Consider the case of the Italian imperfect indicative *amavate* 'you.PL were loving'. Given the VIs in (38), cyclic VI followed by pruning and feature docking will generate the morphosyntactic structure in (39) where all the verbal functional nodes are fused together — in cyclic steps, due to the cyclic nature of VI insertion, an example of fusional morphology:

(38) a. Ø   <--> v^0
    b. Ø   <--> $Voice^0$
    c. Ø   <--> $[\text{-perfective}]_{ASP^0}$
    d. Ø   <--> $[\text{+past}]_{T^0}$
    e. /-v-/   <--> $[\text{-perfective, +past}]_{Mood^0}$

(39)

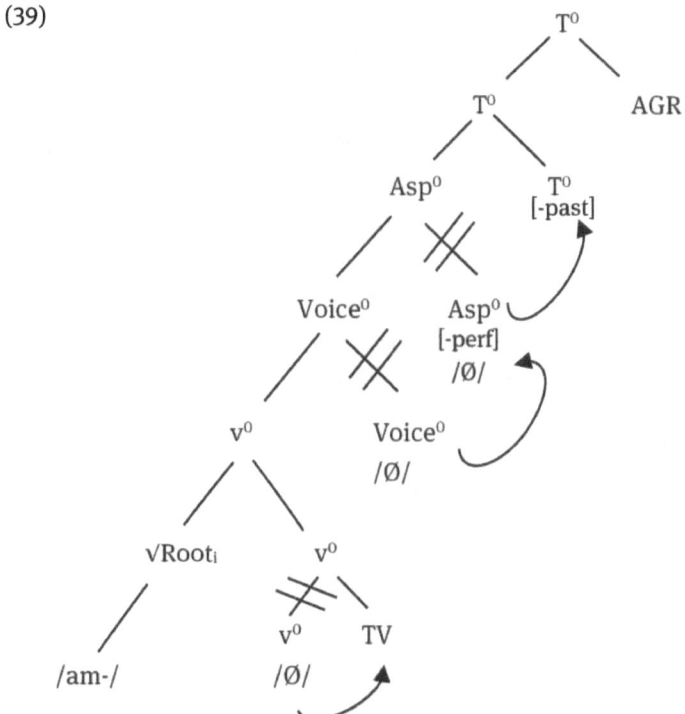

At this point due to the cyclic application of (38e), the exponent /-v-/ is inserted as follows:

(40)

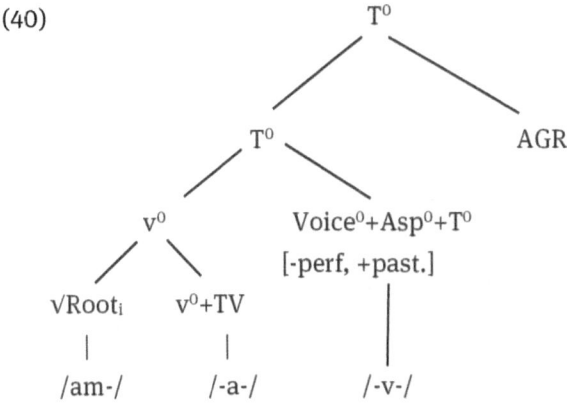

The TV insertion rule (34b) applies, and (41) is generated. For simplicity, we replace the complex fused [Voice⁰+Asp⁰+T⁰] head with T⁰:

(41)

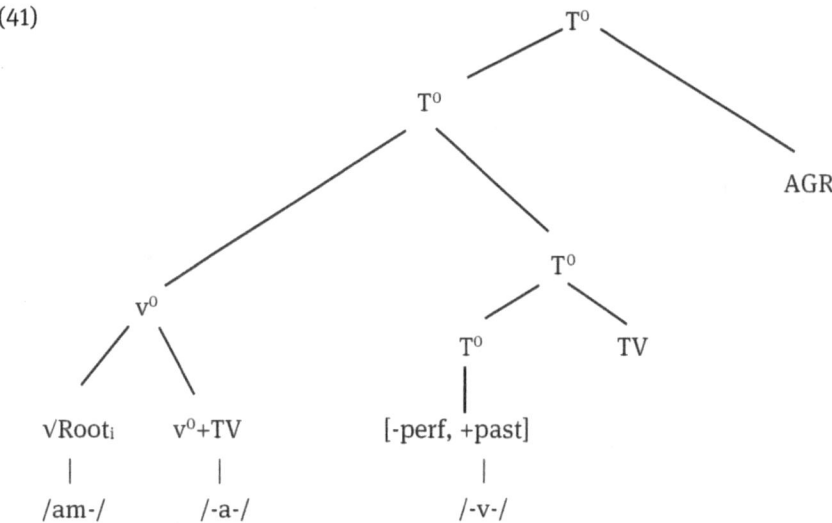

The final application of Vocabulary Insertion for TV and AGR will generate (42):

(42)

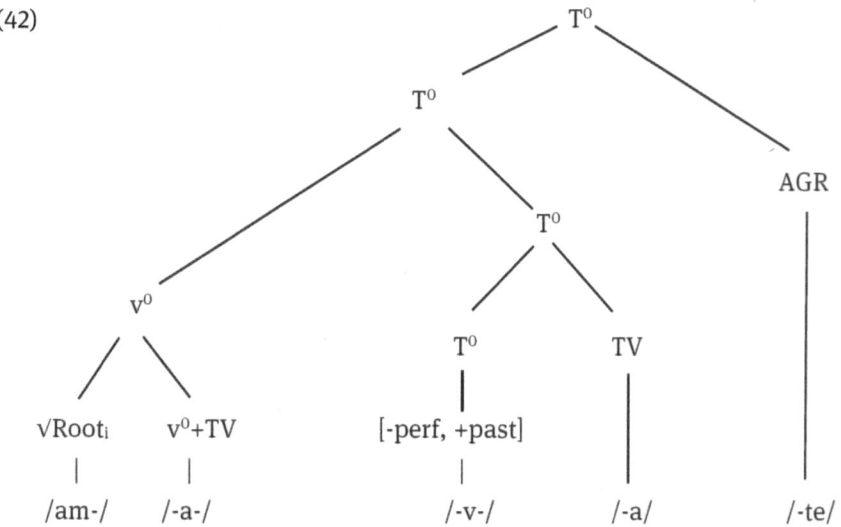

If verbal synthetic forms are due to the cyclic application of head movement which is able to convert the extended functional projection of a verb into a single complex X^0 (i.e., a single word involving a root plus affixes), one can plausibly assume that, in contrast, periphrastic verbal forms — in which similar verbal extended functional projections are broken into different complex X^0 (i.e. different words, auxiliaries and other verbal morphological pieces) — are due to the failure of the application of this operation to certain functional heads. In fact, this approach to periphrasis formation, which was at first formulated in Embick (2000) has been more recently fully developed by Bjorkman (2011), Pietraszko (2016), Fenger (2018, 2020) and Calabrese (2019).[18] In Bjorkman and Pietrasko's works, the failure of functional heads to combine with the verb is due to the action of certain nodes (or better the feature complexes of those nodes) as interveners (Rizzi 1990) in syntactic processes — such as Agree[19] — that lead to head movement. For example, the v-complex may not raise to Tense because (marked) aspect features intervene for the tense feature to be agreed with and checked. In Calabrese's model, in contrast, the failure of head movement is formalized in terms of morphological filters disallowing combinations of functional head features: movement is blocked if such combination may be generated. Fenger proposes that head movement may be blocked by phasal boundaries such as that between the verbal thematic complex which include Aspect and the higher T-C complex (see Bošković 2014, Wurmbrand 2017) — some form of phasal extension would be required to account for the cases where movement crosses these boundaries.

A thorough discussion, comparison and selection among these different theories is far beyond the goals of this paper. What matters for us here is that periphrasis is the result of blocking of head movement. A simple way of implementing this, without taking a stand with respect with above mentioned theories, is to propose that head movement[20] from one head position in the extended functional verb projection to the one directly higher up may be

---

18 An obvious advantage of such approaches over purely lexical ones that assume that periphrastic formation is just due to paradigmatic gaps (see Kiparsky 2004 for example) is that the periphrastic structure, and the subsequent formation of auxiliaries, follows the hierarchial functional structure: it is expected that when there is a higher and lower head, the lower head will end up on the verb, whereas the higher head ends up on the auxiliary.
19 In Bjorkman's system this is done via a version of Agree (Chomsky 2000, 2001), namely Upward Agree (see Merchant 2011, a.o.); in Pietraszko's system this happens through a type of selection, similar to cyclic agree (Béjar & Rezac 2009).
20 Here we are dealing only with head raising. The same blocking could also occur with head lowering, which is not considered here.

parametrized with a parameter allowing or not allowing movement from this position. If higher up movement is blocked, the complex X^0 head that was cyclically contructed up to that point remains stuck there. This leads to a periphrastic formation in which the extended functional projection is split in at least two X^0 complexes-words: a lower one, i.e, the blocked X^0 complex, and a higher one including the higher functional heads of the projection. The head movement parameters may have their deeper grounds in the theories mentioned above, e.g., they may be motivated by morphological constraints on combinations of marked morpho-syntactic features as in Calabrese's approach, and essentially also, in Bjorkman's and Pietraszko's one, or may be the effect of the presence of phasal boundaries as in Fenger's approach, but choosing what are their deeper bases will not be an issue here.

Thus, given the basic syntactic structure in (43), we assume that UG includes a parameter blocking head movement of the Asp [+Prog] head. Therefore, when a complex head reaches this position, it can no longer be head raised to T^0 as in (44):

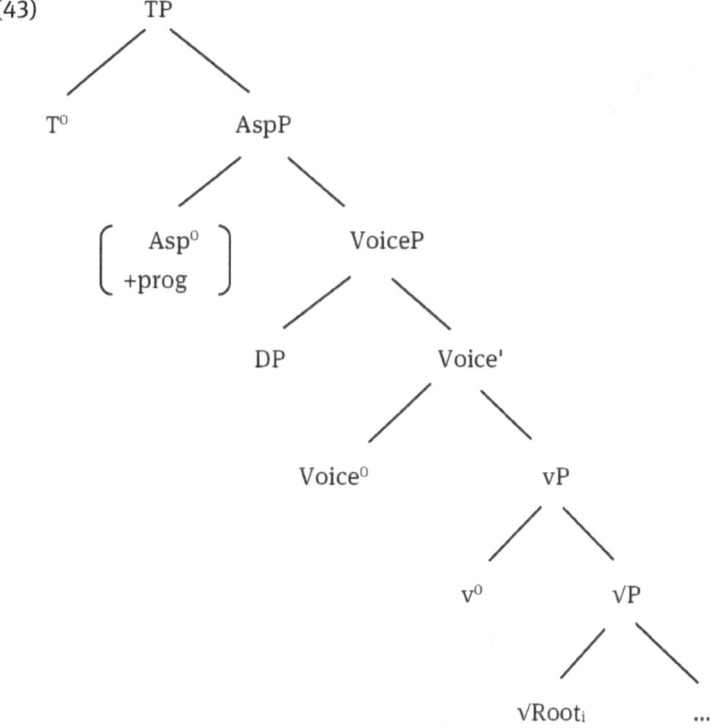

(44)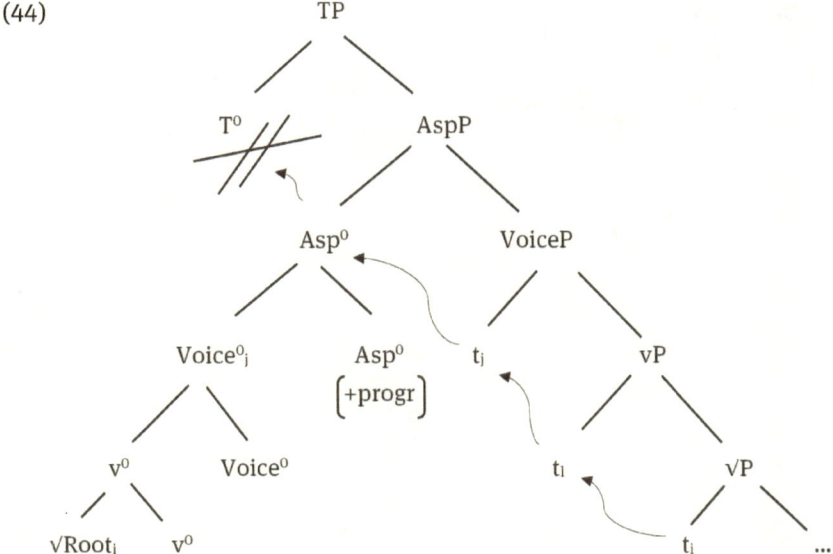

The lower complex X⁰ constituent undergoes pruning and TV and AGR_v insertion as in (45):

(45)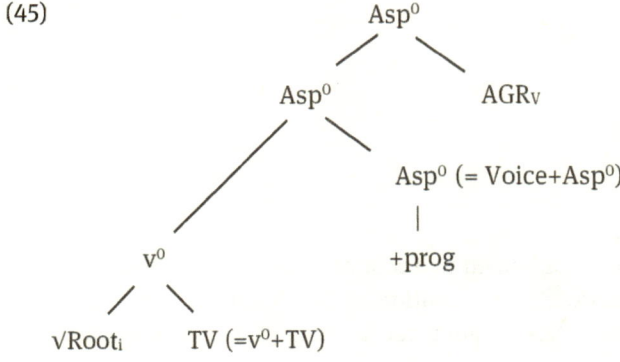

We assume that the gerund marker /-ndo/ cannot be decomposed morphologically. It is a single piece like the suffixal /-re/ of infinitive forms (i.e. *ama-re*, *perde-re*, etc.; see below). This assumption requires the two VIs in (47) and (48). (46) inserts a non-overt Ø for [+prog]_{Asp°}. This triggers pruning of this node and feature floating to the higher AGR, where /-ndo/ is inserted as in (47):

(46) PROGRESSIVE VI
/Ø/ <--> [+prog]$_{Asp^0}$

(47) /-ndo/ <--> [+prog$_{Asp^0}$ + AGR]

(48)
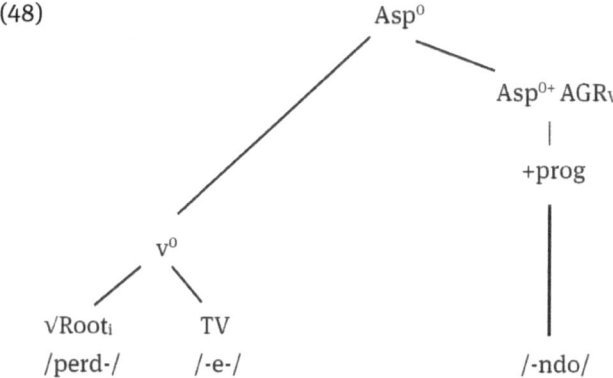

Let us now consider the higher constituent in the structure.

(49)
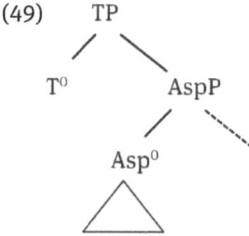

The functional head T^0 is not adjoined to a root or to a complex X^0 containing a root. Therefore, this constituent is in violation of (28). A dummy root — the AUX root — is hence inserted as a "holder" for these functional heads (Bjorkman 2011):

(50)
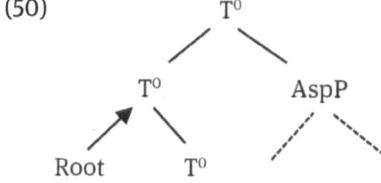

The auxiliary in this case is *stare* (lit. 'stay'). One problem is establishing whether the inserted root in this case is /sta-/ or /st/ + TV /-a-/. If the root is /sta/, the independently motivated rule of hiatus resolution in (51) would account for forms such as *sto* '1sg' (i.e., /sta/+ /-o/→ sto):

(51) V→∅/ __V

The 1st person plural present form *stiamo*, however, shows that the vowel of /sta-/ is actually a thematic vowel insofar as /-ya-/ is the expected allomorph of the thematic vowel in the 1st person plural (see Calabrese 2019). If the stem were /sta/+TV we would expect *sta-ya-mo* in this case as in *tra-ya-mo, tra-e-te* from *tra-e-re* 'pull'.

Note now that there is no v° in the structure in (50) and that therefore there should not be a v° TV. In fact, in many Italian dialects, the thematic vowel is missing in auxiliaries. See for example the following cases that compare the use of *avere* as a lexical verb and as an auxiliary:

(52) Lexical and auxiliary *have* in Sicilian and in Neapolitan
    a. Sicilian

lexical *aviri*	auxiliary
aju	aju
a(i)	a(i)
avi	a
avemu	amu
aviti	ati / atu
annu	annu

    b. Neapolitan

lexical *avé*	auxiliary
aggio	aggiu
aie	ê
ave	a
avimmo	amme
avite	ate
àveno	anno

However, in standard Italian there is indeed a thematic vowel in auxiliary *avere*, so in *avete/avevate* /av-/ is the root and /-e-/ is the expected thematic vowel, which can also be observed when *avere* occurs as a main verb:

(53) avete/avevate una bella casa   (av-e-te/av-e-v-a-te)
'you have/you had a beautiful home'

To account for what happens in this case, Calabrese (2019, 2020a) proposes that this is an instance of an abstract morphomic condition. Abstract morphomic conditions, according to him, introduce ornamental nodes such as Thematic Vowels but also what appears to be syntactically void functional heads. They are the ways in which the outcomes of analogical, or purely morphological, changes are integrated in the PF derivation, and the means by which abstract syntactic structures are converted into surface morpho-phonological forms where one finds pieces that do not have a true syntactic motivation. In the case of the auxiliaries, the morphological structure condition in (55) formally generalizes verb structure to AUX— a purely morphological change — by inserting a syntactically void v⁰ node and therefore the relevant TV. It holds in Italian but not in the Italo-Romance varieties in (52):

(54)

```
                v⁰
               / \
AUX→       AUX   v⁰
```

We can now propose that the auxiliary selection rule is that in (55):

(55) AUX → /st-/ / _____ AspPerf $^{[+prog]}$

The application of (54) to the complex head in (50), as well as the insertion of AGR and TV, and the pruning of null v⁰ due to its null status, will generate (56) in the case of the imperfect forms:

(56)

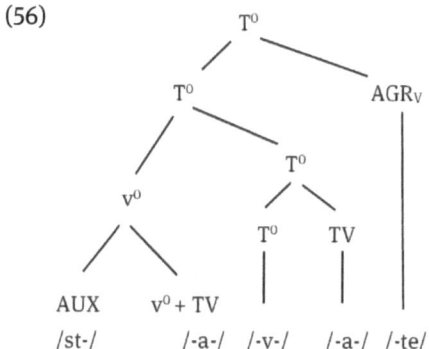

The full periphrastic construction is hence that in (57):

(57)

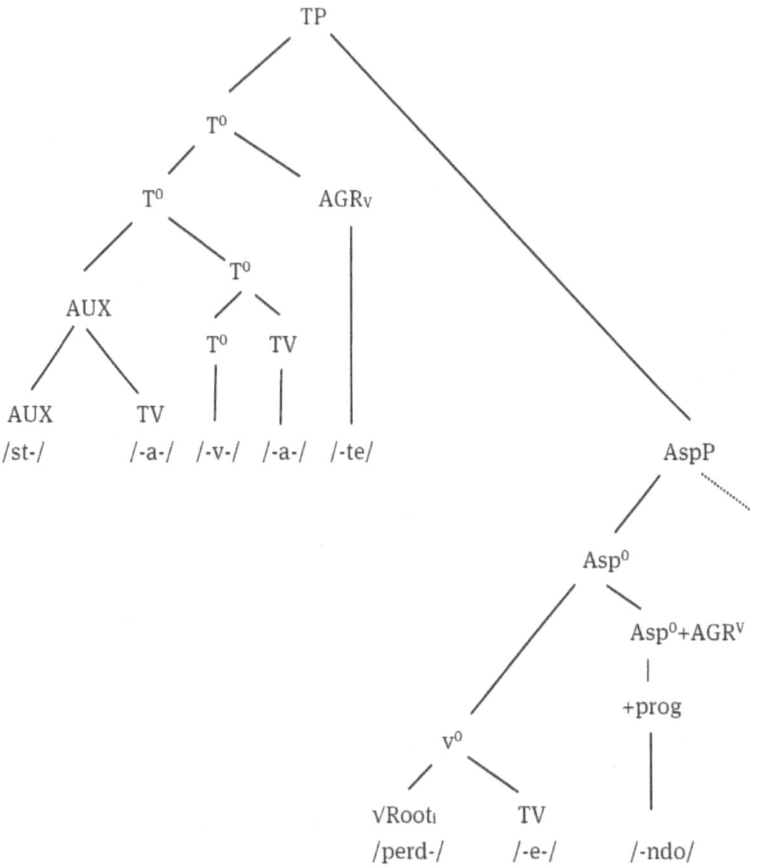

Alternative progressive periphrastic constructions characterized by an infinitive introduced by a simple or complex preposition and possibly a different auxiliary such as *be* ('be at', 'be with', 'be in the middle/midst of', 'do', 'be in the course of', 'be on the way', 'now', 'hold', 'engaged/busy in', 'during', etc.), can be derived in the same way if one assumes that the connecting preposition (the linker) is inserted by the rule in (58) as an instance of ornamental morphology and is therefore devoid of any syntactic and semantic content (see also fn. 1). The structure for the (substandard) Italian progressive periphrasis *stavate a perdere* (you.PL were at losing, 'you were losing') is shown in (59) – see below (cf. § 3.2) on the status of infinitives:

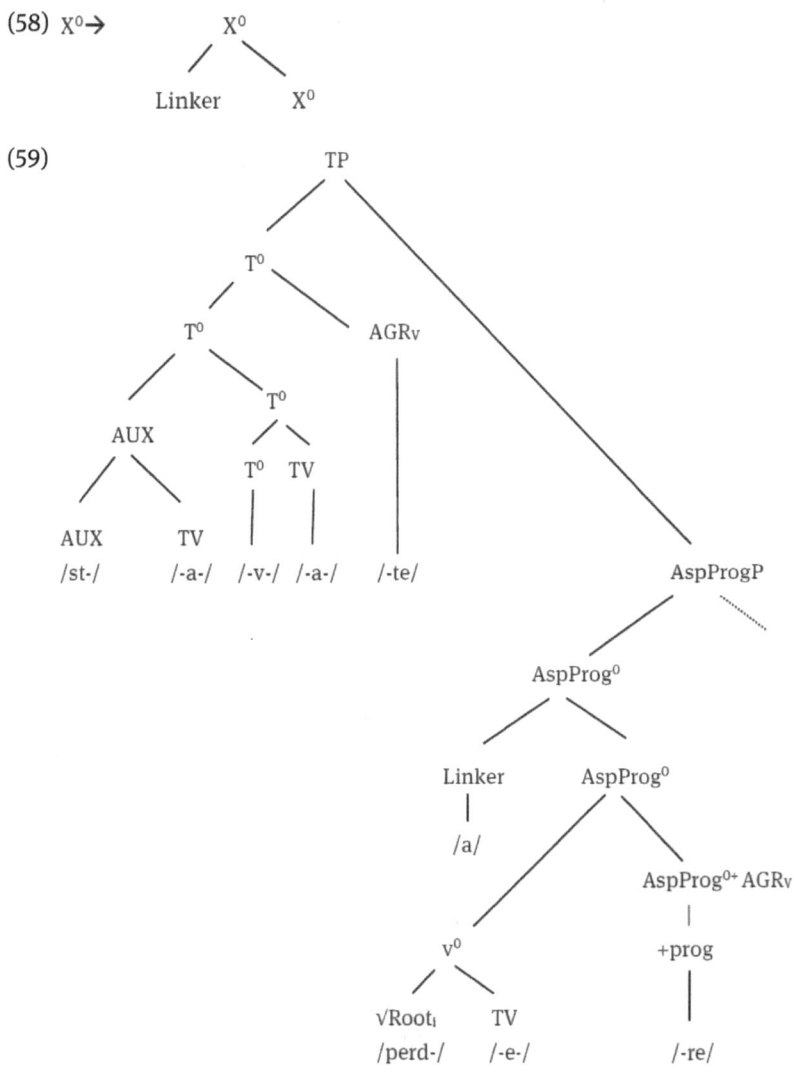

We assume that the Salentino synthetic progressive forms in (60) simply arise from setting the parameter allowing/disallowing head movement of [+progressive]$_{Asp°}$ in this variety. They can then be derived through full cyclic application of head raising (no blocking) with the crucial assumption that the exponent /sta-/ of the progressive is marked as being antitropal, i.e., it appears as a prefix instead of the morphosyntactically expected suffix (cf. (60)):

(60) sta-kumpramu   / sta-kumpravamu
    stay-buy.PRS.1PL / stay-buy.IMP.1PL
    'we are buying' / 'we were buying'

(61)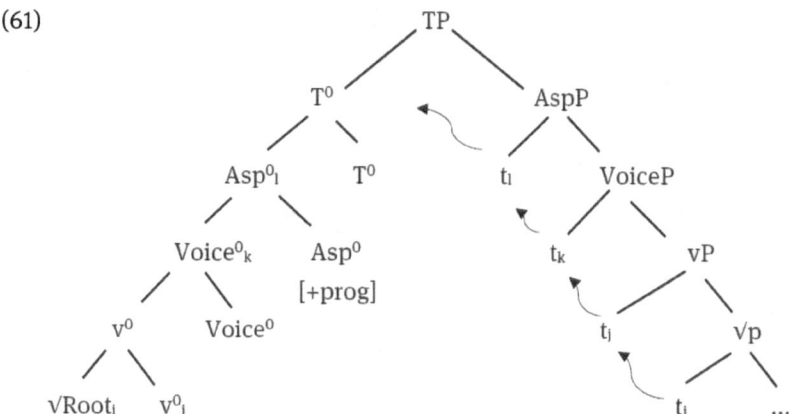

(62) /-sta-/[non-homotropal] <--> [+prog]$_{Asp°}$

Insertion of the relevant TV and pruning of null exponents will generate the surface structure in (63):

(63)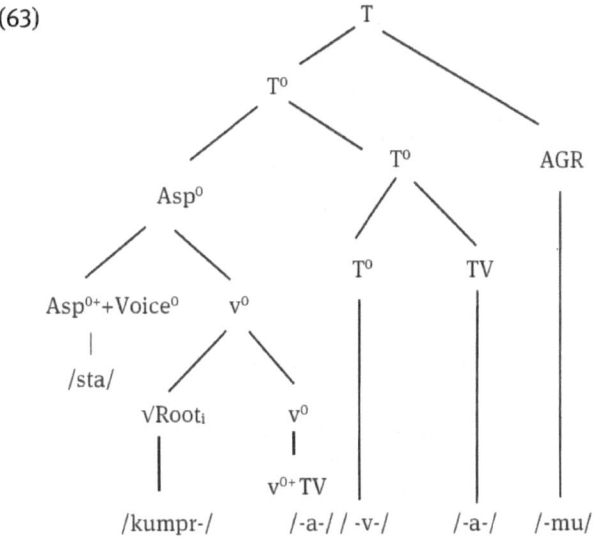

3.2 A morphosyntactic analysis of the Infinitival MVC

Following the model developed above, we can now provide a more explicit morphosyntactic analysis of Infinitival MVC constructions with restructuring. Consider (64):

(64) Lo   andavate   a   mangiare.   (Italian)
     it = go.IMP.2PL to   eat.INF
     'You were going to eat it.'

The sentence in (64) has the basic syntactic structure in (65) in the model developed here. Here V1 is a functional head in the Asp field (cf. § 2), which we label And⁰:

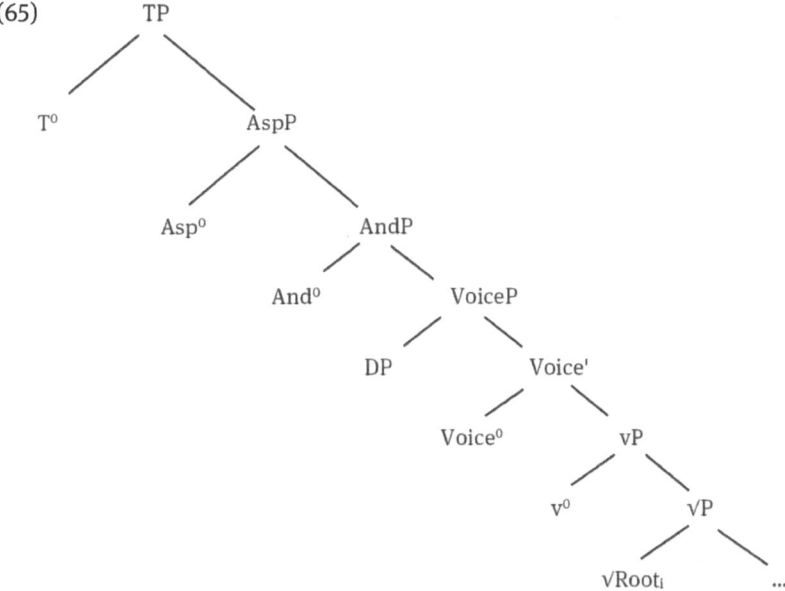

There are two issues to be addressed here before we analyse how (65) is converted to the surface Infinitival MVC in (64). First of all, we need to examine the connecting element /a/ and its morphosyntactic status. As proposed above (cf. § 2), we assume that this element is a linker that is inserted as an instance of ornamental morphology by the rule in (58) repeated as (66). It is thus devoid of any syntactic and semantic content.

(66) X⁰ →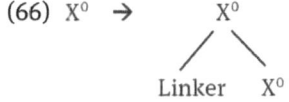

Secondly, we need to understand why V2 is characterized by infinitival morphology: what is the morphological nature of the infinitive? The infinitive, with the gerund, is by definition the "uninflected" verbal form and occurs in a wide variety of embedded constructions. Stowell (1982) suggested a basic distinction between future infinitives like that in (67a) (i.e., constructions in which the embedding predicate requires that the complement be "unrealized" at the time of the matrix event) and propositional infinitives like that in (67b) and (67c) (i.e., constructions in which the embedding predicate does not presuppose or assert anything about the temporality of the embedded event):

(67) a. Carlo ha deciso di leggere quel libro domani.
Carlo has decided of read.INF that book tomorrow
'Carlo decided to read that book tomorrow.'
b. Giorgio ha asserito di essere molto bravo.
Giorgio has stated of be.INF very good
'Giorgio claimed to be very good.'
c. Ritengo Maria essere molto bella.
believe.1SG Maria be.INF very beautiful
'I believe Maria to be very beautiful.'

Wurmbrand (2014) has shown that future infinitives are tenseless but involve a syntactically present future modal *element*, whereas propositional infinitives are TPs that involve a temporal argument corresponding to the attitude holder's NOW. She also adds the category of simultaneous nonattitude infinitives for those that are found in raising and restructuring verbs which can be AspPs if they include embedded (im)perfective or are bare vPs or VP.

(68) Sandra sembra parlar bene il francese. (*infinitive with raising verb*)
Sandra seems speak.INF well the French
'Sandra seems to speak French well.'

(69) a. Mario lo può leggere domani. (*infinitive with restructuring verbs*)
Mario it=can.3SG read.INF tomorrow
'Mario can read it tomorrow.'

b. Giorgio lo deve   comprare   subito.
   Giorgio it=must.3SG buy.INF   immediately
   'Giorgio must buy it immediately.'
c. Giovanni lo ha   cominciato a   cucinare ieri.
   Giovanni it=has started   to cook.INF yesterday
   'Giovanni started cooking it yesterday.'
d. Sandro lo avrebbe   voluto poter   cominciare a fare
   Sandro it=have.COND.3SG wanted can.INF start.INF   to do.INF
   subito.
   immediately
   'Sandro would have liked to be able to sart doing it immediately.'

(70) a. matrix V [CP [TP/FutlP [AspP [vP [VP]]]]]
     b. matrix V   [TP/FutlP [AspP [vP [VP]]]]
     c. matrix V   [AspP [vP [VP]]]
     d. matrix V   [vP [VP]]
     e. matrix V   [VP]

Importantly, for all constructions, Wurmbrand also showed that the different temporal properties of the infinitive do not correlate with a difference between control and ECM/raising. It follows that there is no syntactic functional verbal element, or other syntactic property, that can account for the surface distribution of the infinitive. An alternative, however, is to assume that this distribution is simply determined in the morphological component. Note in particular that all of the infinitival constituents in (70) share the property of being independent morphological words, specifically a verbal complex X^0. As proposed in Calabrese (2019), an important feature of all verbal complexes X^0 is that they are assigned an AGR node which is adjectival in participle forms— analysed as complex Asp^0 heads in Calabrese (2019) — but is otherwise verbal, where verbal AGR_V probes for person and number features, and adjectival AGR_{Adj} probes for gender and number features (and case features in languages with overt morphological case). The rule for AGR insertion proposed in that work is the following:

(71) Given a MP unit U containing v^0, (MP unit =Complex X^0)
     a. Adjoin AGR_{Adj} to its highest X^0 if X^0 is Asp^0
        Otherwise:
     b. Adjoin AGR_V to its highest X^0

We propose that the infinitive is the morphological realization of the AGR$_V$ and that it is therefore sensitive to AGR$_V$ features. In particular, we propose that the AGR properties of inflected verbal forms are associated with the feature [+pronominal], which triggers explicit morphological marking of phi-features. If the AGR is [-pronominal], in contrast, it lacks explicit marking of phi-features, and can co-occur with anaphorically-bound PRO subjects, with overt NPs, and with subjectless structures. The [-pronominal] AGR is realized as the infinitive:[21]

(72) /-re/ <--> [-pronominal]$_{AGR}$

The distribution of infinitives can be captured if one assumes that the presence of [+pronominal] AGR is associated with the presence of a deictic tense, as stated in (73). The feature [-pronominal] occurs as a default when Tense is non-deictic, i.e., anaphorically dependent on the Tense of the matrix verb, or when Tense is simply missing as in the future infinitives or in constructions with restructuring:[22]

(73) Deictic Tense → [+pronominal]$_{AGR}$

Infinitives therefore have a morphosyntactic structure such as that in (74), where X^0 is the highest functional element of the constituents in (70), and can range over different non-Asp^0 heads. This head is eventually fused into a single node with AGR as in the finite present counterpart (see (74)).

---

21 Here we are assuming that the exponent /-re/ of the infinitive cannot be further decomposed. See Cardinaletti & Shlonsky (2004) for a different view.
22 However, if one consider *l'infinitivo sostantivato*, i.e. nominal uses of the infinitive, one can even assume the presence of a TP:

(i) a. L'   aver   Mario vinto   quel concorso   il mese scorso   è una bella cosa.
       the   have.INF   Mario won   that contest   the month last   is a beautiful thing
       'Mario's winning that contest last month is a beautiful thing.'
   b. L'   aver   Mario bevuto   tutto il vino   ieri   è   un grosso problema.
       the   have.INF   Mario drunk   all the wine   yesterday is a   big   problem
       'Mario's drinking all the wine yesterday is a big problem.'

(74)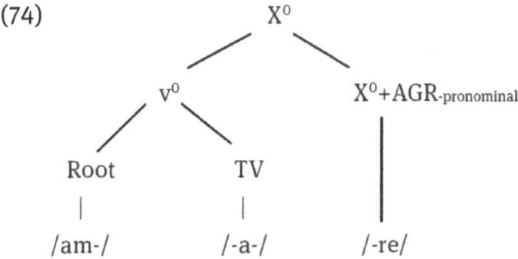

We now finally have all of the machinery to deal with the Infinitival MVC deictical tense. These costructions have all the same basic syntactic structure in (65) where And⁰ selects a VoiceP constituent. As a functional head, And⁰ is targeted by m-word. We propose, however, that head movement of the complex head And⁰ is blocked (as indicated by the sign //) due to the relevant parameter setting as in (75).

(75)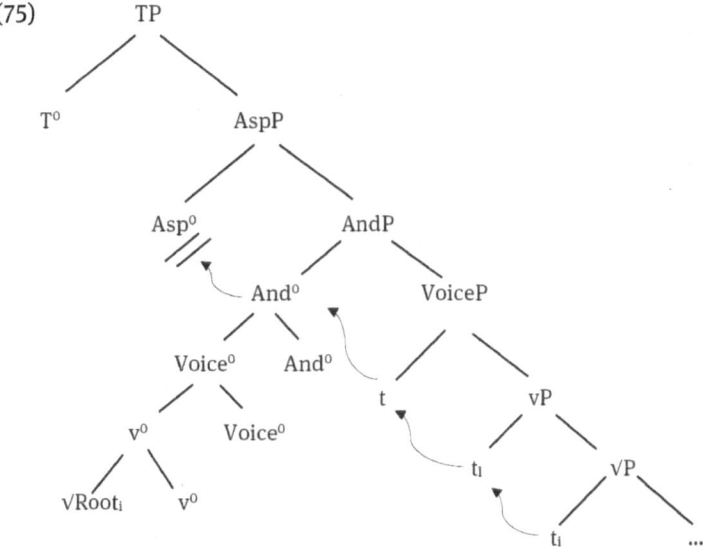

Let us consider the lower complex head in (75). TV and AGR insertion, pruning, and the operations discussed above account for the emergence of infinitive morphology:

(76)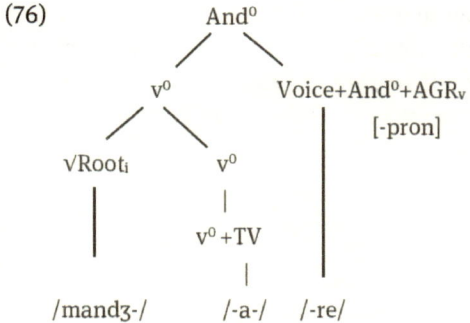

The linker /a/ is inserted as in (77):

(77)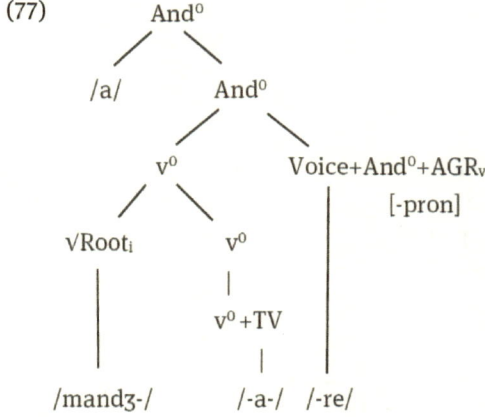

Let us then consider the top part of the structure in (77): Asp⁰ undergoes head movement to T⁰ as in shown in (78).

(78)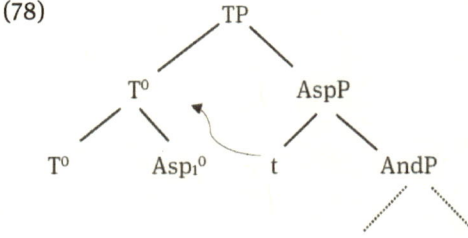

The resulting complex head lacks a root in violation of (28). A dummy AUX root is inserted. The shape of this AUX is determined by the rules in (79), which are sensitive to the different flavours of And⁰ (*andare, passare, venire*, etc.), which percolates upwards to the phrasal projection.

(79) a. AUX→ /AND-/²³ / ___ AndP^A
     b. AUX→ /pass-/ / ___ AndP^P
     c. AUX→ /ven-/   / ___ AndP^v
     etc.

Further v⁰, TV and AGR insertion, along with null node pruning and docking, generates the surface PF string in (80):

(80)
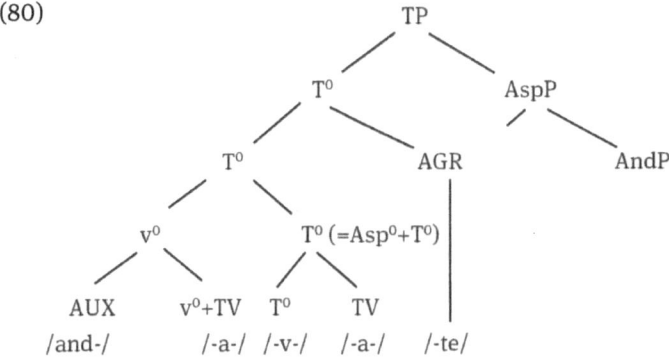

The full surface structure of (64) is displayed in (81):

---

23 This is an abstract root showing the suppletive alternant /vad-/ in the present, otherwise /and-/. See Calabrese (2020b) for an analysis of root suppletion in andative constructions in Salentino dialect of Campi Salentina.

(81)
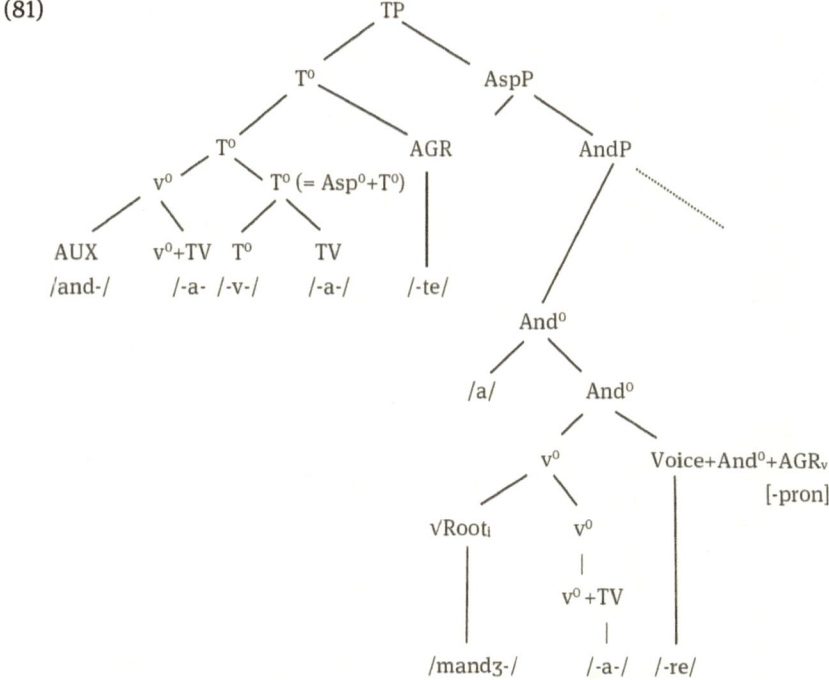

4 Doubly Inflected Constructions

Let us now consider, more specifically, the morphosyntactic patterns that characterize DICs. In some dialects, DIC exhibits a full paradigm, which is often subject to morphological reduction (cf. § 2): this happens in eastern Sicily (e.g. Modica) and Salento (see Manzini & Savoia 2005, I: 689–697). In many southern Italian dialects (in western and central Sicily, as well as in some Barese dialects north of Salento), however, DIC features a defective paradigm (see Cardinaletti & Giusti 2001, Cruschina 2013). We argue that defective paradigm of DIC in these dialects is also the outcome of an impoverishment process yielding a paradigm with a distribution that closely resembles the 'N-pattern' described in Maiden (2004, 2005, 2018).[24] In the tables below, the shaded cells are those in which DIC

---

[24] This is the most widespread defective paradigm in Sicily, but is apparently not the only possible distribution found on the island (see Di Caro 2018, 2019 for the patterns of variation).

is available: as we can see, DIC is not available with the 1st and 2nd persons plural of the present indicative or with the 2nd plural of the imperative, which all feature the allomorphic (arhizotonic) or suppletive roots. The same roots are employed in the imperfect, as well as in the rest of the paradigm, where DIC is systematically absent:

Tab. 1: The paradigm of *viniri* (*vèniri*) 'come' in Mussomeli, Sicily (V2= *pigliari* 'take')

vɪ'nɪrɪ ('vɛnɪrɪ)			Mussomeli		
			present (indicative)	*imperative*	*imperfect (indicative)*
SG	1		'viənnʊ a pɪjjʊ		vi'niva
	2		'viəni a pɪjjɪ		vɪ'nɪvɪ (vi'nivatʊ)
	3		'vɛni a pijja	'viəni/'vɛni (a) pijja	vi'niva
PL	1		*vi'niəmʊ a pijjamʊ		vi'nivamʊ
	2		*vɪ'nɪtɪ a a pijjatɪ		vi'nivavʊ (vɪ'nɪvivʊ)
	3		'viənnʊ a pijjanʊ	*vɪ'nɪtɪ (a) pijjatɪ	vi'nivanʊ

Tab. 2: The paradigm of *passari* 'come (by)' in Mussomeli, Sicily (V2= *pigliari* 'take')

pas'sarɪ			Mussomeli		
			present (indicative)	*imperative*	*imperfect (indicative)*
SG	1		'passʊ a pɪjjʊ		pas'sava
	2		'passɪ a pɪjjɪ		pas'savɪ (pas'savatʊ)
	3		'passa a pijja	'passa (a) pijja	pas'sava
PL	1		*pas'samʊ a pijjamʊ		pas'savamʊ
	2		*pas'satɪ a a pijjatɪ		pas'savavʊ
	3		'passanʊ a pijjanʊ	*pas'satɪ (a) pijjatɪ	pas'savanʊ

Tab. 3: The paradigm of *ìri* 'go' in Mussomeli, Sicily (V2= *pigliari* 'take')

pas'sarı		Mussomeli		
		present (indicative)	imperative	imperfect (indicative)
SG	1	'vajʊ a pıjjʊ		'jıvʊ
	2	'va a pıjjı		'jıʃtı
	3	'va a pijja	'va (a) pijja	'jı
PL	1	*'jamʊ a pijjamʊ		'jamʊ
	2	*'jıtı a a pijjatı		'jıʃtıvʊ
	3	'vannʊ a pijjanʊ	*'jıtı (a) pijjatı	'iərʊ

In the provinces of Bari (BA) and Brindisi (BR), DIC is found with a full paradigm in most dialects (e.g. Alberobello and Cisternino), but a defective DIC is also attested within the same area, as in the dialect of Conversano (Paolo Lorusso p.c., Manzini & Savoia 2005, Andriani 2017):

Tab. 4: Full and defective paradigms in some Barese dialects

full paradigm		defective paradigm
Alberobello (BA)	Cisternino (BR)	Conversano (BA)
'go + fetch'	'go + play'	'go'
vókə ppìgghiə	vò ssòne	vek
vè ppìgghiə	vè ssùənə	ve
vè ppìgghiə	vè ssònə	ve
scì ppəgghiéimə	scì ssunémə	ʃɛm
scì ppəgghiéitə	scì ssunétə	ʃɛt
vàunə ppìgghiənə	vònə ssònənə	van

Crucially, the distribution of DIC in the dialect of Conversano is identical to that found in the Sicilian dialects, where DIC is not available with the 1st and 2nd person plural of the present indicative (i.e. the shaded cells).

At this point we need to account for two major properties of DICs: double inflection and the defective paradigm. As briefly mentioned above (cf. § 2), double inflection arises independently of restructuring. What is special about this set of constructions is the agreement within the extended vP. In other words, DICs involve the assignment of explicit pronominal agreement features to V2. We have already postulated the presence of an AGR$_v$ element in the V2 constituent: it is introduced by the rule in (71). As postulated earlier, this AGR$_v$ is usually assigned the feature [-pronominal] and is hence realized as an infinitive, due to the fact that the V2 constituent lacks a deictic (non-anaphoric) Tense (or lacks this node entirely) (see (70)). If we assume this, then the main feature that characterizes DIC is the fact that the V2 AGR$_v$ is actually assigned the feature [+pronominal]. DICs thus display special morphological behaviour — a [+pronominal] AGR$_v$ in V2, that is, the rule in (82) which is characteristic of these dialects:

(82) Ø→[+pronominal] / [_____]$_{And^o +AGR}$

Let us turn to the question of how the DIC structures are constructed. As assumed earlier, morphological construction operates cyclically from the bottom up, and creates the structure in (83), which is identical to that in (81) except that the lower AGR is assigned the feature [+pronominal] by (82). (Remember that DICs are possible only in the present tense where T^0 has a null exponent in Italo-Romance and therefore undergoes pruning. We use the V1 *passare* to avoid the morphophonological complexities in the verbs *andare* 'go' and *venire* 'come'[25]):

---

[25] *Andare* 'go' requires suppletion (*va* in the present) (see, a.o., Pomino & Remberger 2019). In addition, the independently required morpho-phonological rule of TV deletion before a vowel-initial suffix (TV → Ø / __V) must apply. A further rule deletes the thematic vowel in the 3rd plural in *venire* and *andare*.

(83)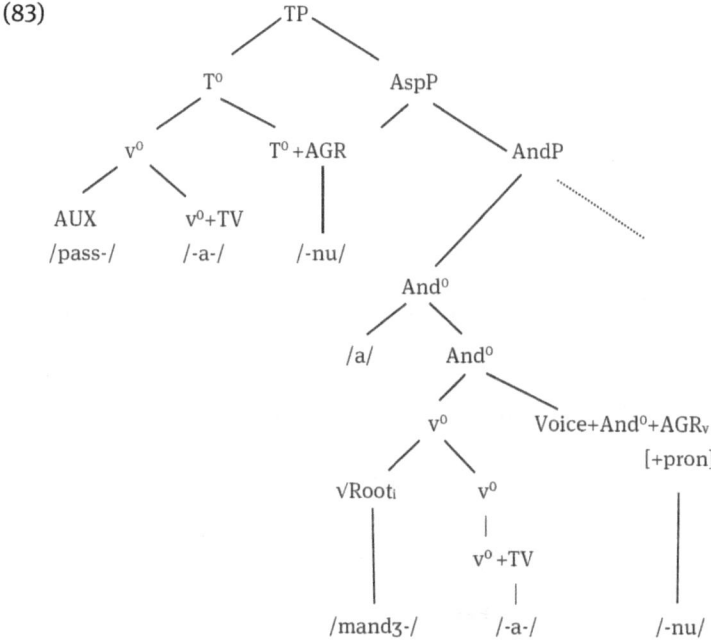

With regard to the defectiveness of the paradigm, we have seen that DICs are often not available in the 1st and 2nd plural. It is not the case, however, that in the dialects with defective paradigms it is impossible to say 'we are going to eat' or 'you (PL) are going to eat'. The issue is rather that the relevant DIC cannot be used for that purpose, and instead a construction where V2 is uninflected, i.e. an infinitive, is used. The actual problem, then, is the use of DIC in the 1st and 2nd plural. We have already drawn a correlation between the defectiveness of DIC and Maiden's N-pattern. Following Calabrese (2019), the special behaviour of the 1st and 2nd plural in the N-pattern can be accounted for by assuming that the regular morphology that appears in these persons is the result of an impoverishment operation. For example, in the case of the present tense of the Italian verb *uscire* 'go out' (*esco, esci, esce, usciamo, uscite, escono*), which presents a case of root alternation, impoverishment deletes the root diacritic that triggers the special ablaut changing *u* to *e* in the present. The assumption is that diacritics are the means through which information about irregular morphological behaviour is represented in morphology; once a diacritic is deleted, regular morphology arises.

Calabrese (2019) in fact shows that impoverishment can be used to account for cases of regularization or morphological levelling in traditional grammars.

For example, in the history of English we see cases of regularization of strong past forms as in (84):

(84) clomb ⇒ climbed
    crope ⇒ crept
    lough ⇒ laughed
    yold ⇒ yielded
    holpen ⇒ helped

The regularization we observe in (84) can be achieved by impoverishing the special root index required for the application of special Vocabulary Items and MP Rules; in other words, the lexical information necessary for their application is made unavailable. Therefore, the regular forms appear. Formally, we can say that *climb* in (84) loses the lexical markings Y and Z that are required for the application of the rules in (86) and (87) (Halle & Marantz 1993):[26]

(85) root^X -> impoverishment → root

(86) [+past] <--> -Ø / root^Y ____ where Root^Z= *sell, tell, climb*

(87) V --> $\begin{pmatrix} +\text{back} \\ +\text{round} \end{pmatrix}$ / [C$_1$ ____ C$_2$]Root^Z [+past] / where root^Y = *beat, drive, bind, …*

This provides us with an account of the changes in (84) (see Calabrese (2019) for more discussion). Let us now consider the following Italian verbal forms where special morphological operations apply in all persons except 1st and 2nd (and in the forms that are always regular: the imperfect and the infinitive): morphophonological rules in (88a–e), insertion of extension /-isk-/ in (88f), suppletion in (88g) and irregular deletion of imperfect marker (88h)).

(88) | 1SG | 2SG | 3SG | 1PL | 2PL | 3PL | |
|---|---|---|---|---|---|---|
| a. venni | venisti | venne | venimmo | veniste | vennero | 'come' (past) |
| b. misi | mettesti | mise | mettemmo | metteste | misero | 'put' (past) |
| c. feci | facesti | fece | facemmo | faceste | fecero | 'do' (past) |
| d. odo | odi | ode | udiamo | udite | odono | 'hear' |

---

26 With this we want to capture the idea that the innovation involves forgetting/not accessing for some reason the information (the diacritic) needed for the application of the rule, which remains the same.

e. esco	esci	esce	usciamo	uscite	escono	'go out'
f. finisco	finisci	finisce	finiamo	finite	finiscono	'finish'
g. vado	vai	va	andiamo	andate	vanno	'go'
h. ero	eri	era	eravamo	eravate	erano	'be' (imperfect)

As discussed in Calabrese (2011, 2012, 2019), the appearance of regular morphology in 1st and 2nd plural can be readily accounted for by assuming that the regularizations we observe in these persons involve repair operations implementing deletion—impoverishment— of featural diacritics. This impoverishment characterizes all Italo-Romance varieties (see Calabrese 2019 for discussion of its origins). For example, the cases in (88) can be accounted for by assuming that they involve impoverishment of the diacritic that triggers contextual allomorpy: morphophonological rules in (88a–f,h) and VIs (for suffixal (88a)) and root suppletion (88g)) (see also Calabrese 2012).

If we adopt this account of the special behaviour of the 1st and 2nd plural, we can then propose the following explanation for the defectiveness observed in DIC constructions. These constructions are characterized by special morphological behaviour—a [+pronominal] AGR in V2. We can therefore say that it is this feature that is impoverished in the context of the 1st and 2nd plural, which accounts for the defectiveness in those persons and for the emergence of the regular infinitival V2 in this case. This is illustrated in (89):

(89) [+pronominal] → Ø / [____, +participant, +plural] $_{And° +AGR}$

Once deleted, the feature [+pronominal] is replaced by its opposite [-pronominal] and AGR is morphologically realized as infinitival (on this specific issue, see also Lorusso 2019).

5 The loss of agreement

Let us now turn to the two final stages of grammaticalization of the MVC, where V1 is morphologically simplified by losing AGR and becomes an uninflected affix-like element. It is important to observe that there are cases in which the absence of an overt agreement marker is purely a surface property of the AGR exponent as in the following case:

(90) va pˈpɛrdu ('go' + 'lose', present indicative; Salentino, Tricase)
va pˈpɛrdi
va pˈpɛrde
ʃamu ppɛrˈdimu
ʃati ppɛrˈditi
vane pˈpɛrdɛnu

In this case the best analysis is one that assumes the presence of a higher AGR node for the andative auxiliary (AGR^1) and the AGR VIs in (91):[27]

(91) a. /-mu/ <--> [+part, +auth, +plur]$_{AGR^1}$
b. /-ti/ <--> [+part, +plur] $_{AGR^1}$
c. /-ti/ <--> [-part, +plur] $_{AGR^1}$
d. /-Ø/ <--> [-plur] $_{AGR^1}$

Table 5 shows the paradigms for the dialects of Putignano (from Ledgeway 2016: 168) and Lecce. If we compare the Campi dialect with those of Putignano and

---

[27] Interestingly, a similar process of affixation with a MVC has been reported for central American varieties of Spanish (Anderson 1979, Fleischman 1982: 116, Schwegler 1990: 146), as shown in the following table:

	standard spanish	selected american dialects
1SG	voy a dormir	yo v(w)adormir
2SG	vas a dormir	tu va:dormir
3SG	va a dormir	el va:dormir
1PL	vamos a dormir	nosotros vamos a dormir
2PL	van a dormir	Uds. va^n a dormir
3PL	van a dormir	ellos va^n a dormir

In Fleischman's (1982: 116) and Schwegler's (1990: 146) description of these data, it is argued that Panamanian speakers have taken 2nd and 3rd person singular as point of departure, assimilating the linking *a* between the two verbs and producing a lengthened vowel. From here the morphologized form seems to (optionally) extend to 1st person singular and, since the final -*n* in *van* is only weakly articulated, it might eventually regularize to the corresponding cells of the paradigm too. Fleischman (1982: 116) additionally provides a list of projected forms, that is the extension of the innovative synthetic form *vadormir* to all persons, including the plural persons. It would be very interesting to verify whether the predicted regularization has since taken place, a task that we leave for future research.

Tricase (see (90)), it emerges that radical reduction inflectional AGR endings has operated in the dialect of Campi, although there is still preservation of exponential suppletion (see Calabrese 2020b for an analysis) in the present, while some more specified inflectional forms are still used in the present forms in the dialects of Tricase and Putignano.

Tab. 5: DIC in the dialects of Putignano (Bari) and Campi (Lecce)

	Putignano (BA)	Campi (LE)
	'go + do'	'go + lose'
present	vɔk a f'fattsu	bba p'pɛrdu
	vɛ f'faʃə	bba p'pɛrdi
	vɛ f'faʃə	bba p'pɛrde
	ʃa fa'ʃeimə	ʃʃa ppɛr'dimu
	ʃa fa'ʃeitə	ʃʃa ppɛr'diti
	vɔn a f'faʃənə	bba p'pɛrdɛnu
past	ʃɛ ffa'ʃevəə	ʃa ppɛr'dia
	ʃɛ ffa'ʃivəə	ʃa ppɛr'dia
	ʃɛ ffa'ʃevəə	ʃa ppɛr'dia
	ʃɛ ffa'ʃemməə	ʃa ppɛr'diamu
	ʃɛ ffa'ʃivəəvəə	ʃa ppɛr'diuvu
	ʃɛ ffa'ʃevəənəə	ʃa ppɛr'dianu

As mentioned in Section 2, a type of radical impoverishment similar to that observed in the dialect of Campi is found in western and central Sicily, but in this case a defective paradigm is the target of the morphological simplification (Cardinaletti & Giusti 2001, 2003, 2019, Cruschina 2013):

(92) 1SG   vaju a pigghiu   / **va** a pigghiu
     2SG   vai a pigghi   / **va** a pigghi
     3SG   va a pigghia   / **va** a pigghia
     3PL   vannu a pigghianu / **va** a pigghianu
     IMPER. 2SG   vannu a pigghianu / **va** pigghia

Recall that in these Sicilian dialects, the impoverished forms are not limited to the verb GO, but are also found with other motion verbs, and that the DIC version with invariant *va* as V1 coexists with the version in which GO displays regular endings.

In some areas of eastern Sicily (e.g. Marina di Ragusa, Acireale) the grammaticalization of V1 appears to have reached the final stage of affix, as discussed in Section 2. The relevant data are repeated below for convenience:

(93) a. **Vo**ppigghju   u   pani.   (Marina di Ragusa, Sicily)
         go+fetch.1SG   the bread   1SG
     b. **Vo**ppigghi   u   pani.   2SG
     c. **Vo**pigghja   u   pani.   3SG   [*full paradigm*] ...
     d. **Vo**ppigghjamu u   pani.   1PL
     e. **Vo**ppigghjati u   pani.   2PL
     f. **Vo**ppigghjanu u   pani.   3PL

(94) a. **O**ccattu   u   giunnali   (Acireale, Sicily)
         go+buy.1SG   the newspaper   1SG
     b. **O**ccatti   u   giunnali.   2SG
     c. **O**ccattunu u   giunnali.   3PL
         ... [*full paradigm*] ...

When AGR morphology is systematically absent, one can assume a systematically phonologically empty AGR, that is, extending (91d) to all persons. We assume, however, that the most adequate analysis is that in which the andative morpheme is simply analysed as a prefix and is thus represented as in (95) (after head movement and AGR insertion):

(95)

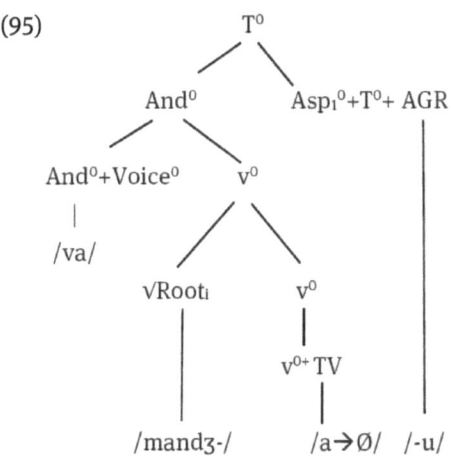

Crucially, the And⁰ exponent in this case must be marked as being antitropal, that is, as a prefix).[28] The structure in (95) is generated by simply allowing head movement to apply to the entire extended projection of v⁰, without blocking. No auxiliary headed by And⁰ would then be created and no AGR would be inserted in the case of V1. Given that free head movement to the highest projection as in (95) is independently required to generate this structure, there is simply no need to assume the presence of phonologically empty AGR in V1: indeed, this account offers a solution that is theoretically more parsimonious.

6 Conclusions

In this paper we have attempted to capture the syntactic and morphological properties and processes that determine the different shades of microvariation in southern Italian MVCs. Concentrating on the cases of restructuring where V1 is a functional verb, we integrated Cinque's (1999) model of functional projections into Distributed Morphology so as to arrive at a syntactic model of word construction. Within this approach, no operation of fusion need be stipulated, but the morphosyntactic features of functional heads are moved upwards

---

28 The prefixal nature of the andative element is confirmed not only by the fact that it can never be separated from the verbal complex, for example by a clitic pronoun (i) or by an adverb (ii), but also by the peculiar position of the andative element in present perfect forms (see (iii)):

(i)   a.   *bba   lu   kkattu
            go   it=   buy.PRS.1SG
     b.   lu   bba   kattu
            it=   go   buy.PRS.1SG
         'I go to buy it.'
(ii)   a.   *bba   sempre   ffatiu,   la   matina.
           go   always   work.PRS.1SG   the   morning
     b.   bba   ffatiu   sempre,   la   matina.
           go   work.PRS.1SG   always   the   morning
         'I always go to work in the morning.'
(iii)   l'addʒu   ʃʃa kkattatu
       it=have.PRS.1SG   go-buy.PTCP
       'I went to buy it.'

In (iii) the andative element appears as a prefix on the past participle below the auxiliary. This periphrastic structure is easily derivable if head movement of the andative head is allowed but not that of the [+Perfect] aspectual head (see Calabrese 2020b for detailed discussion).

cyclically generating complex heads and being available for further vocabulary insertion. Nodes with non-overt exponents are pruned.

Following in particular Calabrese (2019), we accounted for the characteristic properties of several MVCs: the difference between Infinitival MVC and the MVC with double inflection (DIC), the defective paradigm of certain MVCs, and the morphological reduction of the motion V1, which has reached affix status in some constructions. While the infinitive is the morphological realization of a [-pronominal] agreement node lacking phi-features, DIC arises from an identical structure in which AGR is assigned the feature [+pronominal], thus agreeing with V1 in person and number. The special behaviour of the 1st and 2nd plural in the defective paradigms is then accounted for as the result of an operation of impoverishment that applies with these persons. When V1 displays no agreement morphology, we propose that the andative morpheme is simply analysed as a prefix: no independent auxiliary is created and no AGR is inserted.

In southern Italian dialects, all these properties and processes interact and co-exist in different ways, giving rise to a great deal of microvariation. With this study, we thus hope to have contributed to the analysis of microvariation patterns through the tools and insights of formal and theoretical linguistics.

Acknowledgement: We are grateful to Eva-Maria Remberger for her constant support and valuable feedback, and to two anonymous reviewers for their comments and suggestions. We would also like to thank Guglielmo Cinque for helpful discussion and fruitful remarks.

7 References

Anderson, Eric W. 1979. The development of the Romance future tense: Morphologization and a tendency toward analyticity. *Papers in Romance* 1. 21–35.

Andriani, Luigi. 2017. *The syntax of the dialect of Bari*. Cambridge: University of Cambridge dissertation.

Arregi, Karlos & Asia Pietraszko. 2018. Generalized head movement. In Patrick Farrell (ed.), *Proceedings of the LSA, Volume 3*, 5, 1–15. Washington, DC: Linguistic Society of America.

Ascoli, Graziadio I. 1896. Un problema di sintassi comparata dialettale. *Archivio glottologico italiano* 14. 453–468.

Ascoli, Graziadio I. 1901. Appendice all'articolo Un problema di sintassi comparata dialettale. *Archivio glottologico italiano* 15. 221–225.

Baker, Mark. 2010. *The syntax of agreement and concord*. Cambridge: Cambridge University Press.

Béjar, Susana & Milan Rezac 2009. Cyclic agree. *Linguistic Inquiry* 40. 35–73.

Bjorkman, Bronwyn Alma Moore. 2011. *BE-ing default: The morphosyntax of auxiliaries*. Ph.D. dissertation. Cambridge, MA: MIT.
Bobaljik, Jonathan. 2000. The ins and outs of contextual allomorphy. In Kleanthes Grohmann & Caro Struijke (eds.), *Proceedings of the Maryland Mayfest on Morphology 1999*, 35–71. College Park: University of Maryland, Department of Linguistics.
Bon, Noëllie. 2014. *Une Grammaire de la Langue Stieng: Langue en Danger du Cambodge et du Vietnam [A Grammar of the Stieng Language: An Endangered Language in Cambodia and Vietnam]*. Ph.D. dissertation. Lyon: University Lumiere Lyon 2.
Bošković, Željko. 2014. Now I'm a phase, now I'm not a phase: On the variability of phases with extraction and ellipsis. *Linguistic Inquiry* 45. 27–89.
Bybee, Joan, Revere Perkins & William Pagliuca. 1994. *The evolution of grammar: Tense, aspect and modality in the languages of the world*. Chicago: University of Chicago Press.
Calabrese, Andrea. 2008. On absolute and contextual syncretism. Remarks on the structure of paradigms and on how to derive it. In Andrew Nevins & Asef Bachrach (eds.), *The bases of Inflectional Identity*, 156–205. Oxford: Oxford University Press.
Calabrese, Andrea. 2011. Investigations on markedness, syncretism and zero exponence in morphology. *Morphology* 21(2). 283–325.
Calabrese, Andrea. 2012. Allomorphy in the Italian passato remoto: A Distributed Morphology analysis. *Language and Information Society* 18. 1–75.
Calabrese, Andrea. 2019. *Morphophonological investigations: A theory of PF. From syntax to phonology in Italian and Sanskrit verb forms*. Manuscript, University of Connecticut.
Calabrese, Andrea. 2020a. Remarks on the role of the perfect participle in Italian morphology and on its history. To appear in Ian Roberts & Adam Ledgeway (eds.), *Probus*, special issue on Romance Historical Linguistics.
Calabrese, Andrea. 2020b. *The morphosyntax of andative forms in the Campiota vernacular. The synthetic behavior of restructuring roots*. Manuscript, University of Connecticut.
Cardinaletti, Anna & Giuliana Giusti. 2001. Semi-lexical motion verbs in Romance and Germanic. In Norbert Corver & Henk van Riemsdijk (eds.), *Semi-lexical categories. On the function of content words and the content of function words*, 371–414. Berlin: De Gruyter.
Cardinaletti, Anna & Giuliana Giusti. 2003. Motion verbs as functional heads. In Cristina Tortora (ed.), *The syntax of Italian dialects*, 31–49. Oxford & New York: Oxford University Press.
Cardinaletti, Anna & Giuliana Giusti. 2019. Multiple agreement in southern Italian dialects. In Ludovico Franco & Paolo Lorusso (eds.), *Linguistic Variations: Structure and Interpretation. Studies in Honor of M. Rita Manzini*, 125–147. Berlin: De Gruyter.
Cardinaletti, Anna & Ur Shlonsky. 2004. Clitic positions and restructuring in Italian. *Linguistic Inquiry* 35. 519–557.
Chia, Emmanuel N. 1976. *Kom Tenses and Aspects*. Washington, DC: Georgetown University dissertation.
Chomsky, Noam. 2000. Minimalist inquiries: The framework. In Roger Martin, David Michaels & Juan Uriagereka (eds.), *Step by Step: Essays on Minimalist Syntax in Honor of Howard Lasnik*, 89–155. Cambridge, MA: MIT Press.
Chomsky, Noam. 2001. Derivation by phase. In Michael Kenstowicz (ed.), *Ken Hale: A Life in Language*, 1–52. Cambridge, MA: MIT Press.
Christopoulos, Christos. 2018. Restricting the locality of contextual allomorphy. Manuscript, University of Connecticut.

Christopoulos, Christos & Roberto Petrosino. 2017. Greek root allomorphy without spans. In Wm. G. Bennett, Lindsay Hracs & Dennis Ryan Storoshenko (eds.), *Proceedings of the 35th West Coast Conference in Formal Linguistics*, 151–160. Somerville, MA: Cascadilla Proceedings Project.

Cinque, Guglielmo. 1999. *Adverbs and functional heads*. Oxford & New York: Oxford University Press.

Cinque, Guglielmo. 2001. "Restructuring" and functional structure. In Laura Brugè (ed.), *University of Venice Working Papers in Linguistics* 11. 45–127.

Cinque, Guglielmo. 2006. *Restructuring and functional heads*. Oxford & New York: Oxford University Press.

Cinque, Gugliemo. 2017. On the status of functional categories (heads and phrases). *Language and Linguistics* 18(4). 521–576.

Cruschina, Silvio. 2013. Beyond the stem and inflectional morphology: An irregular pattern at the level of periphrasis. In Silvio Cruschina, Martin Maiden & John C. Smith (eds.), *The boundaries of pure morphology. Diachronic and synchronic perspectives*, 262–283. Oxford: Oxford University Press.

Cruschina, Silvio. 2018. The 'go for' construction in Sicilian. In Roberta D'Alessandro & Diego Pescarini (eds.), *Advances in Italian dialectology: Sketches of Italo-Romance grammars*, 292–320. Leiden: Brill.

Cruschina, Silvio. In press. Gone unexpectedly: Pseudo-coordination and the expression of surprise in Sicilian. In Vincenzo Nicolò Di Caro, Giuliana Giusti & Daniel Ross (eds.), *Pseudo-Coordination and Multiple Agreement Constructions*. Amsterdam: John Benjamins.

Cruschina, Silvio & Valentina Bianchi. In press. A surprising association and an unexpected move: Mirative implicatures at the syntax-semantics interface. In Andreas Trotzke & Xavier Villalba (eds.), *Expressive Meaning across Linguistic Levels and Frameworks*. Oxford: Oxford University Press.

Del Prete, Fabio & Giuseppina Todaro. 2020. Building complex events. The case of Sicilian Doubly Inflected Construction. *Natural Language & Linguistic Theory* 38. 1–41.

Di Caro, Vincenzo Nicolò. 2015. Syntactic constructions with motion verbs in some Sicilian dialects: a comparative analysis. MA thesis. Venice: Ca' Foscari University.

Di Caro, Vincenzo Nicolò. 2018. The Inflected Construction in the dialects of Sicily. Parameters of microvariation. In Silvio Cruschina, Adam Ledgeway & Eva-Maria Remberger (eds.), *Italian dialectology at the interfaces*, 63–78. Amsterdam: John Benjamins.

Di Caro, Vincenzo Nicolò. 2019. *Multiple agreement constructions in southern in Italo-Romance. The syntax of Sicilian pseudo-coordination*. Ph.D. dissertation. Venice: Ca' Foscari University of Venice.

Embick, David. 2010. *Localism versus globalism in morphology and phonology*. Cambridge, MA: MIT Press.

Embick, David & Rolf Noyer. 2007. Distributed morphology and the syntax-morphology interface. In Gillian Ramchand & Charles Reiss (eds.), *Oxford Handbook of Linguistic Interfaces*, 289-324. Oxford: Oxford University Press

Fenger, Paula. 2018. Head movement: The view from failure affixation, periphrasis and clitics. Manuscript, University of Connecticut.

Fenger, Paula. 2020. *Words within words: The internal syntax of words*. Ph.D. dissertation. Storrs, CT: University of Connecticut.

Fleischman, Suzanne. 1982. *The future in thought and language. Diachronic evidence from Romance.* Cambridge: Cambridge University Press.
Halle, Morris & Alec Marantz. 1993. Distributed Morphology and the pieces of inflection. In Kenneth Hale & Samuel Jay Keyser (eds.), *The View from Building 20: Essays in linguistics in honor of Sylvain Bromberger*, 111–176. Cambridge, MA: MIT Press.
Harizanov, Boris & Vera Gribanova. 2019. Whither head movement? *Natural Language & Linguistic Theory* 37. 461–522.
Harrison, Sheldon P. 1976. *Mokilese Reference Grammar.* Honolulu: University of Hawaii Press.
Holton, Gary. 2014. Western Pantar. In Antoinette Schapper (ed.), *The Papuan Languages of Timor, Alor and Pantar Vol. 1: Sketch Grammars*, 23–96. Berlin: De Gruyter Mouton.
Kiparsky, Paul. 2004. Blocking and periphrasis in inflectional paradigms. In Geert Booij & Jaap van Marle (eds.), *Yearbook of Morphology 2004*, 113–135. Dordrecht: Springer.
Ledgeway, Adam. 2016. From coordination to subordination: The grammaticalisation of progressive and andative aspect in the dialects of Salento. In Fernanda Pratas, Sandra Pereira & Clara Pinto (eds.), *Coordination and Subordination. Form and Meaning – Selected Papers from CSI Lisbon 2014*, 157–184. Cambridge: Cambridge Publishing Scholars.
Leone, Alfonso. 1973. Vattel'a pesca, vieni a piglialo. *Lingua Nostra* 34. 11–13.
Lorusso, Paolo. 2019. A person split analysis of the progressive forms in some Southern Italian varieties. In Silvio Cruschina, Adam Ledgeway & Eva-Maria Remberger (eds.), *Italian dialectology at the interfaces*, 203–236. Amsterdam: John Benjamins.
MacDonald, Lorna. 1985. *A Grammar of Tauya.* Winnipeg: University of Manitoba dissertation.
Maiden, Martin. 2004. Verb augments and meaninglessness in early Romance morphology. *Studi di grammatica italiana* 22. 1–61.
Maiden, Martin. 2005. Morphological autonomy and diachrony. In Geert Booij & Jaap van Marle (eds.), *Yearbook of Morphology 2004*, 137–175. Dordrecht: Springer.
Maiden, Martin. 2018. *The Romance verb: Morphomic structure and diachrony.* Oxford: Oxford University Press.
Manzini, M. Rita & Leonardo M. Savoia. 2005. *I dialetti italiani e romanci. Morfosintassi generativa.* Alessandria: Edizioni dell'Orso.
Oltra-Massuet, Isabel & Karlos Arregi. 2005. Stress-by-structure in Spanish. *Linguistic Inquiry* 36. 43–84.
Pietraszko, Asia. 2016. The syntax of simple and compound tenses in Ndebele. *Proceedings of the Linguistics Society of America Annual Meeting* 1(18). 1–15.
Pietraszko, Asia. 2018. Auxiliary vs INFL in Bantu. The syntactic and phonological complexity of Ndebele verbs. *Natural Language and Linguistic Theory* 36(1). 265–308.
Pomini, Natascha & Eva-Maria Remberger. 2019. Verbal suppletion in Romance diachrony: The perspective of Distributed Morphology. In Frans Plank & Nigel Vincent (eds.), *Life-Cycle of Suppletion.* Special Issue of the *Transactions of the Philological Society* 117(3). 471–497.
Prins, Maria Clazina. 2011. *A Web of relations: A grammar of rGyalrong Jiǎomùzú (Kyom-kyo) Dialects.* Leiden: Leiden University dissertation.
Pustet, Regina, Juliana Wijaya & Than Than Win. 2006. Progressives in typological perspective. *Languages in Contrast* 6(2). 177–227.
Rizzi, Luigi. 1976. Ristrutturazione. *Rivista di grammatica generativa* 1. 1–54.
Rizzi, Luigi. 1978. A Restructuring Rule in Italian Syntax. In Samuel Jay Keyser (ed.), *Recent transformational studies in European languages*, 113–158. Cambridge, MA: MIT Press.
Rizzi, Luigi. 1990. *Relativized minimality.* Cambridge, MA: MIT Press.

Rohlfs, Gerhard. 1969. *Grammatica storica della lingua italiana e dei suoi dialetti. Vol. 3: Sintassi e formazione delle parole*. Turin: Einaudi.
Schwegler, Armin. 1990. *Analyticity and syntheticity: A diachronic perspective with special reference to Romance Languages*. Berlin & New York: De Gruyter.
Sornicola, Rosanna. 1976. Vado a dire o vaiu a ddico: problema sintattico o problema semantico? *Lingua Nostra* 37. 65–74.
Squartini, Mario. 1998. *Verbal periphrases in Romance*. Berlin: De Gruyter.
Todaro, Giuseppina & Fabio Del Prete. 2018. The morphosyntax-semantics interface and the Sicilian Doubly Inflected Construction. In Silvio Cruschina, Adam Ledgeway & Eva-Maria Remberger (eds.), *Italian dialectology at the interfaces*, 131–154. Amsterdam: John Benjamins.
Wurmbrand, Susanne. 2001. *Infinitives: Restructuring and clause structure*. Berlin: De Gruyter.
Wurmbrand, Susanne. 2004. Two types of restructuring: Lexical vs. functional. *Lingua* 114. 991–1014.
Wurmbrand, Susi. 2014. Tense and aspect in English infinitives. *Linguistic Inquiry* 45(3). 403–447.
Wurmbrand, Susi. 2017. Verb clusters, verb raising, and restructuring. In Martin Everaert & Henk van Riemsdijk (eds.), *The Blackwell companion to syntax 2, Second Edition*. Oxford: Blackwell.

Dalina Kallulli
Issues in the morpho-syntax and semantics of Voice in Romance and beyond

Abstract: This paper reconsiders some issues in the morpho-syntax and semantics of (the category of) Voice, with special reference to Latin and the Modern Romance languages. Crucially, building on my previous work (Kallulli 2007, 2013), specifically on the idea that overt morphological voice markings reflect feature distinctions associated with the little *v* head in the syntax, I show that the special passive, or reflexive morphology (depending on the language) doesn't just bear on the absence of an external argument in the syntax, but on the presence of an 'actor-initiation' feature of the *v* head in syntactic configurations lacking an external argument. This accounts among other things for facts such as the ubiquity of reflexive marking across inherent and non-inherent reflexive verbs (the former being the counterparts of deponents, as I argue), and others, such as the loss of special (i.e. reflexive/non-active) marking in syntactic configurations where such is expected (e.g. so-called "unmarked" anticausatives). The paper also dwells on the 'meaning' of roots, by investigating specifically the deponent and inherent reflexive patterns as found not only in Latin and the modern Romance and Germanic languages, respectively, but also by a comparison with deponent verbs in other languages such as Albanian and Greek, which like Latin have two distinct conjugational paradigms, namely active and non-active. Crucially, by showing that deponent and inherent reflexive verbs are cross-linguistically largely denominal, I develop further the idea in my previous work that deponent verbs do not constitute a form-meaning mismatch; on the contrary, the fact that nominals do not take external arguments straightforwardly accounts for their behaviour. The idea that there is meaning in roots thus does not need to (and cannot) commit one to the acategorial status of roots assumed in extreme constructionist frameworks such as Borer's.

Keywords: voice, *v*, non-active, deponent, reflexive, anticausative, passive

Dalina Kallulli: Universität Wien, Institut für Sprachwissenschaft, Sensengasse 3a, 1090 Wien, Austria, dalina.kallulli@univie.ac.at

https://doi.org/10.1515/9783110719154-007

1 Introduction

In this paper I reconsider some issues in the morpho-syntax and semantics of grammatical voice.[1] Specifically, I discuss voice and voice-related syncretisms and lack of such syncretisms (I will refer to the latter as voice gaps) in arguably different syntactic configurations that have commonly been related to unaccusative syntax (see e.g. Embick 1997, 2000, 2004 and references therein) in languages where such phenomena are extant, such as the well-known "mediopassive" in Latin and Greek, as well as the modern Romance and Germanic languages, which in spite of lacking full conjugational voice paradigms exhibit nonetheless sufficient distinctions relevant to the morphosyntax of voice.

Crucially, building on the idea that overt morphological voice markings reflect feature distinctions associated with the v head in the syntax, I revisit and add to an argument I have made in previous work, namely that the special 'passive', or reflexive morphology (depending on the language) doesn't just bear on the absence of an external argument in the syntax, but on the presence of an 'actor-initiation' feature of the v head in syntactic configurations lacking an external argument. This accounts among other things for facts such as the ubiquity of reflexive marking across reflexive and what I will refer to as pseudo-reflexive predicates (the latter being the counterparts of 'deponent' verbs, as I argue), and others, such as the loss of special (i.e. reflexive/non-active) marking in syntactic configurations where such marking is expected (e.g. so-called "unmarked" anticausatives of the type discussed in Zribi-Hertz 1987 et seq.). Importantly, the paper makes a case for the special ('passive'/reflexive) morphology having among other things a verbalizing function, which in turn relates to the issue of (lack of) canonicity of voice marking in patterns that have widely been described in terms of meaning-form mismatches, as in the case of deponent verbs (see Grestenberger 2014 for a thorough review of analytical approaches).

The rest of this paper is organized as follows. In section 2, I describe the basic patterns that prompt the present inquiry. Section 3 reviews the analytical state-of-the-art and the problems faced by previous approaches. In section 4, building on my previous work I present an alternative analysis, the most far-reaching consequence of which is that it calls into question the extreme constructionist position that roots never project and that they are invariably acategorial.

---

1 Parts of the material presented here also appear in Kallulli (2020).

2 Basic observations: Voice(-related) syncretisms and gaps

It is well-known that in many languages what counts as a 'passive' form does not exclusively correspond to passive syntax the way this phenomenon is described for languages like English or German.[2] To illustrate, in Latin the non-active (as opposed to active) form is used not just in what in English and other languages corresponds to the passive construction, as shown in (1b) vs. (1a), but also in anticausatives and reflexive constructions, as shown in (2) and (3), respectively.[3]

(1) a. Auctor opus laudat.
author$_{NOM}$ work$_{ACC}$ praise$_{3S,PR,NACT}$
'The author praises (his) work.' (Ov. *Pont.* 3, 9, 9)
b. Laudatur Apronius a Trimarchide.
praise$_{3S,PR,NACT}$ Apronius$_{NOM}$ from Trimarchides$_{ABL}$
'Apronius is praised by Trimachides.' (Cic. *Verr.* 2, 3, 155)

(2) Africano illi superiori coronam sibi in convivio ad caput adcommodanti, cum ea saepius rumperetur,
while it$_{NOM,F,SG}$ many.times break$_{3S,SUBJ,IPFV,NACT}$
P. Licinius Varus: "noli mirari" inquit "si non convenit; caput enim magnum est!".
'While Africanus, during the dinner, was putting back again on his own head the crown, since it (the crown) kept on breaking, P. Licinius Varus said: "You shouldn't wonder that it doesn't fit. In fact, you have a big head!"' (Cic. *De orat.* 2, 250)

(3) Abditur Orion.
hide$_{3S,PR,NACT}$ Orion
'Orion hides himself.' (Cic, *Arat.* 462, 26)

---

[2] There is some controversy whether 'passive' form even in English/German should be referred to as such, the argument being that there is no such thing as dedicated passive morphology in these languages either.

[3] The following abbreviations are used in the glosses: ACC = accusative case, ACT = active, AOR = aorist, F = feminine, IPFV = imperfective, NACT = non-active, NOM = nominative case, PR = present tense, PROG = progressive, REFL = reflexive, S = singular, SUBJ = subjunctive.

Similarly, the Albanian and Greek sentences in (4) are ambiguous between a reflexive and a passive interpretation, and those in (5) are ambiguous between an anticausative and a passive interpretation. Notice that in all three languages the form of the verb is non-active (as opposed to active). Indeed, the generalization is that non-active morphology subsumes passive but is not identical with it. Hence, 'passive' form does not entail passive syntax.

(4) a. Fëmija   po   lahet.   (Albanian)
       child.the$_{NOM}$ PROG wash.NACT,IMP,3S
       (i) 'The child is washing itself.'   → reflexive
       (ii) 'The child is being washed.'   → passive
    b. To agori plithike   (mono tu) / (apo ti mitera tu). (Greek)
       the boy   washed.NACT,3S (alone his) / (by the mother his)
       (i) 'The boy washed himself.'   → reflexive
       (ii) 'The boy was washed (by someone).'   → passive

(5) a. Vazoja   *(u) thye   / theu.[4]   (Albanian)
       vase$_{NOM}$ NACT broke.AOR.3S / broke.ACT,AOR.3S
       (i) 'The vase broke.'   → anticausative
       (ii) 'The vase was broken.'   → passive
    b. To   grama **kaike**   / ***ekapse**.   (Albanian)
       The sheet burned.NACT   / burned.ACT
       (i) 'The sheet burned.'   → anticausative
       (ii) 'The sheet was burned.'   → passive

Moreover, as I discuss in Kallulli (2007), in these languages (i.e. Latin, Albanian and Greek) the *by*-phrase diagnostic cannot be applied to distinguish between passives and anticausatives because it also means *from* (i.e. it may also introduce

---

[4] Albanian employs three distinct linguistic means with a fixed distribution to build the non-active paradigm, namely affix (see (4a)), clitic (see (5a)), and auxiliary selection. The distribution of non-active realization in Albanian follows the pattern in (i), taken from Kallulli and Trommer (2011), who also provide a formal analysis of this distribution, as well as further examples:

(i)   **If** the clause contains Perfect:
      express non-active by choice of the auxiliary
      Else: If the clause contains Tense but not Aspect or Admirative:
      express non-active by an inflectional affix
      Else: express non-active by a clitic

the external cause of an event), as the gloss of the Latin example (1b) indicates, and as shown in (6) for Albanian and Greek:

(6) a. Anna **u** dogj nga dielli mbi urë. (Albanian)
Anna NACT burnt.AOR.3S by/from sun.the on bridge
(i) 'Anna burned from the sun on the bridge.'
(ii) 'Anna was burned by the sun on the bridge.'
b. To grama **kaike** apo ti fotia. (Greek)
the sheet burned.NACT by/from the fire
(i) 'The sheet burned from the fire.'
(ii) 'The sheet was burned by the fire.'

Similar syncretisms are also well-known from languages that have no full-fledged morphological voice paradigms, such as the modern Romance and Germanic languages, as the examples in (7) and (8) – which crucially contain a reflexive element – illustrate.

(7) a. Martina *(si) guarda allo specchio. (Italian)
Martina REFL,3 watches in-the mirror
'Martina watches herself in the mirror.' → reflexive
b. Le fragole *(si) mangiano spesso.
the strawberries REFL,3 eat often
'Strawberries are often eaten.' → passive
c. Lo specchio *(si) rompe.
the mirror REFL,3 breaks
'The mirror breaks.' → anticausative

(8) a. Ralf rasiert *(sich). (German)
Ralf shaves REFL,3
'Ralf is shaving/shaves.' → reflexive
b. Dieser Roman liest *(sich) gut.
this novel reads REFL,3 well
'This novel reads well.' → middle
c. Die Tür öffnet *(sich).
the door opens REFL,3
'The door opens.' → anticausative

Moreover, both language types (i.e. Latin/Albanian/Greek on the one hand and modern Romance/Germanic on the other) contain a class of verbs where, unlike in the examples discussed above, the 'marked' morphology (i.e. non-active and/or reflexive, depending on the language) does not seem to bear on some argument-structure alternation such as the active-passive or the causative-anticausative one. Thus, while all the verbs in the examples discussed above can also occur devoid of non-active or reflexive morphology (irrespective of the fact that the interpretations of the sentences they occur in in this 'unmarked' form might differ from the interpretations of the sentences they occur in in their 'marked' form), there are verbs that simply lack an 'unmarked' form altogether (i.e. they cannot occur devoid of non-active or reflexive morphology). To see this, consider the examples in (9) through (14). Crucially, unlike in (9a), (11a) and (13a), the reflexive element in (10a), (12a) and (14a) cannot be said to correspond to a logical argument of the verb, as is evidenced by comparing the grammatical (9b), (11b) and (13b), to the respective (10b), (12b) and (14b), all of which are ungrammatical. The conclusion that the ungrammaticality of (10b), (12b) and (14b) is due to a violation of (some version of) the theta-criterion is therefore imminent.[5]

(9) a. Martina si lava. (Italian)
    Martina REFL,3 washes
    'Martina washes herself.'
  b. Martina lava la camicia
    Martina washes the shirt
    'Martina washes the shirt.'

---

[5] Dutch, which is famous for two morphological classes of reflexives, namely simple *zich* versus complex *zichzelf*, constitutes an interesting case in this context, since pseudo- or 'fake' reflexives (i.e. reflexive elements that cannot be said to instantiate an argument of the verb) are simple, just like reflexive arguments of verbs of bodily grooming such as *comb*, *wash*, *shave* etc. (which are inherently reflexive), and unlike reflexive arguments of non-inherent reflexive verbs such as *hate* or *love*, which are complex. This is interesting because in languages with full-blown conjugational paradigms, a non-inherent reflexive verb bearing non-active morphology can never have a reflexive interpretation (see e.g. Embick 1997, 2004 on reflexives in Greek).
(i)   Jan schaamt zich/ *zichzelf.
    Jan shames REFL,3 REFL.3-SELF
    'John is ashamed (of himself).'
(ii)   Jan haat *zich / zichzelf.
    John hates REFL,3 REFL.3-SELF
    'John hates himself.'

(10) a. Martina si   arrabbia spesso   (Italian)
        Martina REFL,3 angers   often
        'Martina often gets angry.'
    b. *Martina arrabbia spesso Piero
        Martina angers   often Piero
        Intended: 'Martina often angers Piero.'

(11) a. Marina wäscht sich.   (German)
        Martina washes REFL,3
    b. Martina wäscht das Hemd.
        Martina washes the shirt

(12) a. Ich schäme mich.   (German)
        I   shame myself
        'I am ashamed of myself.'
    b. *Ich schäme dich / (die) Martina
        I   shame you / (the) Martina

(13) a. John washed (himself).
    b. John washed the child.

(14) a. John behaved (himself).
    b. *John behaved the child.

The question then arises what the role of the reflexive element in examples such as (10a), (12a) and (14a) is. I have argued in Kallulli (2013) that the reflexive element here is the counterpart of non-active or passive morphology in the class of verbs known from traditional grammars of Latin as 'deponent' verbs.[6] These verbs, which have been traditionally characterized as passive in form but active in meaning, and/or as verbs that do not have an active form (see Grestenberger 2014 for a thorough review of the literature among other things), are illustrated through the verb *hortor* 'I encourage/incite' in (15b) for Latin, which as Grestenberger (2018) notes, can only appear with passive morphology (there is no

---

6 This argument is further strengthened by the fact that, as an anonymous reviewer remarks, "the class of deponents in Latin is non-homogenous and unstable, with several verbs often alternating between the two forms" (e.g. *elucubro/elucubror* 'burn the midnight oil'), and thus reminiscent of the optionality of the reflexive element in certain pseudo-reflexive verbs, such as *to behave (oneself)* in English.

hortō), but is syntactically active and transitive like *amō*, but which unlike the passive form of *amō*, namely *amor* 'I am loved', never means *'I am encouraged'. This amounts to saying that deponent verbs do not passivize.[7] The Albanian examples in (16) further illustrate the point that deponents do not have formally 'active' counterparts.

(15)   Pres.act.   Pres.pass.
      a. alternating   am-**ō**   am-**or**
                         'I love'   'I am loved'
      b. deponent   hort-**or**
                                          'I encourage'

(16)   Non-active   Active   (Albanian)
      a. *dergj-***em**   a'. **dergj*
         'I linger'
      b. *përgjigj-***em**   b'. **përgjigj*
         'I answer'
      c. *kreno-h-***em**   c'. **kreno-j*
         'I take pride in'
      d. *lig-***em**   d'. **lig*
         'I weaken'
      e. *pendo-h-***em**   e'. **pendo-j*
         'I regret'

On top of the voice(-related) syncretisms and the alleged meaning-form mismatch described above, languages also systematically display what I will refer to as voice gaps, which will be defined here as cases in which the expected voice-related syncretism does not obtain. For instance, unlike in (5b), where the verb 'burn' can only bear non-active morphology both in the passive and in the anticausative alternation, the verb does not – indeed it cannot – appear in the non-

---

[7] Grestenberger (2014, 2018) notes however that there is a rather small set of deponent verbs that do passivize. I postpone the discussion of these verbs to section 4. Interestingly, the anonymous reviewer remarks that even *hortor* is also found in the active, and may also occur in passive constructions (e.g. *ab amicis hortaretur* 'after the enemy had been ordered', and *hoste hortato*, which due to the fact that no context is provided, is unfortunately untranslatable). Crucially, these rather few instances occur in restricted sources describing the grammar of Latin, as the reviewer also acknowledges. Be it as it may, this amounts to further evidence for the morphological instability of deponents (see also note 6).

active form in the anticausative frame in Greek, as seen in (17a).⁸ Similarly, unlike the verb 'open' in (8c), the verb *zerbrechen* 'to break' is not marked (i.e. it cannot co-occur with a reflexive element) in the anticausative frame in German.

(17) a. *I porta espase / *espasike.* (Greek)
the door broke.ACT / broke.NACT
'The door broke.'
b. *Das Fenster zerbrach (*sich).* (German)
the window broke REFL,3
'The window broke.'

Interestingly though, sometimes the two forms (i.e. marked and unmarked) co-exist within one and the same language even for one and the same verb, as the Albanian examples in (18) illustrate:⁹

(18) a. *Dritarja u kris.* (Albanian)
window.the$_{NOM}$ NACT crack.AOR.3S
(i) 'The window cracked.'
(ii) 'The window was cracked.'
b. *Dritarja krisi.*
window.the$_{NOM}$ cracked.ACT,AOR.3S
(i) 'The window cracked.'
(ii) *'The window was cracked.'

Note that while the sentence in (18a) containing a 'marked' (i.e. formally non-active) verb is ambiguous between an anticausative and a passive interpretation, the minimally different (18b) containing an 'unmarked' (i.e. formally active) verb lacks a passive interpretation. Crucially, however, unlike what has sometimes been claimed for Romance (cf. Zribi-Hertz 1987 for French, Bentley 2006 for Italian, Cennamo et al. 2015 for Latin and Old Norse Icelandic) but also denied (cf. Martin and Schäfer 2014), under their anticausative interpretation the morphologically different anticausative variants in (18a) and (18b) are fully synonymous (i.e., the choice is not dependent on other parameters, such as aspectual value etc., as has been argued for other languages by the authors cited above).

---

8 Note, however, that the existence of deponents and pseudo-reflexives can in principle also be described as instantiating a voice gap, since their 'unmarked' alternants do not exist. Yet, I will reserve this term only for the cases where the special ('marked') morphology fails to appear.
9 This pattern also exists in Greek.

In the next section I review the analytical state-of-the-art on the phenomena described in this section, and point out the problems that these previous analyses face.

3 Analytical state-of-the-art

An influential proposal that incorporates robust generalizations and insights from a long tradition of work on argument structure is the one in Embick (1997) et seq. (Embick 2000, 2004). For Embick, the source of the syncretism between (alternating and non-alternating) unaccusatives, passives and reflexives (as in *John combed himself*, a construction which as noted earlier may involve non-active morphology in the relevant languages), is a particular syntactic property, namely the lack of an external argument. That is, what these distinct syntactic constructions have in common, is that they all lack an external argument, and it is precisely this syntactic property that the syncretic morphology (dubbed "u-syncretism") is sensitive to or reflects. In other words, while the computational system generates passives, unaccusatives and reflexives, each fully specified for the distinct features that differentiate these constructions, the morphological elements may be underspecified with respect to the syntactic environment in which they appear.

Embick's concrete implementation of the u-syncretism is stated in terms of the realization of the functional head *v* in a particular structural environment. Using –X to refer to the feature or property associated with non-active morphology, the representation of this is as shown in (19):

(19) v ↔ v – X/_ no external argument

In a similar spirit but different implementation, adopting a late insertion view of morphology and building on the idea of underspecification and a 'flavors-of-v^0' approach, in Kallulli (2007) I argue that the passive or anticausative morphology is just inserted into ("realizes") a v^0 containing the [- ext(ernal) arg(ument)] feature, which like the other features I postulate there (see below) is a privative one in that system. The difference between English on the one hand and Albanian/Greek on the other is that English has a special morpheme that realizes the [$_v$ [+act], [-ext arg]] bundle (namely, the passive morpheme) and a different morpheme that realizes the [*v* [+cause], [-ext arg]] bundle (namely, the anticausative).[10] Albanian, on the other hand, has just one morpheme that realizes [-ext arg] *v*⁰s, namely, the non-active morphology. In Albanian, the absence of a passive/anticausative distinction is then just a syncretism in the *v*⁰ morphology (reminiscent of Embick's "u-syncretism").

An obvious problem for both of the approaches above is the fact that since the absence of the external argument does *not* entail non-active morphology, as was illustrated by (17a) and (18b) for Greek and Albanian respectively, the correlation between non-active and lack of an external argument is at best an imperfect one. In other words, the lack of an external argument cannot be what triggers non-active, irrespective of whether this idea is implemented as in Embick (2004), who explicitly argues against the view that [- ext arg] is a syntactico-semantic feature, or as in Kallulli (2007), where I argue in favor of such a view. Thus, the question of what exactly non-active/passive morphology relates to persists, as does the question of why voice gaps arise only with anticausatives (and/or non-alternating unaccusatives) but not with passives.

Another problem for Embick (1997, 2000, 2004), which he however considers a special strength of his underspecification approach, concerns deponent verbs, to which he basically assigns a class feature, namely *passive*. More specifically, Embick argues that with deponents, unlike in genuine (i.e. syntactic) passivization and reflexivization contexts, this feature does not show up on a functional head (i.e. *v*⁰) but rather on a root, where subcategorization information and interpretation are not affected.

In spite of the fact that the background of Embick's approach to the morphosyntax of voice is a realizational framework, namely the framework of Distributed Morphology (Halle and Marantz 1993) according to which inflectional items are post-syntactic realizations of functional heads, Embick's approach to deponents is conceptually eerily similar to lexicalist approaches such as the one in Kiparsky (2004:121-122),[11] who suggests that "passive inflection in Latin is a conjugational feature – we'll call it [±Passive] – which can be lexically specified, for verb stems as well as for inflectional endings, or left unspecified", and who further goes on to state that "[+Passive] inflections trigger one or more of the operations on the verb's argument structure [...] forming passives, as well as possibly reflexives,

---

[10] The system of privative features in Kallulli (2007) is given in Tab. 1 (see section 4). My arguments for the primitives I postulate there involve evidence from both English and languages with non-active voice paradigms such as Albanian, Greek and Latin.
[11] See also Sadler and Spencer (2001).

reciprocals, and inchoatives, depending on further, partly idiosyncratic, properties of the verb". The question then also for Embick is what, if anything, enables the appearance of this class feature on roots? This question becomes even more pressing in view of generalizations like those drawn in work by Xu, Aronoff and Anshen (2007) on deponents in Latin, Kallulli (2013) on deponents in Albanian, and Zombolou and Alexiadou (2014) on deponents in Greek, which have prompted what may be referred to as 'spurious semantic deponency' approaches, according to which there is no mismatch.[12] Under these approaches, the morphological exponent faithfully realizes a certain abstract semantic property, i.e. deponent verbs in all these languages can form a semantically defined natural class with other, more obvious instances of non-active morphology after all. For instance, in Kallulli (2013) I have argued that the fact that cross-linguistically deponents are overwhelmingly denominal crucially evidences the canonicity of the non-active form for this class of verbs, since nouns typically lack external arguments.[13] I will indeed defend this proposal here, but before presenting further details, I would like to summarize another recent influential proposal, namely the one in Grestenberger (2014, 2018), who also provides arguments against spurious semantic deponency approaches.

Based on Grestenberger (2014), Grestenberger (2018) provides the definition of deponency in (20):

(20) Definition of deponency

In an active/non-active voice system, a deponent is a verb with an agent subject that appears in a syntactically active context and is morphologically non-active.

Thus, Grestenberger argues that deponent verbs, as a lexical property, project an agent DP *within* the VP (as opposed to vP). Thus, there is an agent, the clause is transitive, but the context for morphological realization of active exponence (see (21)) is not present (which is what leads Müller (2016) to classify Grestenberger's approach as a 'spurious morpho-syntactic' one).[14]

---

12 The term 'spurious semantic deponency' is due to Gereon Müller, class lectures at the University of Vienna, summer semester 2016.
13 In Kallulli (2013) I argue that this is also largely the case for pseudo-reflexives in modern Romance and Germanic; i.e. like deponents, pseudo-reflexives are cross-linguistically overwhelmingly denominal.
14 In Grestenberger's system, *v* in (21) – which is Grestenberger's system as presented in Müller (2016) – corresponds to Voice. As Müller (2016) notes, Grestenberger's approach belongs to the

(21) Post-syntactic rules of morphological exponence:
   a. *v* triggers non-active morphology if it does not have an agentive DP as its specifier
   b. *v* triggers active morphology if it has an agentive DP as its specifier.

More specifically, Grestenberger argues that the low agent of deponents is the outcome of a diachronic reanalysis process by which a self-benefactive argument, which is merged below VoiceP as given in (22a), is reanalyzed as an agent, as shown in (22b), where the boxed DP is the one undergoing the reanalysis. The resulting deponent structure is given in (23).[15]

(22)

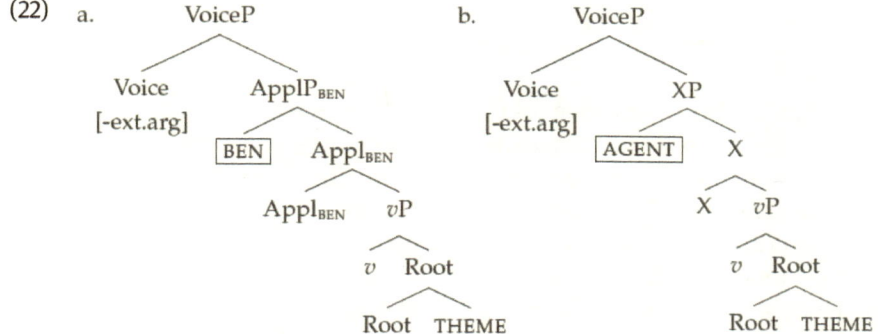

---

class of spurious morpho-syntactic approaches to deponency because non-active morphological realization is tied to the abstract morpho-syntactic property of *v* devoid of a DP specifier, and it is this abstract property that characterizes regular passive verbs and deponent verbs as a natural class. Thus, strictly speaking there is no mismatch between form and function, even though Grestenberger herself classifies her approach as involving a genuine mismatch given her contention that the agent of deponents is merged low (i.e. not in Spec of *v*P, the canonical position where agents are externally merged).

15 Note that self-benefactive arguments always occur with non-active morphology in languages like Latin and Greek. For details, see Grestenberger (2014, 2018).

(23) Deponent:

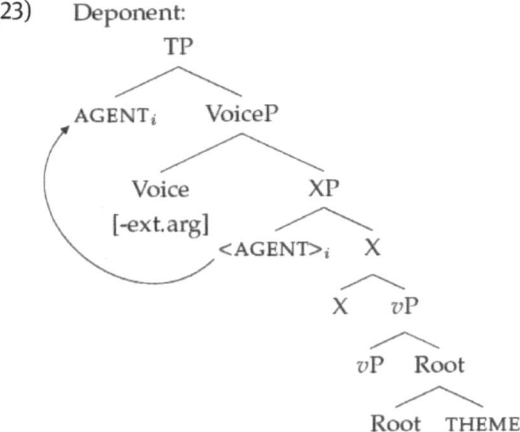

The Albanian data in (24) seem to lend support to Grestenberger's approach. Specifically, in (24a), with the non-active verb *lutem* 'I beg', Eva (who bears nominative case) is the beggar and Ben (who bears dative) the one being begged. In (24b), with the active verb *lus* 'I beg', again (nominative) Eva is the beggar and Ben, which crucially bears accusative here, is the one being begged. While the two sentences feel synonymous, there is a sense in which Anna in (24a) – note the existence of non-active morphology here – feels more 'affected' than in (24b), i.e. as if she is pleading with Ben, thus reflecting a sense of self-beneficial implication. Under Grestenberger's approach, this 'affectedness' effect could be said to have been lost over time (at least with certain verbs), resulting in the same unmarked agent reading as in (24b), but with the non-active morphology as a sort of diachronic remnant.[16]

(24) a. *Eva   iu   lut   Benit   (për muaj   me rradhë).*
     Eva_NOM CL,3S,DAT.NACT begged Ben_DAT for months on end
     'Eva begged Ben (for months on end).'
   b. *Eva   e   luti   Benin   (për muaj   me rradhë).*
     Eva_NOM CL,3S,ACC begged.ACT,3S Ben_ACC for months on end).
     'Eva begged Ben (for months on end).'

---

16 Incidentally, Laura Grestenberger (personal communication) confirms that 'beg' and 'ask' are definitely verbs that show up as deponents in Ancient Greek and Sanskrit (mostly with accusative objects).

A potentially problematic aspect of Grestenberger's approach for data such as these however lies in her statement that "the non-active morphology of deponents cannot be motivated in terms of the *synchronic* canonical functions of non-active morphology. That is, synchronically they do not fall into any of the categories listed [...] (reflexive, self-benefactive, anticausative, etc)". At least in Albanian, deponents, which in this language are incompatible with objects bearing accusative case, they actually do seem to fall into some such category associated with the synchronic canonical functions of non-active morphology (namely: self-benefactive). In other words, the pattern observed in (24a) vs. (24b) seems to be productive, as also replicated in (25a) vs. (25b).

(25) a. *Mendohem*   *(për)   të ardhmen.
       ponder.1S,PR,NACT for   future.the_ACC
       'I ponder/think about the future.'
    b. *Mendoj*   (për)   të ardhmen.
       think.1S,PR,ACT about   future.the_ACC
       'I think about the future.'

A solution to this tension might be that the synchronic analysis of data such as (24a) and (25a) might be different from the languages Grestenberger scrutinizes, especially in view of the 'affectedness' ingredient in these examples as opposed to (24b) and (25b), respectively. Coupled with the productivity of the pattern (i.e. the alternation) illustrated here, and the fact that deponents in Albanian are incompatible with accusative objects, it seems reasonable to assume that Grestenberger (2018) wouldn't have to analyze cases like (24a) and (25a) as deponents at all, because they are not agentive; recall her definition of deponency in (20). It is precisely in terms of (lack of) agency that my approach to deponents differs from Grestenberger's. Specifically, I maintain that Grestenberger's definition of deponency is too narrow in that not all deponents can be conceived of as agentive predications. I discuss this issue among others in the next section.

4 Reanalyzing non-active morphology

In section 3, I mentioned that an obvious problem for the approaches in Embick (1997, 2000, 2004) and Kallulli (2007) is the fact that since the absence of the external argument does *not* entail non-active morphology, as was illustrated by (17a) and (18b) for Greek and Albanian respectively (though the pattern extends to the so-called "non-marked" anticausatives in languages with no full-fledged voice paradigms), the correlation between non-active and lack of an external argument is at best an imperfect one. In other words, the lack of an external argument cannot be what triggers non-active (and/or reflexive for the relevant anticausative cases in Italian/modern Romance and German). Thus, the question of what exactly non-active (and/or reflexive) morphology relates to persists, as does the question of why voice gaps (in the sense defined in section 2 and as used throughout this paper) arise only with anticausatives (and/or non-alternating unaccusatives) but not with passives.[17]

Building on my previous work, I contend that non-active morphology is (being) reanalyzed as realizing Kallulli's (2007) feature [+activity] in the context of the feature [-external argument], a view that is crucially corroborated by developmental evidence.[18] Furthermore, I contend that the emergence of voice gaps with anticausatives is due to this arguably ongoing process of reanalysis of non-active (and/or reflexive) morphology – note crucially that anticausatives do not have an [+activity] feature in v^0 (see footnote 10 and Kallulli 2007 for further details).

My claim that non-active morphology is being reanalyzed as realizing the feature [+activity] in the context of [-external argument] implies that the non-active form is the base form from which voice gaps develop. Crucial evidence for this claim comes from deponents, as I discuss next.

Firstly, though 'transitive' deponents (i.e. deponents that combine with objects bearing accusative case) exist both in Latin, Greek and other languages with voice paradigms (for details, see Grestenberger 2014, 2018), which is the main if not sole argument motivating the view that syntactically they are not unaccusative, not all languages that have deponent verbs have transitive deponents. Thus, in Albanian there are no transitive deponents, as already mentioned. Secondly,

---

17 The anonymous reviewer points out that the claim that (morphological) voice gaps do not arise with passives seems to be contradicted by data in contemporary Brazilian Portuguese, where (citing examples from Cyrino 2013:287) "the active voice may occur in both anticausative (*a janela fechou* 'the window closed') and passive function (*o carro está pintando* 'the car is being painted')". Notice, however, that the latter example (*o carro está pintando* 'the car is being painted') is perfectly analogous to the English construction where the progressive is used with a passive function *The house was building for years*, which in Kallulli (2009), I have indeed taken as corroborating evidence for the view defended here, namely that non-active and/or reflexive morphology is (being) reanalyzed as realizing Kallulli's (2007) feature [+activity] in the context of the feature [-external argument].

18 Thus, for instance, Tsimpli (2006) and Fotiadou and Tsimpli (2010) report that the developing L1 grammar shows evidence for multiple ambiguities in the interpretation of non-active and active morphology on the same verb in Greek, while the adult data shows less ambiguous interpretations.

as Flobert (1975: 590) notes, most of the oldest deponents in Latin are intransitive, a fact that is itself in need of explanation and that might be construed to reveal the true (unaccusative) nature of this class of verbs.[19] Similarly, the fact that intransitive deponents in Modern Greek far outnumber transitive deponents and the fact that the majority of transitive deponents are thematically experiencers (Zombolou 2012), also speaks for their unaccusative nature.[20] Thirdly, the fact that deponents just like their fake reflexive counterparts in modern Romance and Germanic are largely denominal (see Kallulli 2013 and references therein) also points to their unaccusative nature, given that nouns lack external arguments.[21] Finally, though deponents cannot always combine with prepositional phrases indicating the presence of an agent or external cause of an event, some verbs that are clearly derived from such deponents with no causative semantics (compare (26a) to (27a) below) can however transitivize, as shown in (27b) which contrasts with (27c).

(26) a. *Dielli u   duk   (*nga   Zoti / qielli).*
       sun   NACT   appeared   from/by   God / sky
       'The Sun appeared *(by/from God / the sky).'
    b. *Krenohem   (*nga   djali)   / për / me djalin.*
       am.proud.PR.NACT   from/by   son.the.NOM / for / with son.the.ACC
       'I am proud of my son.'

(27) a. *Në   rregull, po   zhdukem   atëhere.*
       in   order   PROG disappear.NACT   then
       'OK, I (will) disappear then'
    b. *I   zhduka   gjurmët.*
       CL,3PL,ACC   disappear   traces
       'I made the traces / evidence disappear'
       (I.e. 'I destroyed the evidence'.)
    c. **Duk   diellin   / gjurmët.*
       appear.ACT   sun.the   / traces.the
       'I make the sun/the traces (i.e. evidence) appear'

---

19 On the emergence and development of 'active' deponents in Latin see also Cennamo (2008), who notes among other things that full activization of deponents in this language is attested from the 7th century onwards.
20 Zombolou (2012) reports that 70% of all deponent verbs in this language are intransitive and only 18% out of 100% combine with an object bearing accusative case.
21 See Kallulli (2013) for further arguments that fake reflexives of the type illustrated in (10a), (12a) and (14a) are the counterparts of deponents.

The very same transitivization process as in (27b) is also attested with fake reflexives among others in Italian, as illustrated in (28); note in particular the transitivity parallelism between the Albanian (27b) and the Italian (28c) as opposed to the intransitivity of (27c) and (28b), respectively.[22]

(28) a. *quando   Dio   *(si)   vergogna   degli   uomini   e   gli   uomini   *(si)*
      when   God   REFL   shamed   of-the   men   and   the   men   REFL
      vergognano   di   Dio
      shamed   of   God
      'when God is ashamed of men and men are ashamed of God'
   b. **Gli   uomini   hanno   vergognato   il   Dio*
      the   men   have   shamed   the   God
      'Men have put God to shame.'
   c. *Gli   uomini   hanno   svergonato   il   Dio*
      the   men   have   shamed   the   God
      'Men have put God to shame.'

Taken together, these facts suggest that the function of non-active morphology in deponents and, accordingly, of reflexive morphology in languages that do not have full-fledged voice paradigms, is that of a verbalizer, i.e. verbalizing nominal roots, an idea which is also theoretically appealing, since what we know about nouns is that just like unaccusative (and passive) verbs, they lack external arguments, thus making the appearance of non-active/reflexive morphology seem canonical rather than non-canonical. One question that arises, however, concerns the so-called "transitive" (Embick 1997 et seq.) deponents of the *sequor* 'I follow' type, which as mentioned can combine with an accusative object (and which Grestenberger argues to be truly "agentive"). Following a suggestion originally due to Embick (1997), which he however eventually discards, but which has more recently been picked up in Alexiadou (2013), Kallulli (2013) and Zombolou and Alexiadou (2014), I uphold that transitive non-alternating nonactive verbs can be analyzed synchronically as experiencer verbs (note that according to Pesetsky (1995) experiencer arguments are arguments of the root), specifically as dyadic

---

22 The fact that the prefix *zh-* in the Albanian *zhduka* in (27b) and the Italian *s-* in *svergognato* in (28c) do not have the same 'meaning' in these contexts is of course tangential to the fact that is crucial to the point at hand, namely that both obviously have a transitivizing function.

unaccusative (stative) psych predicates.²³ As mentioned earlier, this line of reasoning has however been newly rejected in Grestenberger (2014, 2018), who contends that there is indeed a small class of truly agentive deponents. Grestenberger's main arguments are the following. First, reiterating Embick's observations which eventually led him to discard the idea that transitive deponents are psych verbs, she points out that with some psych-verbs, both an agentive and a psychological reading is possible in Modern Greek. Under what she refers to as "the agentive reading", as in (29a) which contains an animate subject, the object does not have to be clitic doubled, while under the psychological reading in (29b) (note that the subject is inanimate), the object needs to be clitic doubled.

(29) a. *I   Maria   enohli   ton   Petro.*
       the Maria$_{NOM}$ bothers the Petro$_{ACC}$
       'Maria bothers Petro.'
   b. *Ta epipla   *?(ton)   enohlun ton   Petro.*
       the furniture$_{NOM}$ him$_{CL,ACC}$ bothers the$_{ACC}$ Petro
       'The furniture bothers Petro.'

Transitive agentive deponents like *hriazome* 'need' pattern with the so-called "agentive" reading and do not require clitic doubling, as shown in (30). Grestenberger takes this to indicate that the subject of *hriazome* is therefore an agent rather than a cause/theme.

(30) *I   Maria   hriazete   ton   Petro.*
      the Maria$_{NOM}$ needs   the$_{NOM}$ Petro
      'Maria needs Petros.'

While these judgments seem clearer for some Greek speakers than for others, all they show is that the distinction between animate and inanimate subjects has some bearing on clitic doubling of the object.²⁴ Jumping from these data to the conclusion that the contrast between (29a) and (30) on the one hand versus (29b) on the other is due to agentivity of the subject in the former is unwarranted, since Maria could equally well be an actor unintentionally causing bother to Petro.

---

23 Cf. also Zombolou (2012), who points out that the subject of the majority of transitive deponents in Modern Greek (transitive deponents combining with an accusative object make up 18% of deponents in this language) are experiencers.
24 I thank Artemis Alexiadou (personal communication) for discussing these data with me.

Likewise, in (30) Maria might indeed need Petro without intending or even wanting to. In other words, what these examples show, is just that clitic doubling of the object is affected by the (in)animacy of the subject but they can certainly not be used as a test for agentivity, since participants capable of willful agency might always act unintentionally.[25] Similarly, Embick's observation reiterated by Grestenberger that transitive deponents pattern as non-psych verbs in triggering clitic left-dislocation is not any more conclusive of the agentivity of transitive deponents. Secondly, as I have pointed out in a different context in Kallulli (2007), Grestenberger's claim that so-called "agent-oriented" adverbs expressing intention or volition only modify agentive predicates is cross-linguistically contradicted by data like those in (31) for Italian and (32) for German, which specifically demonstrate that unaccusative syntax is not incompatible with such adverbs:

(31) a. *Gianni è caduto / *ha caduto apposta.* (Italian)
       Gianni is fallen / has fallen on.purpose
   b. *Gianni è rotolato / *ha rotolato giù apposta.*
       Gianni is rolled / has rolled down on.purpose
   (Folli and Harley 2006)

(32) *Peter ist / *hat absichtlich eingeschlafen.* (German)
     Peter is / has deliberately fallen.asleep
     'Peter fell asleep on purpose.'

Grestenberger's strongest argument for the agentive status of (transitive) deponents comes from languages like Vedic and in some cases Ancient Greek, which have a trivalent voice system, where one can distinguish among other things between deponents and passives on the basis of morphology. In other words, Grestenberger's strongest argument is that there are languages in which deponents may passivize. While the data she provides from Vedic (and Ancient Greek) seem to indicate this, these data have the potential to destroy Grestenberger's own system, since one would have to assume a Passive head on top of the voice head, which makes these languages similar to English, German or Hebrew (cf. Alexiadou 2013 and Alexiadou et al. 2015), but which in turn contradict her own observation that there are no deponents in English/German. In even more recent work, Grestenberger (forthcoming) argues however that these languages do not have a higher Passive head, and that what looks like a passive suffix, is situated between

---

25 For details on (animate) actors versus (intentional) agents and their representation, see Demirdache (1997) and Kallulli (2006, 2007).

the root and the Voice head, in the position where we usually find *v* (verbalizing morphology). In other words, the passive head in such trivalent languages selects roots rather than *v* or Voice, and seems to suppress the projection of higher arguments, i.e. agents. While Grestenberger maintains that this holds as a diagnostic of agentivity in deponents because this passive suffix blocks the projection of both non-deponent and deponent agentive verbs alike, note that she thus directly provides independent evidence for my central claim in this paper, namely the existence of verbalizing voice morphology close to the root, which moreover seems rather similar in function to non-active and/or reflexive morphology in deponents (and elsewhere) in that it blocks the projection of higher arguments.[26] Note also that my claim that non-active and/or reflexive morphology can on top of other things also function as a verbalizer (specifically in the case of deponents and/or fake reflexives), fills in a gap in the voice typology provided in Schäfer (2016) given in (33). According to this picture, (33a) generates so-called "SE-reflexives" such as (the Romance and Germanic counterparts of) *wash oneself*, which are semantically and syntactically transitive predicates.[27] In contrast, the semantically intransitive but syntactically transitive structure in (33b) generates SE marked anticausatives as in Romance and/or Germanic, with the reflexive marker being an expletive argument. (33c) and (33d) are self-explanatory: (33c) refers to the general passive voice, introduces an external argument θ-role but lacks a D-feature, and the external argument must remain implicit but can be taken up via by-phrase; (33d) refers to the Voice head for marked anticausatives in languages like Greek (e.g. (6b)), with the expletive not introducing a θ-role. (33d) differs from the active expletive Voice in (33b), as it does not project a specifier.

(33) a. [$_{TP}$ *T* [$_{VoiceP}$ DP$_{AGENT}$ *Voice* [$_{vP}$ *v* SE$_{PATIENT}$]]]
　　b. [$_{TP}$ *T* [$_{VoiceP}$ SE$_{EXPL}$ *Voice* [$_{vP}$ *v* DP$_{THEME}$]]]
　　c. Thematic passive Voice
　　d. Non-thematic (expletive) passive Voice

It is important to note that the fact that deponents are largely denominal, does not entail that if a verb is denominal, it is deponent (i.e. there is an implication, but there is no equivalence). Crucially, as Xu, Aronoff and Anshen (2007:139)

---

[26] Grestenberger provides one more argument from agent nouns for her claim that deponents are agentive predicates. Since the discussion of this issue is rather complex, and the evidence is confounding and therefore non-conclusive, I will for reasons of space not dwell on it here.
[27] Note that this does not include fake reflexives.

point out for Latin deponents but the point is more general (see Kallulli 2013), Latin denominal or deadjectival verbs differ in form depending on whether they have a causative sense: "[t]hose with causative senses tend to be active, while those that fall into general non-causative semantic categories such as 'to act or to be x', 'to act like y', 'to give or make (with a sense of creation) z', 'to use z', and 'to get z' tend to assume deponent forms". This is precisely why non-active rather than active morphology is used as a default verbalizer in these (non-causative) contexts, but this does not mean that active morphology cannot be used as a verbalizer in other contexts, such as causative ones, where indeed it is the default one. This notion of 'defaultness' is closely tied to Kallulli's (2007) system summarized in Tab. 1 below; recall that the primitive features in this system are privative:

Tab. 1: The system of privative features (Kallulli 2007)

	Features in v^0	
a.	[+activity]	Ben ate the apple.
b.	[+activity] [-external argument]	The apple was eaten (by Ben).
c.	[+cause]	The pressure cracked the window.
d.	[+cause] [-external argument]	The window cracked (from the pressure).
e.	[+cause] [+activity]	John cleaned the table.
f.	[+cause] [+activity] [-external argument]	The table was cleaned (by John).
g.	[-external argument]	John arrived.

The primitive feature *activity*, which is a shorthand for *actor-initiation*, is for the discussion at hand particularly relevant, not least with respect to the voice gap patterns discussed earlier – recall for instance the formal opposition between the (marked) anticausative (18a) and the (unmarked) anticausative in (18b), as well as the (spurious) optionality of the reflexive marker in Romance (Zribi-Hertz 1987, Martin and Schäfer 2014). If, as I contend, non-active (and the analogous reflexive) morphology is being reanalysed as relating to the [+activity] feature in syntactic configurations lacking an external argument, anticausatives start dropping non-active/reflexive marking, as they don't have an [+activity] feature, as discussed at length in Kallulli (2007). This view is corroborated by the fact that non-alternating unaccusatives such as *arrive*, or *die* tend to be morphologically active cross-linguistically. This reanalysis accounts among other things for the fact that cross-linguistically reflexive markers abound in being used to instantiate the relevant voice distinctions that involve the feature [+activity], since a reflexive marker must at some point have related in terms of lexical content to an actor-initiation (i.e. activity) feature.

5 Conclusion

In this paper, I have reconsidered some well-known facts on grammatical voice and the evolution of the voice system from Latin and Latin-like languages such as Albanian and Greek, to the modern Romance (and Germanic) languages, which instantiate the relevant relations among other things through the use of reflexive pronouns or clitics. In particular, I have shown that non-active voice can sometimes function as a verbalizer, specifically on 'deponent' roots, which are nominal. Thus, a far-reaching conclusion is that at least some roots seem to be categorial, and their category and other selectional features (such as non-causative semantics) relevant for Merge.

Finally, the "voice syncretism" approach predicts that deponents should also be able to have a passive reading, because both deponents and regular passives have Voice [-ext.arg] and get non-active morphology, which is corroborated in the philological tradition, as it has sometimes been claimed that though rare, there are some passive readings of deponents in Latin.[28]

Acknowledgement: For questions, comments, and discussion on the material presented here I thank the audience of Romanistentag 2017, Laura Grestenberger, Stefan Schumacher, an anonymous reviewer, and the editors of the present volume.

6 References

Alexiadou, Artemis. 2013. Where is non-active morphology? In Müller, Stefan (ed.), *Proceedings of the 20th International Conference on Head-Driven Phrase Structure Grammar*, 244–262. Stanford, CA: CSLI Publications.

---

[28] I thank Laura Grestenberger (personal communication) for pointing this out to me.

Alexiadou, Artemis, Elena Anagnostopoulou & Florian Schäfer. 2015. *External arguments in transitivity alternations*. Oxford: Oxford University Press.
Bentley, Delia. 2006. *Split intransitivity in Italian*. Berlin: De Gruyter.
Cennamo, Michela. 2008. The rise and development of analytic perfects in Italo-Romance. In Thórhallur Eythórsson (ed.), *Grammatical change and linguistic theory: The Rosendal papers*, 115–142. Amsterdam: John Benjamins.
Cennamo, Michela, Thórhallur Eythórsson & Jóhanna Barðdal. 2015. Semantic and (morpho)syntactic constraints on anticausativization: Evidence from Latin and Old Norse-Icelandic. *Linguistics* 53(4). 677–729.
Cicero: De oratore: Kumaniecki, Kazimierz (ed.). 1995. M. Tulli Ciceronis scripta quae manserunt omnia, 3. Leipzig: Teubner.
Cicero: In C. Verrem orationes sex: Klotz, Alfredus (ed.). 1923. M. Tulli Ciceronis scripta quae manserunt omnia, 5. Leipzig: Teubner.
Cyrino, Sonia. 2013. Argument promotion and se-constructions in Brazilian Portuguese. In Elly van Gelderen, Michaela Cennamo & Jóhanna Barðdal (eds.), *Argument structure in flux. The Naples-Capri papers*, 284–306. Amsterdam/Philadelphia: John Benjamins.
Demirdache, Hamida. 1997. Out of control in St'at'imcets Salish and event (de) composition. In Amaya Mendikoetxea & Myriam Uribe-Etxebarria (eds.), *Theoretical Issues at the Morphology - Syntax Interface. International Journal of Basque Linguistics and Philology*, Vol. XL, 97–143. Bilbao: Universidad del País Vasco.
Embick, David. 1997. *Voice and the interfaces of syntax*. Ph.D. dissertation. Philadelphia, PA: University of Pennsylvania.
Embick, David. 2000. Features, syntax, and categories in the Latin perfect. *Linguistic Inquiry* 31. 185–230.
Embick, David. 2004. Unaccusative syntax and verbal alternations. In Artemis Alexiadou, Elena Anagnostopoulou & Martin Everaert (eds.), *The unaccusativity puzzle*, 137–158. Oxford: Oxford University Press.
Flobert, P. 1975. *Les verbes déponents Latin des origines à Charlemagne*. Paris: Les Belles Lettres.
Folli, Raffaella and Heidi Harley. 2006. Waltzing Matilda around and around: On the licensing of directed-motion resultatives. *Studia Linguistica* 60(2). 1–35.
Fotiadou, Giorgia & Tsimpli, Ianthi Maria. 2010. On the L1 acquisition of passives and reflexives in Greek: Does frequency count? *Lingua* 120(11). 2605–2626.
Grestenberger, Laura. 2014. *Feature mismatch: Deponency in Indo-European*. Ph.D. dissertation, Cambridge, MA: Harvard University.
Grestenberger, Laura. 2018. Deponency in finite and non-finite contexts. *Language* 94(3). 487–526.
Grestenberger, Laura. Forthcoming. Two types of passive? Voice morphology and "low passives" in Vedic Sanskrit and Ancient Greek. In Kleanthes K. Grohmann, Akemi Matsuya & Eva-Maria Remberger (eds.), *Passives Cross-Linguistically: Theoretical and Experimental Approaches*. Leiden: Brill.
Halle, Morris & Alec Marantz. 1993. Distributed Morphology and the pieces of inflection. In Ken Hale & Samuel Jay Keyser (eds.), *The View from Building 20: Essays in linguistics in honor of Sylvain Bromberger*, 111–176. Cambridge, MA: MIT Press.
Kallulli, Dalina. 2006. Unaccusatives with dative causers and experiencers: a unified account. In Daniel Hole, André Meinunger & Werner Abraham (eds.), *Datives and other cases*, 271–301. Amsterdam: John Benjamins.

Kallulli, Dalina. 2007. Rethinking the passive/anticausative distinction. *Linguistic Inquiry* 38(4). 770–780.
Kallulli, Dalina. 2009. (Non-)Blocking in the voice system. *Language Typology and Universals* 62(4). 269–284.
Kallulli, Dalina. 2013. (Non-)canonical passives and reflexives: deponents and their like. In Artemis Alexiadou & Florian Schäfer (eds.), *Non-canonical passives*, 337–358. Amsterdam/Philadelphia: John Benjamins.
Kallulli, Dalina. 2020. Voice morphology (mis)behaving itself. In Bárány, András, Theresa Biberauer, Jamie Douglas & Sten Vikner (eds.), *Syntactic architecture and its consequences III: Inside syntax*. Language Science Press.
Kallulli, Dalina & Jochen Trommer. 2011. Closest c-command, agree and impoverishment: The morphosyntax of non-active voice in Albanian. *Acta Linguistica Hungarica* 58(3). 277–296.
Kiparsky, Paul. 2004. Blocking and periphrasis in inflectional paradigms. In Geert Booij & Jaap van Marle (eds.), *Yearbook of Morphology* 2004, 113–135. Dordrecht: Springer.
Martin, Fabienne & Florian Schäfer. 2014. Anticausatives compete but do not differ in meaning: A French case study. Actes du 4e CMLF. (Available open source at: https://www.shs-conferences.org/articles/shsconf/abs/2014/05/shsconf_cmlf14_01245/shsconf_cmlf14_01245.html)
Müller, Gereon. 2016. Introductory seminar on morphology: Current approaches to inflectional morphology. Course taught at the University of Vienna, summer semester.
Ovid: Epistulae ex Ponto: Richmond, John A. (ed.). 1990. P. Ovidi Nasoni ex Ponto libri quattuor. Leipzig: Teubner.
Pesetsky, David. 1995. *Zero Syntax: Experiencers and Cascades*. Cambridge, MA: MIT Press.
Sadler Louisa & Andrew Spencer. 2000. Syntax as an exponent of morphological features. In Geert Booij & Jaap van Marle (eds.), *Yearbook of Morphology* 2000, 71–96. Dordrecht: Springer
Schäfer, Florian. 2016. Two types of argument expletives: Evidence from by-phrases and object-drop. Handout of paper presented at the Workshop on Impersonality and Correlated Phenomena: Diachronic and Synchronic Perspectives, University of Salzburg, Salzburg, Austria, 10–11 November.
Tsimpli, Ianthi Maria. 2006. The acquisition of voice and transitivity alternations in Greek as native and second language. In Sharon Unsworth, Teresa Parodi, Antonella Sorace & Martha Young-Scholten (eds.), *Paths of Development in L1 and L2 acquisition*, 15–55. Amsterdam: John Benjamins.
Xu, Zheng, Mark Aronoff and Frank Anshen. 2007. Deponency in Latin. In Matthew Baerman, Greville Corbett, Dunstan Brown & Andrew Hippisley (eds.), *Deponency and morphological mismatches*, 127–143. Oxford University Press.
Zombolou, Katerina. 2012. The canonical function of deponents in Greek. Paper presented at the 15th International Morphology Meeting, Vienna.
Zombolou, Katerina and Artemis Alexiadou. 2014. The canonical function of the deponent verbs in Modern Greek. In Franz Rainer, Francesco Gardani Hans Christian Luschützky, & Wolfgang U. Dressler (eds.), Morphology and Meaning. Selected Papers from the 15th International Morphology Meeting, Vienna, February 2012. 331–44. Benjamins.
Zribi-Hertz, Anne. 1987. La réflexivité ergative en français moderne. *Le Français Moderne* 55. 23–54.

Barbara Schirakowski
What constrains the formation of Spanish nominalized infinitives?

A case study on transitive base verbs and event interpretations

Abstract: This contribution investigates the most nominal type of Spanish nominalized infinitives which represents a rather marginal means of event nominalization. Based on an acceptability judgment experiment on transitive base verbs, it will be shown that the distribution of NI is determined by the interaction of two variables: argument realization and event interpretation. The event structure of the verbal base is represented in Ramchand's (2008) decompositional model. The analysis reveals that Spanish NI are not as sensitive to event structure as sometimes assumed, but that only the higher argument of the base verb can be realized as a PP-argument. Furthermore, a preference for generic interpretations is attested for the NI under investigation.

Keywords: nominalized infinitive, argument realization, event type, judgment data

1 Introduction

The term *nominalized infinitive* (NI) usually refers to a number of constructions in which an infinitive is preceded by a determiner. Spanish NI come in different subtypes which can be distinguished by their syntactic properties (cf. a.o. de Miguel 1996, Pérez Vázquez 2002, Plann 1981, Ramírez 2003, Yoon & Bonet-Farran 1991). Based on argument realization, it is possible to identify at least three different forms: In the most nominal use, the NI can realize an argument of the base verb as a PP headed by the preposition *de* (henceforth PP_{de}) or a possessive determiner, (1). In a more verbal use, it allows for a direct object, (2), and in the sentential form, it represents a full argument clause that licenses not only an object, but also a subject, (3).

Barbara Schirakowski: Freie Universität Berlin, Institut für Romanische Philologie, Habelschwerdter Allee 45, 14195 Berlin, Germany, barbara.schirakowski@fu-berlin.de

https://doi.org/10.1515/9783110719154-008

(1) a. el   cantar   de los pájaros
       the sing.INF of the birds
       'the singing of the birds'
    b. su   cantar
       POSS   sing.INF
       'their singing'

(2)   el   cantar   una copla
       the sing.INF a song
       '(the) singing a song'

(3)   El   cantar   yo La Traviata [...]   (Yoon & Bonet-Farran 1991: 353)
       the sing.INF I   la traviata
       'that I sing La Traviata [...]'

Previous studies on NI have focused on their internal syntax and the (in-)compatibility of verbal and nominal projections within the same configuration. Differences between forms like (1), (2) and (3) are usually attributed to the locus at which the verbal structure is nominalized and the category of the nominalizer, which can be an N-/n-head or a determiner, (1) vs. (2) and (3) (cf. e.g. Iordăchioaia & Soare 2015 for the distinction between n- and D-based nominalizations). Less attention has been paid to the individual subtypes and the factors that determine their distribution. This study focuses on the most nominal form of NI and argument realization by means of a PP_{de}, i.e. forms such as (1)a, which are event-denoting nominalizations that can alternate with deverbal nouns in a limited number of contexts, (4).

(4)   Le disgustaba {el lamentar / la lamentación} de sus hijos.
       'He disliked the complaining of his children.'

NI represent a rather marginal means of nominalization, which is often criticized in terms of style and usually occurs in certain registers more typical of written language (e.g. Torres Cacoullos 2009). Unlike verbal NI, forms of the nominal type seem to show restrictions regarding the base verb. Previous studies have addressed the relevance of the arity and the situation aspect of the base verb since, in their most typical uses, NI are built on intransitive and atelic verbs, (5).[1]

(5) el   pausado caminar   de las tortugas   (Rodríguez Espiñeira 2008: 143)
     the slow   walk.INF   of the turtles

Some authors have stated that NI cannot be built on transitive and telic verbs (e.g. Hernanz 1999, Rodríguez Espiñeira 2008), (6)a and (7)a. However, this generalization appears too coarse-grained as transitive base verbs seem to yield different acceptability values depending on which argument is mapped onto the PP_{de}. NI that realize the higher argument of the base appear more felicitous than forms in which the lower argument is realized, cf. (6)b.[2] Telic base verbs are not entirely ruled out either, but seem to be well-formed as long as the event is presented as temporally unbounded, for instance, due to the presence of an aspectual modifier like *continuous* and/or a plural argument as in (7)b.

(6) a. *el escribir   de una novela
         the write.INF of a novel
     b. el escribir   de Juan
        el write.INF   of Juan

(7) a. *el llegar   de Juan
         the arrive.INF of Juan
     b. el continuo   llegar   de víctimas
        the continuous arrive.INF of victims

Therefore, the first aim of this contribution is reviewing the compatibility of NI with different verb classes and options of argument realization. I will adopt Ramchand's (2008) syntactic model of the split VP in order to represent verbal event and argument structure within NI. This approach adopts the common assumption that eventive nominalizations embed a VP which contains a verbal predicate

---

[1] For referring to the two levels of verbal aspect, i.e. the telic/atelic distinction and the perfective/imperfective distinction, I will use Smith's (1997) terminology and speak of *situation aspect* vs. *viewpoint aspect*.
[2] As arguments are distinguished solely by their position in the event structure (cf. 3.2 for details), I will speak of *higher argument* to refer to the argument that corresponds to the subject of the active clause and of *lower argument* to refer to the argument that corresponds to the direct object.

and its arguments (cf. Alexiadou, Haegeman & Stavrou 2007: 515ff. for an overview of different [DP[NP[VP]]]-models).

The second factor that will be addressed concerns the external distribution of NI, i.e. their distribution as event nominals in different contexts. This issue has only been considered rather informally so far (but see Fábregas & Varela 2006) and it has been noted that NI only allow for a restricted number of eventive interpretations. Here, we will focus on the distinction between episodic and generic event readings which has rather recently made its way into studies on the semantics of deverbal nominalizations (cf. e.g. Iordăchioaia & Soare 2015, Soare 2017). The main proposal of this study is that the formation of NI is not entirely restricted to certain verbal bases but determined by the interaction of two factors: argument realization and event interpretation. This claim is supported by an acceptability judgment experiment on transitive base verbs. The results show that NI built on these bases are most acceptable when the higher argument is realized as a PP_{de} and the NI receives a generic interpretation as in (8).

(8) El escribir de este autor es realmente obsesivo.
The write.INF of this author is really obsessive.

The study is organized as follows. Section 2 introduces Ramchand's (2008) decompositional model. In section 3, the model will be applied to NI in order to reach finer subgeneralizations regarding their compatibility with different event structures and variants of argument realization. Section 4 provides an overview of interpretational possibilities for NI. Section 5 presents the acceptability judgment experiment. Section 6 summarizes and discusses the results.

2 Verbal event structure and the split VP

In Ramchand's (2008) model, cf. figure 1, verbal predicates are decomposed into up to three subevental components and the V-node is replaced by three functional heads and their projections. Init is a stative head and stands for causation. Proc represents change and is the core of any dynamic predicate while res denotes the final state that can emerge as the result of the event denoted by proc.

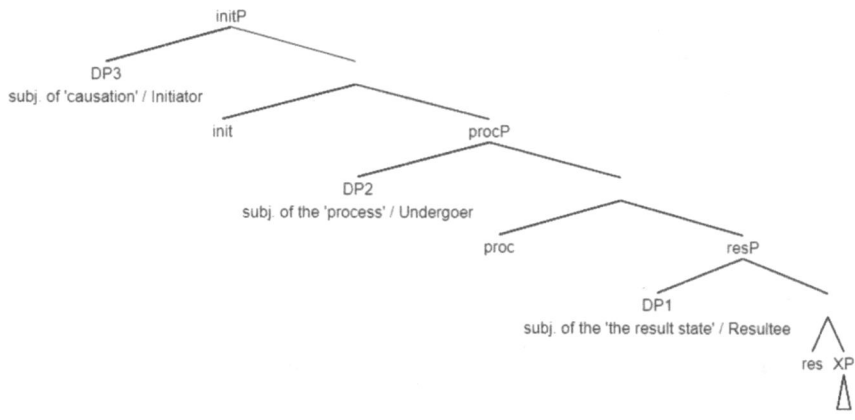

Fig. 1: The split VP (cf. Ramchand 2008: 39)

Crucially, init, proc and res are not only the labels for the subevental heads, but also refer to the features for which a root (or an affix) can be lexically specified. Thus, event and argument structure are represented syntactically, but the lexicon is not totally void of categorical information. Roots or affixes are specified for one, two or all three of the features init, proc and res. The feature specification determines which part(s) of a potentially complex event the item can lexicalize and accounts for its syntactic and aspectual behavior.

Any dynamic verb is minimally specified for a proc-feature, (9). The presence of init depends on the availability of the causative-inchoative alternation. Verbs that cannot be causativized are lexically specified for init, (10). Verbs that can be causativized lack this feature, (9).

(9) a. roll: [proc]
   b. The ball rolled. / Ben rolled the ball.

(10) a. dance: [$init_i$, $proc_i$]
   b. Anna danced / *Michael danced Anna.

The presence or absence of a res-feature determines situation aspect and concerns the Vendlerian (1957) distinction between Achievements, Accomplishments and Activities. Verbs that are specified for a res-feature are obligatorily telic and punctual, i.e. Achievements, (11), whereas verbs that lack this feature denote durative events and can be telic (Accomplishments) or atelic (Activities) depending on the referential properties of their argument and/or the exact configuration in which they are inserted, (12).[3] Finally, stative verbs are specified for an init-feature only since they do not express change and, thus, no resultative meaning either, (13).

(11) a. break: [$proc_i$, res_i]
    b. The vase broke {in two seconds / *for two seconds}.

(12) a. eat: [init, proc]
    b. Mary ate porridge {*in ten minutes / for ten minutes}.
    c. Mary ate a pizza {in ten minutes / *for ten minutes}.

(13) a. love: [init]
    b. Katherine loves Michael.

The possible combinations of the three features init, proc and res yield five major verb classes, cf. table 1. More fine-grained distinctions of subclasses arise – among other things – from the possibility of coindexation (see further below).

Tab. 1: verb classes (cf. Ramchand 2008: 108)

lexical feature(s) of a verbal root	coindexation of lexical features	example
1. [init, proc]		eat, push
	[$init_i$, $proc_i$,]	dance, sleep
2. [init, proc, res]		give, throw
	[init, $proc_i$, res_i]	find, kill
	[$init_i$, $proc_i$, res_i]	arrive, die
3. [proc, res]	[$proc_i$, res_i]	break, crash
4. [proc]		change, roll
5. [init]		hate, love

---

[3] There are numerous distributional diagnostics and entailment tests for distinguishing between atelic and telic expressions (cf. Dowty 1979: 60 for an overview). In the following, I will use the time adverbial test according to which atelic predicates can be combined with time span adverbials of the type *FOR x time*, whereas telic predicates are compatible with time frame adverbials of the type *IN x time*.

Arguments are identified via their position in the configurational structure. Each subevent licenses a DP in its specifier position. InitP licenses the external argument (the Initiator), (14). ProcP introduces the entity which undergoes change (the Undergoer), (15), and the resP introduces the entity which comes to hold a final state (the Resultee), (16). Furthermore, argument roles can be composite as Ramchand assumes a copy theory of movement. The information that the same DP can be the subject of more than one subevent is represented by the indices in the lexical entry of the corresponding verb (cf. table 1, column 2). Two or all three lexical features can be coindexed thus determining the arity of the verb. *Give* in (16), for instance, lexicalizes all three subevents each of which has a different subject. Thus, *give* is a three-place predicate. *Arrive* in (17) is also specified for init, proc and res, In this case, however, all three features are coindexed thus representing that *the train* is both Initiator, Undergoer and Resultee of the event. Hence, there is only one argument and the verb is intransitive.

(14)   *Katherine* drove the car.

(15)   *The prices* have changed. / The merchants have changed *the prices*.

(16) a. John gave *Peter* the ball.
     b. give: [init, proc, res]

(17) a. *The train* arrived.
     b. arrive: [init$_i$, proc$_i$, res$_i$]

The complement position of each eventive head can be occupied by an argument that further describes the corresponding subevent. The complement position of proc can be occupied by a so-called Path. In Ramchand's model, Paths are all XPs that can delimit the event depending on whether they provide a mereological structure. Thus, the notion of Path also applies to object-DPs of verbs like *eat*. In (12)b, the direct object refers to an unbounded mass (*porridge*) which yields an atelic VP. In (12)c, the object referent is a bounded individual (*a pizza*) which yields a telic VP. Direct objects of verbs like *push*, on the other hand, are Undergoers, i.e. subjects of spec, procP. They cannot delimit the event regardless of whether they denote an unbounded mass as in (18)a or a bounded individual as in (18)b.

(18) a. The machine pushed sand {for two hours / *in two hours}.
     b. The machine pushed the cart {for two hours / *in two hours}.

Under the view that (a-)telicity and argument realization might be relevant factors in determining the well-formedness of NI, two aspects stand out: First, telicity that emerges from properties of an object-DP is represented differently from telicity that is part of verb meaning proper. The latter is the case with verbs specified for a res-feature like *arrive* or *find*. Second, the well-known distinction between internal arguments that can evoke telicity and those that cannot (a.o. Dowty 1979, Krifka 1989, Verkuyl 1972) is represented within the syntactic configuration.

3 Verb classes and argument realization with NI

Ramchand's approach will be adopted in order to clarify which parts of a potentially complex event can be lexicalized by a NI. A similar approach has been followed for other types of deverbal nominalizations in Romance e.g. by Fábregas (2010), Sleeman & Brito (2010) and Jaque Hidalgo & Martín García (2012). The data presented in the following come from previous studies on NI that have addressed the (in-)compatibility with certain individual verb classes. It will become clear that NI show a preference for init-proc-structures, but that their formation is not entirely restricted to these subevents.[4]

---

[4] The only verb class that will not be considered are pure init-verbs since NI with a PP_{de}-argument cannot be built on verbs belonging to this class, (1) and (2). I have no principled explanation as to what this restriction might be attributed to, but it appears to be related to the lexicalization process some nominal NI underwent. Torres Cacoullos (2009: 1686) has shown in a diachronic study that the first NI that were fully lexicalized as nouns and lost their event and argument structure, appeared with stative verbs, (3).

(1)   el   estar   (*de María)
       the be.present.INF of María

(2)   el   saber   (*de inglés) / el   saber   inglés (*de María)
       the know.INF of English / the know.INF English of María
       (Fábregas & Varela 2006: 24)

(3)   *el poder* 'power', *el saber* 'knowledge, wisdom', *el sentir* 'opinion, feeling'

3.1 Intransitive base verbs

In the most typical case, NI are built on init$_1$, proc$_1$-structures. It has been noticed that they show a preference for emission-of-sound verbs (e.g. Rodríguez Espiñeira 2008), (19), and for verbs of movement (e.g. NGLE 2009: §26.3k), (20). However, there do not seem to be any systematic constraints that block the formation of NI on init$_1$-proc$_1$-verbs that lexicalize different concepts, cf. (21) and (22).

(19) el misterioso crujir de la madera.
      the mysterious creak.INF of the wood
      (Fábregas & Varela 2006: 25)

(20) el caminar pausado de la gente
      the walk.INF slow of the people
      (NGLE 2009: §26.3ñ)

(21) el sangrar del niño
      the bleed.INF of the child
      (Fábregas & Varela 2006: 26)

(22) el trabajar de Juan en el campo
      the work.INF of Juan in the field
      (Alexiadou 2010: 504)

NI built on pure proc-structures are exemplified in (23)a and (24)a. Since these verbs participate in the causative-inchoative alternation, it cannot be deduced from the surface structure whether the PP-argument corresponds to the sole argument of the intransitive alternant or the lower argument of the transitive alternant. This is particularly the case when the intransitive and the transitive alternant of the base verb are morphologically identical, cf. (23)b and (24)b.

(23) a. el subir de los precios
         the rise.INF of the prices
      b. Los precios están subiendo. / Los comerciantes han subido los precios.
         The prices are rising. / The merchants have raised the prices.

(24) a. el hervir de la leche
         the cook.INF of the milk

b. La leche está hirviendo. / María está hirviendo la leche.
   The milk is cooking. / Maria is cooking the milk.

Under the assumption that NI allow for atelic base verbs only, they should not occur with init$_i$-proc$_i$-res$_i$-verbs or proc$_i$-res$_i$-verbs as both classes are obligatorily telic. Initially, this assumption is supported by examples such as (25)a and (26)a.[5] However, other NI built on the same verbs are judged as acceptable. In these cases, the event is presented as temporally unbounded, which appears to save the construction. In (25)b, an iterative-unbounded interpretation emerges because the event is repeated on every item in the plural set and the number of items is not specified. In (26)b, the event is iterated on the same individual. Still, the NI is coerced into an unbounded reading due to the aspectual modifier *constante*. This is also why the NI can combine with an adverbial of the type *FOR x time* despite having a telic base verb (cf. Ramchand 2008: 31 for event repetition independent of the event type).

(25) a. *El   caer   de Constantinopla se produjo en 1453.
       The fall.INF of Constantinople happened in 1453.
       (Hernanz 1999: 2346)
    b. Había presenciado el   caer   de las bombas.
       He had witnessed the fall.INF of the bombs.
       (Skydsgaard 1977: 1050)

(26) a. *El llegar   tarde de Juan nos preocupó a todos.
       The arrive.INF late of Juan had us all worried.
       (de Miguel 1996: 42)
    b. el constante llegar   tarde de Juan durante seis años
       the constant arrive.INF late of Juan during six years
       (Alexiadou 2010: 505)

It seems that although NI show a preference for init$_i$-proc$_i$-structures, they can lexicalize, in principle, the full array of subevental components, including a resP, as long as an unbounded event interpretation becomes available.

---

[5] Acceptability markings are adopted from the corresponding sources if not noted otherwise.

3.2 Transitive base verbs

As shown in table 1 above, all five verb classes identified in Ramchand's system can yield transitive versions. We will concentrate on init-proc-verbs since they do not participate in the causative-inchoative alternation and are flexible with regard to telicity. It has already been shown that these verbs come in two versions depending on the lower argument, which can be a Path or an Undergoer.

If the lower argument is a Path, it could be relevant whether it is bounded or unbounded as some authors attribute the unacceptability of NI with transitive base verbs to telicity effects (e.g. Pérez Vázquez 2002: 153). NI that realize a bounded Path as a PP$_{de}$ are usually considered unacceptable, cf. (27) and (28). However, the same appears to hold true for NI with an unbounded Path-argument like a bare plural noun as in (28) and (29).

(27) *el construir de una casa
 the build.INF of a house
 (Pérez Vázquez 2007: 84)

(28) *ese afilar del cuchillo
 this sharpen.INF of the knife
 (de Miguel 1996: 49)

(29) *el leer de novelas románticas
 the read.INF of romantic novels
 (NGLE 2009: §26.3j)

(30) *ese leer de libros
 this read.INF of books
 (de Miguel 1996: 49)

If the lower argument is an Undergoer, telicity does not come into play. Yet, NI built on init-proc-verbs that select an Undergoer are often considered unacceptable as well, (31) and (32), but cf. (33) for a counter-example.

(31) *el masticar de(l) chicle
 the chew.INF of (the) gum
 (Pérez Vázquez 2002: 84)

(32) *el amasar   de la harina
    the knead.INF of the dough
    (Pérez Vázquez 2002: 84)

(33) el   constante murmurar de palabras obscenas
    the constant mutter.INF of obscene words
    (Plann 1981: 229)

Hence, telicity and the structural position of the lower argument do not seem to be decisive in determining an NI's acceptability. It rather appears that realization of the lower argument is generally disfavored, regardless of its aspectual contribution. This finding brings up the question of whether transitive base verbs are ruled out per se or whether they are possible when the higher instead of the lower argument is mapped onto the PP$_{de}$. This possibility should exist with base verbs that show the unspecified object alternation in finite verbs (cf. Levin 1993: 33). In these cases, the lower argument (the Undergoer or Path) can remain unexpressed (also in non-generic contexts) and the verb shows a transitive and an intransitive alternant, (34).

(34) a. Anna is reading a novel.
    b. Anna is reading.

Data presented in Hernanz (1999) suggest that the higher argument cannot be realized as a PP$_{de}$ either. However, (35)a and (36)a do not convincingly support this generalization since the respective base verbs do not allow the unspecified object alternation in the first place, (35)b and (36)b. Assuming that the possibility of realizing only the higher argument in the finite verb correlates with the possibility of realizing only the higher argument in the nominalized structure, the unacceptability of (35)a and (36)a is expected and not due to the NI.

(35) a. *el destruir   de los romanos
       the destroy.INF of the Romans
    b. ?/* Los romanos destruyen.
       The Romans destroy.
       (Hernanz 1999: 2345)

(36) a. un ordenar   del general
       an order.INF of the general

b. ?/* El general ordena.
   The general orders.
   (Hernanz 1999: 2345)

The situation is different when focusing on base verbs that do allow the unspecified object alternation. Without further annotations, Ramírez (2003), Demonte & Varela (1998) and Plann (1981) present examples in which the higher argument appears as a PP$_{de}$, (37), (38) and (39). Interestingly, in Plann's example, the NI is marked unacceptable although the base verb *pintar* 'to draw' allows the lower argument to remain unexpressed. In the following, it will become clear that in the latter case the unacceptability can be attributed to the episodic reading triggered by the matrix predicate *vio* 'he/she saw'.

(37) Aquel escribir de Gabriel explica su fama.
     this write.INF of Gabriel explains his fame.
     (Ramírez 2003: 117)

(38) El mirar de la mujer es agradable.
     the glance.INF of the woman is pleasant.
     (Demonte & Varela 1998: 151)[6]

(39) *Vio el pintar del maestro.
     He/she watched the paint.INF of the master
     (Plann 1981: 237)

The data, thus, indicate that the formation of NI is not primarily restricted by verb class, but rather by argument realization. Transitive init-proc-structures might be possible bases for the formation of NI as long as the higher and not the lower argument appears as a PP$_{de}$. However, argument realization appears not to be the only relevant factor. The NI presented in (37) and (38) show a generic event reading. Only (39) comes with an unambiguous episodic interpretation. Thus, I hypothesize that NI can lexicalize in principle all event components and whatever argument occupies the highest specifier position, but that further restrictions apply from the way the event is perspectivized.

---

[6] *La mujer* 'the woman' has to be interpreted as the Initiator, i.e. the person watching and not the person being watched since Demonte & Varela (1998) themselves note that NI can only realize the argument that corresponds to the subject of the active clause.

4 Interpretational possibilities of NI

This section discusses the question of why NI might tend towards generic readings and shows how generic and episodic event interpretations can be distinguished within the domain of deverbal nominalizations. NI built on intransitive verbs can refer to both event episodes and to event kinds, (40)a and b.

(40) El murmurar de los alumnos
 the whisper.INF of the students
 a. está continuando aún.
  is going on still.
 b. es una mala costumbre.
  is a bad habit.

Since transitives are usually not considered as bases for NI, their interpretational possibilities are unknown. In the remainder of this study, I will pursue the hypothesis that NI built on transitives are specialized on generic interpretations and, thus, more limited in their distribution than NI built on intransitives. Under this view, the unacceptability of (39) presented in 3.2 above is not owed to the verb class nor to argument realization, but to the episodic event interpretation triggered by the matrix predicate.

4.1 NI as unbounded expressions and genericity

It has been noted in the previous sections that an unbounded event interpretation appears to improve or even save the acceptability of an otherwise odd NI. In the following, we will therefore take a brief look at different manifestations of (un-)boundedness. It has been observed in numerous studies that the distinction between telic and atelic situation aspect and perfective and imperfective viewpoint aspect in the verbal domain parallels the distinction between count nouns and mass nouns in the nominal domain and that countability can, thus, be viewed as a nominal correlate to verbal aspect (a.o. Jackendoff 1991, Krifka 1989, Mourelatos 1978). With regard to verbal aspect, we have seen that the telic / atelic distinction is only partially relevant for the well-formedness of NI. Therefore, we will concentrate on viewpoint aspect.

Various authors have claimed that NI are imperfective nominalizations that present the event from an internal perspective as ongoing (cf. de Miguel 1996, Demonte & Varela 1998 for Spanish, Ehrich 1991 for NI in German). As NI cannot be morphologically or syntactically marked for viewpoint aspect, its identification depends on distributional criteria (cf. e.g. Ferret & Villoing 2012). It has been suggested that imperfective nominalizations cannot be embedded under expressions that refer to the completion of the event. Demonte & Varela (1998) have noted that NI are infelicitous with matrix predicates that refer to its temporal extension, beginning or endpoint, (41). Similarly, Ferret & Villoing claim that a nominalization is imperfective if it cannot be embedded under the preposition *after*. Spanish NI do not appear well-formed as the complement of *después de*, (42).

(41) Aquel corretear   majestuoso de su tía
      this run.around.INF queenly of their aunt
      {*duró toda la tarde / *comenzó hace muy poco / *ya ha finalizado}.
      {lasted the whole afternoon / has begun only recently / has already stopped.}
      (Demonte & Varela 1998: 149)

(42) ? después del subir   de los precios
        after   the rise.INF of the prices

Furthermore, it has been observed that the possibility of pluralizing a nominalization correlates, among other things, with aspectual properties of the verbal structure.[7] It has been argued that nominalizations that can be pluralized tend towards perfective interpretations (e.g. Knittel 2011), whereas nominalizations that behave (more) like mass nouns and cannot be pluralized show a preference for imperfective readings (cf. Iordăchioaia & Soare 2008). With the exception of fully lexicalized forms such as *el deber / los deberes* 'the duty / the duties', NI cannot be pluralized and even show further properties typical of mass nouns such as the ability to combine with quantifiers like *tanto* 'so much' in the singular form, (43).

(43) a. el trinar   de los pájaros / *lo-s trinar-es   de los pájaros
        the warble.INF of the birds   the.PL warble.INF-PL of the birds

---

[7] There is, however, an ongoing debate about whether the relevant correlation is between situation aspect, i.e. the telic / atelic distinction, and countability or between viewpoint aspect, i.e. the perfective / imperfective distinction, and countability (for a summary e.g. Meinschaefer 2016).

b. con tanto   gritar   de los chiquillos
   with so much scream.INF of the little ones
   (Demonte & Varela 1998: 147)

Thus, NI cannot refer to countable instantiations of events and display properties considered typical of imperfective nominalizations. This is where genericity comes into play. It has been noted that generic sentences present events as temporally unbounded (for an overview cf. Mari, Beyssade & Del Prete 2013: 41ff.). They are, for instance, usually odd when combined with a definite temporal expression as in (44). Furthermore, it is well-known that in languages like Spanish that can mark the perfective-imperfective distinction morphologically, the imperfective form is not only used for imperfective episodic readings, but also for expressing genericity, (45)a and b. Similarly, nominalizations that tend towards imperfective interpretations of event episodes might also show a preference for generic readings.

(44)   Los perros ladran (? hoy).
        Dogs bark (today).

(45)   Juan conducía   un coche deportivo.
        Juan drive.IMPF.3SG a sports car.
   a. ≈ 'Juan was driving a sports car.'
   b. ≈ 'Juan used to drive a sports car.'
        (cf. Mari et al. 2013: 41, 48)

4.2 Distinguishing episodic and generic event readings

The semantic literature usually distinguishes between (at least) two types of genericity depending on whether the locus is the DP or the clause (cf. Krifka et al. 1995). Since genericity on the DP-level is not marked by any particular morphosyntactic means, we will briefly review a number of contexts in which a nominalization can only receive a generic or an episodic interpretation. The literature has provided a number of tests to identify generic expressions (a.o. Carlson 2011, Krifka et al. 1995). It has been noted that certain kind-level predicates such as the copula structures in (46) do not only impose an eventive, but also a generic interpretation on their subject argument.

(46) ser {una mala costumbre / un tipo de suceso / un evento común}
to be {a bad habit / a type of event / a common event}

Furthermore, a matrix predicate can be modified in a way that the only possible interpretation of its DP-argument is a generic one. (47)a, for instance, is ambiguous with respect to the event interpretation, but insertion of an adverb such as *normalmente* or a verbal periphrasis with *soler* yield a generic reading, (47)b and c.

(47) El ladrar de los perros
 the barking of the dogs
 a. me molesta.
 bothers me
 b. normalmente me molesta.
 normally bothers me
 c. suele molestarme.
 usually bothers me

Reversely, certain matrix predicates impose an episodic event interpretation on their argument. This is, for example, the case with progressive periphrases of the type *estar* + gerund in Spanish. This observation also concerns the DP-level since the subject of a sentence with a progressive verb form can only be interpreted episodically, (48).

(48) El ladrar de los perros me está molestando.
 The barking of the dogs is bothering me.

Episodic interpretations also arise when the event-denoting nominalization is modified by a definite temporal expression. The German *ung*-nominalization in (49), for instance, only allows for an episodic interpretation due to the modifier *gestrig*, cf. (49)a vs. b.

(49) Die gestrige Räumung von Häusern
 The yesterday.ADJ vacating of houses
 a. war mühsam.
 was arduous.
 b. *ist weit verbreitet.
 is very common.
 (Ehrich 1991: 450)

Contexts of this type were used for the experimental study to elicit unambiguous episodic or generic event interpretations of the NI and test for their compatibility with one or the other reading.

5 Acceptability judgment experiment

The acceptability judgment task was designed to pursue the two hypotheses laid out in the previous two sections.
- NI can be built on transitive base verbs as long as the higher and the not the lower argument of the init-proc-structure is realized as a PP_{de}.
- NI that instantiate this type of structure have a preference for generic interpretations.

The experimental approach was chosen considering that judgment data provide a suitable means for detecting fine-grained differences between expressions that are rather marginal and might fail to appear in corpora in sufficient numbers. Furthermore, clear distinctions between generic and episodic readings can be drawn only when the NI is embedded under a matrix predicate that imposes one or the other interpretation on its argument.

5.1 Design and material

The experiment was based on a two-factorial design with two levels for each factor: argument realization (lower vs. higher argument) and event interpretation (episodic reading vs. generic). (50) exemplifies a concrete token set instantiating the four conditions.

(50) a. *lower argument / episodic*
En la Antártida, el cazar de ballenas está continuando durante toda la temporada porque las ballenas grises ya no se consideran como animales en peligro de extinción.
In Antarctica, the hunt.INF of whales is going on for the entire season because the grey whales are not considered threatened to become extinct anymore.
b. *lower argument / generic*
Japón ha recibido fuertes críticas de varias organizaciones medioambientales que consideran el cazar de ballenas como un negocio cruel.

Japan was severely criticized by various environmental organizations which consider the hunt.INF of whales a cruel business.

c. *higher argument / episodic*
Todavía continúa el cazar de las leonas. Están intentando separar una cebra de su manada.
The hunt.INF of the lionesses is still going on. They are trying to separate a zebra from its herd.

d. *higher argument / generic*
El cazar de las leonas es rápido y eficaz. Atrapan a su víctima con una aceleración enorme y un salto final.
The hunt.INF of the lionesses is quick and efficient. They catch their victim by accelerating enormously and with a final jump.

The material consists of twelve token sets, i.e. 48 items like the one presented in (50). All NI were built on transitive verbs that show the unspecified object alternation. They were chosen based on Moliner's (2001) dictionary in which verbs that fulfill this criterion are labelled *transitivos absolutos*. In some cases, the argument in the PP-position had to be varied with regard to definiteness and/or number in order to disambiguate between interpretation as higher or lower argument and/or to support the intended event reading. A bare plural noun was chosen, for instance, for the lower argument in (50)a and b, whereas a full DP was chosen for the higher argument in (50)c and d as bare plurals cannot be subjects of clauses with transitive verbs in Spanish (cf. table 2 in the appendix for all combinations of infinitive and argument lexemes). Matrix predicates and contexts were chosen to support an episodic or generic interpretation of the NI in the best possible way. For episodic readings, the NI were subjects of durational verbs like *continuar*, (50)a, or complements of perception verbs such as *escuchar* or *observar*. For generic readings, the NI occurred as the subjects of copula structures of the type *ser* + event noun or *ser* + adjective as in (50)b and d.

5.2 Procedure and participants

The experiment was based on a within-subject design. The material was counterbalanced and, thus, distributed onto four lists following a Latin-square design. Filler items were added to the experimental items in a ratio of 1,5: 1 so that every participant had to rate 30 items, 18 fillers and 12 experimental stimuli. The stimuli were presented in a pseudo-randomized order alternating experimental items and fillers in an irregular fashion. Acceptability was measured on a seven-point Likert scale on which 1 was labelled "does not fit at all into the context" and 7 stood for "fits perfectly into the context". The participants were 16 monolingual speakers of Castilian Spanish from the Madrid or Salamanca region. Participants were recruited in university contexts and could enter a raffle for a gift certificate. The study was carried out as a web-based experiment using *surveyguizmo*. The statistical analysis was performed with R studio (R Core Team 2018) using Bonferroni correction and a Wilcoxon signed-rang test as a non-parametric significance test suitable for within-subject designs. Additionally, a Generalized Linear Mixed Model (GLMM) was performed to take further variables into account that might have influenced acceptability.

5.3 Results

We start by comparing the different event interpretations for both variants of argument realization. With realization of the lower argument, the difference between episodic (mdn = 3) and generic (mdn = 2,5) readings did not have a significant effect on the acceptability of the NI (W = 985,5, p > 0,05). With realization of the higher argument, the situation was slightly different. These forms received higher acceptability values in generic readings (mdn = 4) than in episodic interpretations (mdn = 3). However, the difference did not turn out to be significant (W = 1414, 5, p > 0,05). We continue by comparing the argument realization variants in each reading. In episodic interpretations, realization of the higher argument and realization of the lower argument reached similar acceptability ratings (W = 1100, p > 0,05). A highly significant difference was found only in generic interpretations. When referring to event kinds, realization of the higher argument was strongly preferred over realization of the lower argument (W = 713, p < 0,001).

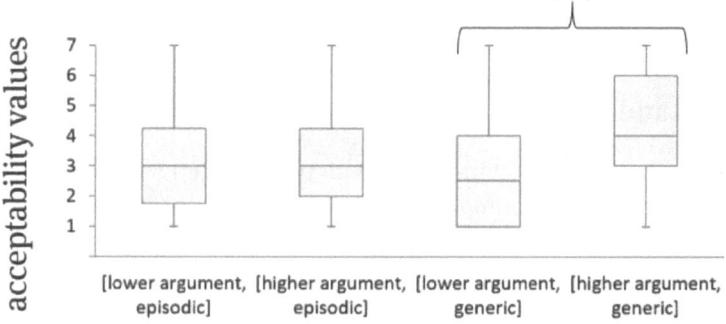

Fig. 2: Experimental results (n = 192)

To perform a GLMM, I used lme4 (Bates et al. 2015) and transformed the acceptability ratings of each participant into z-scores prior to fitting the model (Schütze & Sprouse 2013). As fixed effects, argument realization, event reading and the interaction of argument realization and event reading were included. As random effects, I added a random intercept for each item, i.e. for each of the 48 experimental stimuli. P-values were obtained by pairwise comparisons of models using anovas. The interaction between argument realization and event reading survived as the most significant predictor (χ^2= 5,96, df = 1, p < 0,05) and the model containing a random intercept for individual items was significantly better than a linear model without this random factor (χ^2= 4,86, df = 1, p < 0,05) (cf. table 3 in the appendix for a model summary).

Visual inspection of the experimental items revealed the following: NI built on *masticar* 'to chew' obtained higher acceptability ratings than NI built on other base verbs. Interestingly, this result was found with both realization of the higher and realization of the lower argument, cf. (51)a and b. Crucially, in both cases, the NI can be reinterpreted as an emission-of-sound-event as it is embedded under the perception verb *escuchar* 'to listen'. This finding supports the claim made in previous studies that NI show a preference for referring to directly perceptible events. Event perceptibility can, thus, be viewed as a further context-related factor (independent of the generic-episodic distinction) that influences the acceptability of this type of nominalization.

(51) a. Escuchando el masticar de Ramón, se nota que todavía no se ha acostumbrado a su aparato dental tras la operación.
Listening to the chew.INF of Ramón, one notices that he has not yet gotten used to his braces after the surgery.
b. Todo estaba muy tranquilo en la sala de lectura. El único sonido que es oía era el masticar de chicle.
Everything was very quiet in the reading room. The only sound that was heard was the chew.INF of gum.

6 Conclusion

This case study has been dedicated to identifying the factors that determine the occurrence of the most nominal type of Spanish NI. Focusing on transitive base verbs, it was shown that the factors argument realization and event interpretation are inter-dependent on each other. NI that realize the higher argument are relatively acceptable in generic readings. This result might relate to the simultaneous availability of a manner interpretation, (52), which is also considered typical for NI built on intransitive base verbs (cf. Hernanz 1999, Di Tullio 2001) and which is not available in generic contexts in which the lower argument is realized, (53).

(52) a. El cocinar de este jefe siempre es un espectáculo.
The cook.INF of this chef is always a spectacular event.
b. ≈ el modo en que cocina
the way in which he cooks

(53) El cocinar de estas setas es algo complicado.
The cook.INF of these mushrooms is somewhat complicated.

I tentatively assume that NI built on transitives are specialized on expressing how the event is typically carried out by the referent of the highest argument and that the manner interpretation is, thus, associated with the init-subevent.

On a more general level, it seems noteworthy that NI cannot be analyzed in terms of categorical (un)grammaticality, but rather in terms of graded acceptability. This result brings up the question about the distribution of NI in comparison to deverbal nouns. It is not entirely clear to what extent the existence or lack of a competing structure influences an item's acceptability (cf. Fanselow 2007: 357). With regard to transitive base verbs and argument realization, it is doubtful whether NI of the nominal type and deverbal nouns even compete with each other as the latter usually allow for realization of the lower argument and, in fact, often prefer this variant, cf. (54)a. Competition might rather concern deverbal nouns and more verbal uses of the NI in which the lower argument appears adjacent to the infinitive as in (54)b. However, these NI show a clear preference for generic readings (cf. Schirakowski 2016), which is not expected for deverbal nouns, but typical of (more) verbally structured nominalizations (cf. a.o. Iordăchioaia & Soare 2015).

(54) a. la cocción {de (las) setas / ?del jefe}
the cooking of {(the) mushrooms / the chef}
b. el cocinar (las) setas
the cook.INF (the) mushrooms

Generalizations regarding the distribution of NI and deverbal nouns can only be drawn with great caution in any case. First, unlike NI, deverbal nouns do not always have fully transparent meanings. Second, Spanish possesses a broad range of nominalizing affixes which contribute to the aspectual properties and interpretational possibilities of the nominal in question. Further comparisons are, therefore, left for future research.

Acknowledgement: Many thanks are due to the anonymous reviewer and the editors of this volume for valuable comments on an earlier version of this paper. I am also grateful to Josefa Martín García and Judith Meinschaefer for discussing the experimental stimuli. The presented results are based on my dissertation (Schirakowski 2016). All remaining errors are, of course, mine.

7 Appendix

Tab. 2: Experimental material (infinitive and argument lexemes)

Infinitive	lower argument	higher argument
1. *estudiar* 'study'	el vocabulario 'the vocabulary'	Juan
2. *escribir* 'write'	un guión 'a script'	*los niños* 'the children'
		este autor 'this author'
3. *comer* 'eat'	kikos 'toasted corn'	*el niño* 'the child'
	la verdura 'the vegetables'	*sus hijos* 'their children'
4. *leer* 'read'	el capítulo 'the chapter'	Pablo
	una novela 'a novel'	el niño 'the child'
5. *celebrar* 'celebrate'	*los músicos* 'the musicians'	el cumpleaños 'the birthday'
6. *pintar* 'draw, paint'	el/un cuadro 'the/a picture'	el artista 'the artist'
7. *beber* 'drink'	agua embotellada 'bottled water'	Iván
8. *limpiar* 'clean'	el baño 'the bathroom'	Clara
9. *cocinar* 'cook'	las/estas setas 'the/these mushrooms'	el/este jefe 'the/this chef'
10. *cazar* 'hunt'	ballenas 'whales'	*las leonas* 'the lionesses'
11. *masticar* 'chew'	chicle 'gum'	Ramón
12. *saquear* 'plunder'	casas 'houses'	los militares 'the soldiers'

Tab. 3: Model summary

fixed effects	estimate	standard error	t-value
interaction: argument realization + event reading	0.78945	0.32736	2.412

random effects	variance	standard deviation	
experimental item	0.1428	0.3779	
residual	0.7149	0.8455	

8 References

Alexiadou, Artemis. 2010. Nominalizations: A probe into the architecture of grammar part I: The nominalization puzzle. *Language and Linguistics Compass* 4. 496–511.
Alexiadou, Artemis, Liliane M. V. Haegeman & Melita Stavrou. 2007. *Noun phrase in the generative perspective*. Berlin & New York: De Gruyter.
Bates, Douglas, Martin Maechler, Ben Bolker & Steve Walker. 2015. Fitting linear mixed-effects models using lme4. *Journal of Statistical Software* 67. 1–48.
Carlson, Gregory N. 2011. Genericity. In Claudia Maienborn, Klaus von Heusinger & Paul H. Portner (eds.), *Semantics. An international handbook of natural language meaning*, 1153–1185. Berlin: De Gruyter.
Demonte, Violeta & Soledad Varela. 1998. Spanish event infinitives. From lexical semantics to syntax-morphology. In Amaya Mendikoetxea & Myriam Uribe-Etxebarria (eds.), *Theoretical issues at the morphology-syntax interface. Supplement of the International Journal of Basque Linguistics and Philology*, 145–169. Bilbao: Universidad del País Vasco.
Di Tullio, Ángela L. 2001. El infinitivo nominal y la lectura de manera: Una cuestión de combinación. *Anales del Instituto de Lingüística de la Universidad de Cuyo* 22–23. 97–113.
Dowty, David. 1979. *Word meaning and Montague grammar*. Dordrecht: Reidel.
Ehrich, Veronika. 1991. Nominalisierungen. In Arnim von Stechow & Dieter Wunderlich (eds.), *Semantik. Ein internationales Handbuch der zeitgenössischen Forschung*, 441–458. Berlin & New York: De Gruyter.
Fábregas, Antonio. 2010. A syntactic account of affix rivalry in Spanish nominalizations. In Artemis Alexiadou & Monika Rathert (eds.), *The syntax of nominalizations across languages and frameworks*, 67–92. Berlin & New York: De Gruyter.
Fábregas, Antonio & Soledad Varela. 2006. Verb classes with eventive infinitives in Spanish. In Nuria Sagarra & Almeida J. Torribio (eds.), *Selected proceedings of the 9th Hispanic Linguistics Symposium*, November 10–13, 2005, 24–33. Somerville, MA: Cascadilla Proceedings Project.
Fanselow, Gisbert. 2007. Carrots – perfect as vegetables, but please not as a main dish. *Theoretical Linguistics* 33. 353–367.
Ferret, Karen & Florence Villoing. 2012. L'aspect grammatical dans les nominalisations en français. Les déverbaux en -*age* et -*ée*. *Lexique* 20. 73–127.

Hernanz, M. Lluïsa. 1999. El infinitivo. In Ignacio Bosque & Violeta Demonte (eds.), *Gramática descriptiva de la lengua española*, Vol. 2, 2197–2356. Madrid: Espasa Calpe.
Iordăchioaia, Gianina & Elena Soare. 2008. Two kinds of event plurals: Evidence from Romanian nominalizations. *Empirical Issues in Syntax and Semantics* 7. 193–216.
Iordăchioaia, Gianina & Elena Soare. 2015. Deverbal nominalization with the down operator. In Enoch O. Aboh, Jeannette C. Schaeffer & Petra Sleeman (eds.), *Romance Languages and Linguistic Theory 2013. Selected papers from "Going Romance" Amsterdam 2013*, November 28–30, 2013, 223–238. Amsterdam: Benjamins.
Jackendoff, Ray. 1991. Parts and boundaries. *Cognition* 41. 9–45.
Jaque Hidalgo, Matías & Josefa Martín García. 2012. Configurational constraints on non-eventive nominalizations. *Nordlyd* 39. 113–140.
Knittel, Marie Laurence. 2011. French event nominals and number inflection. *Recherches Linguistiques de Vincennes* 40. 127–148.
Krifka, Manfred. 1989. *Nominalreferenz und Zeitkonstitution. Zur Semantik von Massentermen, Pluraltermen und Aspektklassen*. München: Fink.
Krifka, Manfred, Francis J. Pelletier, Gregory N. Carlson, Alice ter Meulen, Gennaro Chierchia & Godehard Link. 1995. Genericity: An introduction. In Gregory N. Carlson & Francis J. Pelletier (eds.), *The Generic Book*, 1–24. Chicago: Chicago University Press.
Levin, Beth. 1993. *English verb classes and alternations: a preliminary investigation*. Chicago: University of Chicago Press.
Mari, Alda, Claire Beyssade & Fabio Del Prete. 2013. Introduction. In Alda Mari, Claire Beyssade & Fabio Del Prete (eds.), *Genericity*, 1–92. Oxford: Oxford University Press.
Meinschaefer, Judith. 2016. Nominalizations. In Susann Fischer & Christoph Gabriel (eds.), *Manual of grammatical interfaces in Romance*, 391–418. Berlin: De Gruyter.
Miguel, Elena de. 1996. Nominal infinitives in Spanish: An aspectual constraint. *The Canadian Journal of Linguistics* 41. 29–53.
Moliner, María. 2001. *Diccionario de uso de español*. Madrid: Gredos.
Mourelatos, Alexander P. 1978. Events, processes and states. *Linguistics and Philosophy* 2, 415–434.
NGLE = Asociación de Academias de la Lengua Española 2009. *Nueva gramática de la lengua española. Sintaxis II*. Madrid: Espasa Libros.
Pérez Vázquez, Mª Enriqueta. 2002. A mixed extended projection: The nominalized infinitive in Spanish and Italian. *Quaderni del Laboratorio di Linguistica* 14. 143–158.
Pérez Vázquez, Mª Enriqueta. 2007. *El infinitivo y su sujeto en español*. Bologna: Gedit.
Plann, Susan. 1981. The two *el*+infinitive constructions in Spanish. *Linguistic Analysis* 7. 203–240.
R Core Team. 2018. *R: A language and environment for statistical computing*. Vienna, Austria: R Foundation for Statistical Computing. https://www.r-project.org. (31 May, 2019.)
Ramchand, Gillian C. 2008. *Verb meaning and the lexicon. A first-phase syntax*. Cambridge: Cambridge University Press.
Ramírez, Carlos J. 2003. The Spanish nominalized infinitives: A proposal for a classification. *Toronto Working Papers in Linguistics* 21. 117–133.
Rodríguez Espiñeira, María José. 2008. El infinitivo como categoría híbrida o ambivalente. In María José Rodríguez Espiñeira & Jesús Pena Seijas (eds.), *Categorización lingüística y límites intercategoriales*, 127–148. Santiago de Compostela: Universidade de Santiago de Compostela.

Schirakowski, Barbara. 2016. *Nominalisierte Infinitive im Spanischen. Eine empirische Untersuchung anhand von Akzeptabilitätsurteilen*. Dissertation. Berlin: Freie Universität Berlin.

Schütze, Carson T. & Jon Sprouse. 2013. Judgment data. In Robert J. Podesva & Devyani Sharma (eds.), *Research methods in linguistics*, 27–50. Cambridge: Cambridge University Press.

Skydsgaard, Sven. 1977. *La combinatoria sintáctica del infinitivo español*, Vol. 2. Madrid: Castalia.

Sleeman, Petra & Ana Maria Brito. 2010. Aspect and argument structure of deverbal nominalizations: A split vP analysis. In Artemis Alexiadou & Monika Rathert (eds.), *The syntax of nominalizations across languages and frameworks*, 199–218. Berlin & New York: De Gruyter Mouton.

Smith, Carlota S. 1997. *The parameter of aspect*. Dordrecht et al.: Kluwer.

Soare, Elena. 2017. Generic, habitual and episodic events in Romanian nominalizations. In Maria Bloch-Trojnar & Anna Malicka-Kleparska (eds.), *Aspect and valency in nominals*, 285–300. Berlin & Boston: De Gruyter.

Torres Cacoullos, Rena. 2009. Las nominalizaciones de infinitivo. In Concepción Company (ed.), *Sintaxis histórica del español. La frase nominal*, Vol. 2, 1673–1738. México: Fondo de Cultura Económica y Universidad Nacional Autónoma de México.

Vendler, Zeno. 1957. Verbs and times. *The Philosophical Review* 66. 143–160.

Verkuyl, Hendrik J. 1972. *On the compositional nature of the aspects*. Dordrecht: Reidel.

Yoon, James H. & Neus Bonet-Farran. 1991. The ambivalent nature of Spanish infinitives. In Dieter Wanner & Douglas Kibbee (eds.), *New analyses in Romance linguistics*, 353–370. Amsterdam: Benjamins.

Lena Baunaz and Genoveva Puskás
Complementizer functional sequence: the contribution of Italo-Romance

Abstract: In this paper, we discuss the realization of complementizers in different Romance languages. We show that some Italo-Romance varieties exhibit two forms of complementizers, which select for indicative versus subjunctive embedded clauses. We show that the constraints on the licensing of these two complementizers are determined by properties of the matrix selecting predicate. While all embedding verbs have a sentient feature, only verbs embedding subjunctive clauses also exhibit an emotive feature. We propose that in French and standard Italian, the same verbs select for the same complementizers. However, in these languages, 'indicative' and 'subjunctive' complementizers are syncretic.

Keywords: complementizer, indicative, subjunctive, sentient, emotive, syncretism.

1 Introduction

The aim of this paper is to discuss, based on the specific phenomenon of subjunctive selection, how syntax and semantics contribute to a linguistic model of human language. While most researchers have lived with the idea that semantics accounts for *meanings* and that syntax, quite independently, accounts for *sentence structure*, we believe that the two are interconnected in the way linguistic knowledge and linguistic output is built.

The question of subjunctive selection is particularly relevant in this respect. It has indeed been claimed by many to be a purely semantic phenomenon, in that it involves giving access to alternative worlds or to non-presupposed contents of various kinds. While we do integrate the semantic notion of access to "non-realistic" bases, we also question the role and nature of the complementizers, and hence of selection and selecting verbs, a syntactic notion.

Lena Baunaz: University of Zürich, Romanisches Seminar, Zürichbergstrasse 8, 8032 Zürich, Switzerland, lena.baunaz@gmail.com
Genoveva Puskás: University of Geneva, Faculty of Letters, Linguistics Dept, 5, rue de Candolle, 1211 Geneva 4, Switzerland, genoveva.puskas@unige.ch

https://doi.org/10.1515/9783110719154-009

Our proposal is based on recent work in what has become known as *nanosyntax*. Given that we assume a lexical decomposition that takes features to be atomic parts of the sentence, whatever surfaces in a sentence (including subjunctive marking) is the product of (iterative) syntactic operations on sub-morphemic units; syntactic selection of subjunctive clauses fares along with other (syntactic) processes and is assumed to follow from (an ordered set of) features.

In this paper, we wish to answer the following questions:
i. What role do complementizers play in the selection of the subjunctive mood (vs. indicative) in embedded clauses?
ii. What licenses these complementizers?

The point we would like to make is that the selection of subjunctive mood exhibits different morpho-syntactic realizations in the embedded clause but is triggered in a similar way cross-linguistically. To support this claim, we use data from French and Italo-Romance dialects.

Our paper is organized as follows: We first briefly introduce our theoretical framework and our main hypotheses. In section 3, we examine the distribution of indicative and subjunctive licensing complementizers in various Italo-Romance dialects and reach the conclusion that in languages where this distinction is not morphologically marked, we have cases of syncretism. In section 4, we turn to the question of the licensing of the complementizer forms themselves. We argue that the criterion for selecting the subjunctive mood in French is *emotivity*, while the selection of the indicative is neutral w.r.t. emotion. We also set grammatical diagnostics in favor of the existence of the two classes (see Baunaz 2017). In section 5, we further decompose the notion of *emotive* and show how different predicates select for different complementizers via the *emotive* feature. Section 6 is our conclusion.

2 Background

Since our analysis of the subjunctive complementation phenomenon involves both the sentence and the word-internal levels, our analysis is rooted within the more general cartographic framework (Rizzi 1997, 2004, 2013, Cinque 1999, a.o), and ventures into the world of its most direct descendant, nanosyntax (Starke 2009, 2011, Caha 2009, Baunaz and Lander 2018a, a.o). In this section, we first briefly introduce our theoretical assumptions, as well as the methodology behind our nanosyntactic analysis.

2.1 Cartography

We follow cartographers (see Rizzi 1997, 2004, 2013; Cinque 1999, Cinque and Rizzi 2008/2010 a.o) in assuming (i) a strict syntax-semantics mapping (i.e. syntax is the vehicle for expressing (grammatical) semantics by means of a rigidly ordered structure of syntactico-semantic features); (ii) simplicity of projections; (iii) each syntactico-semantic feature is an independent head that projects, in line with the "one feature – one head" principle (Cinque & Rizzi 2008: 50, see also Kayne 2005: ch.12). The approach leads to the extremely detailed syntactic structures that have emerged from the cartographic research program.

2.2 Nanosyntax (NS)

This paper is set within the nanosyntactic approach to grammar (NS).[1] According to NS, morphemes are decomposable into discrete atomic features, which are merged recursively in a syntactic functional sequence (fseq) assumed to be invariable across languages (Caha 2009; Starke 2009, 2011). NS is thus an advocate of the *morphology is syntax* approach: morphemes are built in syntax.

The atomic features that are used to build morphemes consist of syntactico-semantic features. NS advocates for a strict syntax-semantics mapping, i.e., (grammatical) semantics is syntacticized: typically features encoding number, person, case (...) are 'split' into primitive features like *singular, plural, dual, 1p* (= speaker), *2p* (= hearer), *3p, nominative, accusative, dative*, or *path, source, goal* etc. Since both morphology and grammatical semantics are syntacticized, NS refers to the syntactic module as *Syntax-Morphology-Semantics* module (SMS). SMS is the component of the language faculty where grammatical features are merged into a hierarchy according to the universal and invariable fseq.

As just said, this theory advocates that the atoms are combined and merged *in* syntax. The lexicon in NS is thus post-syntactic. As such a lexical entry is minimally a single morpheme with its own syntactic structure. Once a morpheme is built, it is stored in the lexicon. A lexical entry is thus used to store a syntactic structure that is linked to phonological and CONCEPTUAL (extra-grammatical) information, as schematized in (1). The syntactic structure that is stored in the lexical entry in (1) is called a lexical structure.

(1)   Lexical entry: </phonology/ ⇔ syntax ⇔ CONCEPT>

---

[1] This section builds on Baunaz & Lander (2018a) to which we refer the reader for further details.

Minimally a lexical entry is thus a single morpheme (but a hierarchically organized set of features). [2]

In order to uncover the true nature of a fseq, NS has various tools, two of which are syncretism and containment. The two are methodologically complementary and are discussed in what follows.

2.2.1 Syncretism

Caha 2009 claims that syncretism helps establish the linear ordering of a fseq. His approach to syncretism is based on the idea that (syntactic) heads are cumulative. He defines this phenomenon as "a surface conflation of two distinct morphosyntactic structures" (Caha 2009: 6),[3] meaning that it systematically targets adjacent regions in a paradigm – and hence, in a fseq[4]. Caha 2009 exemplifies this idea with a fine-grained study of the (nominative-accusative) Case system cross-linguistically (based on Blake 1994). Consider his example from Russian (Caha 2009: 12):

Tab. 1: Paradigm of Russian Case declension

	'window' (SG)	'teacher' (PL)	'one hundred'
Nominative	okn-o	učitel-ja	st-o
Accusative	okn-o	učitel-ej	st-o
Genitive	okn-a	učitel-ej	st-a
Dative	okn-u	učitel-am	st-a
Instrumental	okn-om	učitelami	st-a

---

2 A morpheme is thus the smallest unit pairing a phonology ('sound') and a CONCEPTUAL information ('meaning'). This pairing is achieved once the syntactic derivation reaches the point of lexicalization. Note that, whereas languages share all the same basic ingredients that serve them to build structures (i.e. the atomic features), they vary as to how they 'lexically' package the fseq.
3 Baunaz, de Clercq, Lander and Haegeman 2018:330 define syncretism as "The phenomenon whereby multiple grammatical distinctions in a *paradigm* are *lexicalized* by a single *phonological exponent*".
4 On this issue, see also Caha 2010, 2013; Taraldsen 2009; Pantcheva 2011; De Clercq 2013, 2018; Lander 2015; Lander and Haegeman 2018, Baunaz 2015, 2016, 2017, 2018; Baunaz and Lander 2017, 2018a,b a.o.

Table 1 shows that Russian has Case syncretism in NOM/ACC, ACC/GEN and GEN/DAT/INS. The shaded areas highlight the fact that these five cases can be grouped together according to syncretism patterns. Once this is done, we see that syncretism involves only contiguous regions (or cells). Expanding to many more languages and cases, Caha shows that the case sequence can be organized in a single invariant order cross-linguistically, where attested syncretisms are systematically in adjacent cells (2i). His generalization is given in (2ii):

(2) Universal Case Contiguity (Caha 2009, 49)
 (i) Non-accidental case syncretism targets contiguous regions in a sequence invariant across languages.
 (ii) The Case sequence is: NOM-ACC-GEN-DAT-INS-COM

(2) predicts when syncretisms are possible: two non-adjacent cases in a paradigm should never be syncretic, i.e. NOM and GEN should never be syncretic to the exclusion of ACC for instance. This adjacency effect had also been stated in terms of the *ABA-theorem, i.e., the fact that so-called ABA patterns are never found cross-linguistically (Bobaljik 2007, 2012; Caha 2009). For example, if A is NOM and GEN and B is ACC, we should never find a syncretism pattern with NOM and GEN to the exclusion of ACC. Caha's research has showed that this is cross-linguistically valid.

This generalization about syncretism had been extended to all types of syncretism patterns and becomes a tool to discover the atoms of the SMS module (i.e. syntax). Indeed, attested syncretisms cross-linguistically help identify the fine-grained atoms which build morphemes and help discover how these atoms are (linearly) ordered, since they tell us which feature sits next to which other feature in the fseq.[5,6]

Although syncretism facts can determine what the *linear* order of features is in a fseq, they do not determine their *hierarchical* order. In other words, there is,

---

[5] An important feature of nanosyntactic research is that it favors detailed, typologically adequate empirical investigations. Not all languages will show syncretism, so a cross-linguistic approach is required. In other words, to build generalizations about language universals, NS advocates for sampling diversity. This allows to uncover the inventory of atoms in the fseq and to see how this fseq is packaged into different lexical items across individual languages.
[6] Overall, the understanding of *syncretism* in NS is somewhat more constrained than in many other frameworks. NS looks at the structure of functional morphemes, and their syncretism patterns, in order to detect the underlying fseq, with syncretism always being highly constrained by adjacency of the respective grammatical features in the sequence. This is the understanding of the term that we will use from now on.

at this point, no way to decide whether nominative hierarchically dominates (and hence includes) accusative in the fseq or the other way round.

2.2.2 Containment

What may help determine the hierarchical organization of features is the study of morphological and semantic containment relations. They provide particularly clear glimpses into internal structure (see also Fábregas 2009, Pantcheva 2011 a.o). Morphological containment, which determines the hierarchy of nominative and accusative, for example, is attested in Finnish (Caha 2009: 115):

(3) A subset of Finnish singular cases
Bear, sg
Nom karhu
Acc karhu-n
Gen karhu-n

Nominative is morphologically contained in accusative; accusative and genitive are syncretic. A similar process can isolate the relation between e.g. accusative and genitive in other languages.

In this paper, morphological containment is not discussed and we refer the reader to Baunaz and Lander (2018a) for details. As we will show below, semantic considerations (i.e. semantic compositionality) can play a role in building up functional sequences and in determining the hierarchical relation between the components of the fseq. [7]

---

[7] Working on the hierarchy of *event* features, Ramchand (2008) argues for a strong isomorphism between syntax, semantics and morphology. She proposes that (dynamic) verbs are decomposed into subparts, where "each projection corresponds to a subevent with its own predicational subject position, and linked by the generalized 'leads- to' or 'cause' relation" (Ramchand 2008: 118). She argues that the events denoted by a predicate can be decomposed into sub-events. Crucially each sub-event of a predicate is associated with a specific syntactic head forming a functional sequence (fseq), compositionally. She gives a number of semantic arguments in support of the way her hierarchy in (i) is built.

(i) [$_{initP}$ DP3 init [$_{procP}$ DP2 proc [$_{resP}$ DP1 res [XP]]]] [Ramchand 2008, 118 (3)]

An initiation, for instance, can be seen as the causing sub-event; it may include the sub-events associated with the feature Process and Result. Hence in terms of structure, initiation can be

2.2.3 A note on apparent circularity

On the surface, the nanosyntactic enterprise may seem to lead to circular reasoning, as has been pointed out by a reviewer. Indeed, the theory appears to postulate hierarchical structures, and use morphological evidence to identify hierarchies, using these findings as a proof for the existence of hierarchical structures. However, nanosyntactic theory is explanation driven, and searches to find deep-rooted motivations for linguistic phenomena. Its methodology therefore starts from observations about syncretisms: one area of the linguistic field appears to exhibit syncretisms (in other words, we observe one lexical form, which is associated with different functions). Research in this area will aim at explaining why such syncretisms are possible, under a strong assumption that it is not accidental and that linguistic systems are coherent and organized. The method to approach such a *why* question is first to decompose the target items into morphological/semantic discrete units which will show the overlapping functions of the syncretic items. However, this is clearly not yet an explanation. The next step is to identify containment relations, that is, which properties (be they morphologically identifiable or only semantically manifest) are common to the various forms – in which case they are at the core of the syncretic element – and which one are additional. If a feature α is a property of both forms A and B, and β characterizes only B, then having β entails having α, but not vice-versa. We can thus establish a hierarchy in which $<\alpha, \beta>$ is a subset of $<\alpha>$ (in terms of tree diagram representations, in means that α occurs lower than β, since all structure will minimally contain α). Crucially, as mentioned above (see footnote 5), a descriptively adequate hierarchy can only be based on cross-linguistic investigation, which will provide a large inventory of atomic properties to be built into a universal functional sequence. The explanatory power of such an approach lies in the fact that syncretisms occur because smaller units, which have a more "core" property can be enriched with more "peripheral" properties. Clearly, a deep explanation of how linguistic knowledge is organized in the brain – and whether it indeed reflects the organization of deep cognitive properties of human beings – is necessary, but the approach brings us one step closer to that enterprise in providing a reasoned account of linguistic mechanisms as (i) feature-based, (ii) recursive and (iii) universally valid.

---

thought of as being built on top of the features Process and Result (in other words, a result necessarily requires a process, which in turn necessarily requires a cause).

2.2.4 Lexicalization and the Superset Principle

As we saw above, a lexical entry may correspond to various grammatical functions, that is, to various (hierarchically related) portions of the fseq. For instance, in French, *que* can be a complementizer, a relative pronoun, or an interrogative pronoun. In NS a lexical entry is an element of the lexicon, which is composed of: (i) a phonological representation, (ii) a syntactic structure (i.e. a Lexical tree) and (iii) conceptual information. Lexicalization is the process by which a feature (or set of features) is associated with a phonological representation within a syntactically constrained structure. An example of lexical entry for French *que* is given in (4) below:

(4) Lexical entry < /kə/ ⇔ [Comp [Rel [Wh]]] ⇔ que>

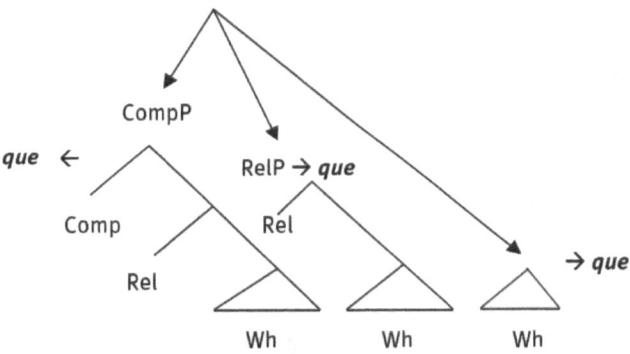

The lexical entry in (4) shows that the phonological string /kə/ corresponds to the lexicalization of the feature [wh], but also of the fseq encoding the features [rel] and [wh] which stand in a hierarchical relation *rel>wh*, as well as of the fseq encoding the features [comp], [rel] and [wh], where comp dominates *rel* (which dominates *wh*), the relative hierarchical relations having been determined by morphological and/or semantic containment relations.

Lexicalization is regulated by different principles, among which the Superset Principle. The latter allows for a Syntactic-tree to be lexicalized by a Lexical-tree drawn from the lexicon as long as that Lexical-tree is similar in size (or bigger) than the Syntactic-tree. Therefore, in our example, a single Lexical entry may apply in multiple syntactic environments, and enable to lexicalize different (related) Syntactic-trees:

(5) Lexical entry < /kə/ ⇔ [Comp [Rel [Wh]]] ⇔ que>[8]

2.2.5 Hypotheses

Given what has been laid out in section 1 and 2, our working hypotheses are the following:
i. Given locality principles, the modal connection between the matrix predicate and the embedded subjunctive clause is mediated by the complementizer. Complementizers may be syncretic.
ii. Given that embedded subjunctives occur in selected contexts, some (sub)-component of the matrix predicate is associated with subjunctive. This component will be responsible for the selection of the relevant complementizer.

3 Complementizers as clause selecting elements

Embedded clauses are introduced by a complementizer. We observe that languages vary as to the array of complementizers licensing subjunctive or indicative embedded clauses. However, based on comparative data from French and Italian dialects, we propose that complementizers are complex elements, with different sub-components relating to subjunctive/indicative, and that they may exhibit syncretism.[9]

3.1 Dual complementizer systems

French and standard Italian do not show any surface difference in the complementizer selecting indicative (*a* examples) or subjunctive (*b* examples) embedded clauses. Both are realized as *que* in French and *che* in Italian:

---

8 We thank Eric Lander for inspiring us with this drawing.
9 A reviewer notes that in old French and standard Italian, the complementizer introducing subjunctive clauses can be deleted/left unpronounced. Although there seems to be some co-occurrence of subjunctive marking and complementizer deletion in Romance, this is not systematic (only a subset of subjunctives seems to allow for deletion), suggesting that there might be only an indirect correlation between the two phenomena. This is supported by the fact that English, e.g. allows for complementizer deletion with indicative. This remains to be investigated.

(6) a. Léon pense que Georges **écrit** des poèmes. (French)
    Leon thinks that Georges writes.IND poems
  b. Léon souhaite que Georges **écrive** des poèmes.
    Léon wishes that Georges write.SUBJ poems

(7) a. Penso che Maria **verrà**. (Italian)
    I think that Maria will.come
  b. Voglio che Maria **venga**.
    I want that Maria come.SUBJ

As opposed to French and standard Italian, Italo-Greek dialects have dual complementizer systems (see Ledgeway 2005, 2006, 2013, a.o, Manzini & Savoia 2003, 2011). (Examples (8) and (9) are taken from Ledgeway 2006):[10]

(8) a. Pensu **ca** vèni. (S. Calabria)
    'I think that he'll come.'
  b. Vogghiu **mu** (mi) mangia.
    'I want that_MOOD he eat.'

(9) a. Pistèo **tí** pái. (Calabria, Bova)
    'I think that he will go.'
  b. θèlo **na** pái.
    'I want that_MOOD he go.'

Verbs like *think* generally appear with a complementizer of the QUIA/QUID type (*a* examples), while verbs like *want* select for a complementizer of the MODO type, as in (*b* examples), sometimes considered as a mood particle. The Calabria

---

10 In addition to these dialects, another Standard Romance language, Romanian, also exhibits a dual complementizer system:

(i) Maria   crede   ca   Ion   a   plecat.
    Mary   believe.3SG   that   John   has.3SG left
    'Mary believes that John left.'
(ii) Maria   vrea   **să**   plece   Ion.
     Mary   wants   SUBJ   leave.3SG   John
     'Mary wants John to leave.'
     (Cotfas 2011: 27)

dialect selects for complementizers cognate with Modern Greek (MG) *oti* and *na*, as shown in (10).

(10) a. Nomizo   oti   efije   noris   (MG)
      think.1SG that.C1 left.3SG early
      'I think that he left early'
      (Roussou 2010: 593)
   b. Thelo   **na**   liso   to provlima.
      want.1SG   that.C2 solve.1SG the problem
      'I want that I solve the problem'
      (Roussou 2010: 583)

Similar facts have been observed for unrelated languages like Fongbe (Niger Congo), in (11) (see Lefebvre and Brousseau 2002; Damonte 2002 a.o).

(11) a. Kɔ́kú   lìn   ɖɔ̀   Àsíbá   gbà   mɔ́tò ɔ́.   (Fongbe)
      Koku think that Asiba destroy car DEF.
      'Koku thinks that Asiba destroyed the car'.
      (=(3b) in Lefebvre 1992)
   b. Ùn   jló   **ní/nú**   à ní wá.   (Fongbe)
      1SG want that$_{MOOD}$ 2SG come
      'I want you to come.' [Lit.: 'I want that you come.']
      (from Lefebvre and Brousseau 2002: 116,117)

Manzini and Savoia (2003) observe that many Romance varieties actually distinguish between at least two complementizers of the QUIA/QUID type. This is the case for instance in the dialects of Guglionesi and Ardaùli exemplified in (12) and (13). In both dialects, *ka* lexicalizes the default complementizer of embedded declaratives (generally in the indicative), as in (12a) and (13a); *kə /ki* introduces embedded declarative clauses dependent on verbs like *want*, which typically require the subjunctive in other Romance varieties (12b) and (13b).

(12) a. 'm ɔnnə ' dəttə   **ka**   vɛ   'krɛ   (Guglionesi, Molise)
      to me they.have said that he.comes tomorrow
   b. 'vujjə **kə** vɛnnə 'krɛ
      I.want that he.come tomorrow
      (Manzini and Savoia 2003, (5a,b))

(13) a. 'm anta 'nau **ka** eniði ɣraza (Ardaùli, Sardinia)
me they.have told that he.comes tomorrow
b. 'kɛrdzɔ **ki** 'ɛndzɛðɛ ain'nɔɣɛ
I.want that he.comes here
(Manzini and Savoia 2003, (6a,b))

The predicates *pensu*, *pistèo* are epistemic verbs, while *vogghiu*, *θèlo* belong to the class of desiderative verbs, which typically embed subjunctive clauses in languages that have such morphological marking (see examples 6, 7 above). We will therefore adopt the idea that *ka*, *tí* are complementizers selecting for an 'indicative' clause, while *mu*, *na* are complementizers selecting a 'subjunctive' clause.[11] In these dialects, mood distinction correlates with complementizer selection, but tends not to appear as verbal morphology, due to morphological erosion (see Ledgeway 2005 about Southern Italian dialects). However, the differentiated marking on the complementizers as well as the semantics of the embedded clauses suggest that subjunctive as a mood is at play.

Where these languages mark a distinction between two forms, which broadly correlate with the indicative vs. subjunctive mood of the embedded clause, languages like French and Italian do not. Table 1 below illustrates the two cases:

Tab. 2: Complementizer forms in Romance languages

	Guglionesi Comp QUIA/QUID	Ardaùli (Sardinian) CompQUIA/QUID	French CompQUIA/QUID	Italian CompQUIA/QUID
Indicative	ka	ka	kə	ke
Subjunctive	kə	ki	kə	ke

This suggests that French *que* and Italian *che* have two variants in one form, and that these languages show syncretism in the comp-system. This also suggests a more fine-grained hierarchy in the complementizer domain.

---

[11] For the purpose of this paper, particles *mu/mi/na* are considered as complementizers. See Giannakidou (2009) for discussion on Modern Greek. See Rohlfs (1969), Calabrese (1993), as well as Ledgeway (2005, 2006, 2013) and references cited there for discussion on Southern Italian *mu/mi/na*.

3.2 The internal structure of complementizers

Building on recent work by Baunaz (2015, 2016, 2018) and Baunaz & Lander (2017, 2018b,c), we propose that complementizers are not simplex heads, but complex constructions. Recall that in NS, syncretism, and lack thereof, can help establish linear ordering. Accordingly, since que_{ind} and que_{subj} are syncretic, they must (probably) occupy adjacent cells in a paradigm table. The question that remains to be answered is: in what hierarchy do they stand in (14)?

(14) $Comp_{ind} > Comp_{subj}$ or $Comp_{subj} > Comp_{ind}$?

To answer this question, we must look in more detail at other complementizers.

3.3 Italo-Romance dialects and relative complementizers

Complementizers also occur as heads of relative clauses. In French and Italian, the relative complementizer is syncretic with the declarative complementizer: *que/che*, respectively. Interestingly Manzini and Savoia observe that some Italian dialects may display two forms of relative complementizer: appositive and restrictive.

The syncretism obtained in the Italo-Romance dialects can be arranged in the table here, where restrictive relative can be syncretic with appositive relative and $Comp_{subj}$ (Sonnino, Dorgali) or with $Comp_{ind}$ (Guardaregia and Làconi). The appositive relative can be syncretic with $Comp_{subj}$, but never with $Comp_{ind}$ to the exclusion of restrictive relative.[12]

---

[12] Ardaùli appears to be an exception to the rather general pattern shown here, in that it realizes $Comp_{ind}$ as *ka*, $Rel_{restrictive}$ as *ki*, $Rel_{appositive}$ as *ka* and $Comp_{subj}$ as *ki*. Although it seems to offer a problematic counterexample, a closer scrutiny of the data may reveal more subtle differences.

Tab. 3: Paradigm of complementizers in Italo-Romance dialects

	Comp$_{ind}$	Rel$_{restrictive}$	Rel$_{appositive}$	Comp$_{subj}$
Sonnino	ka	ke	ke	ke
Dorgali	ka	ki	ki	ki
Guardiaregia	ka	ka	ke	ke
Làconi	ka	ka	tʃi	tʃi
Villa San Giovanni	ka	ki	ki	mi

Similar patterns are found cross linguistically (table 4).

Tab. 4: Paradigm of complementizers in various languages

	Comp$_{ind}$	Rel$_{restrictive}$	Rel$_{appositive}$	Comp$_{subj}$
M. Greek	oti	pu	pu	na
Bulgarian	če	deto	deto	da
Romanian	că	ce / care	care	să
Polish	że	że / co	co	by
English	that	that	that	that
French	kə	kə	kə	kə
Italian	ke	ke	ke	ke

Based on Baunaz (2016, 2018), we adopt a fseq in which Comp$_{subj}$ is at the bottom of the hierarchy. We propose that Comp$_{subj}$ merges with the lower part of the structure to form the complex element CompP$_{subj}$.

As for the relative complementizers, again, two hierarchical patterns may arise:

(15) a. Comp$_{ind}$ | Rel$_{restrictive}$ | Rel$_{appositive}$ | Comp$_{subj}$
 b. Comp$_{ind}$ > Rel$_{restrictive}$ > Rel$_{appositive}$ > Comp$_{subj}$

In the Villa San Giovanni dialect, syncretism is found only in the relative complementizers. The data is compatible with both (15a) and (15b). However, in Guardiaregia in Table 3, Comp$_{subj}$ spells out as *ke*, Rel$_{appositive}$ also spells out as *ke*, but

Rel$_{restrictive}$ spells out as *ka*. Syncretism arises with Comp$_{subj}$ and Rel$_{appositive}$. We conclude that appositive Rel merges with CompP$_{subj}$ to form the complex element RelP$_{appositive}$. Then restrictive Rel is merged.

Similarly, in Sonnino, Comp$_{subj}$ merges with Rel$_{appositive}$ and spells out as *ke*. In addition, when Rel$_{restrictive}$ merges, RelP$_{restrictive}$ also spells out as *ke* (where Guardiaregia spells out *ka*). Finally, Comp$_{ind}$ is spelled out as *ka* in the two dialects. Thus, both Guardaregia and Sonnino speak in favour of hierarchy (15b):

(16) a. Giardaregia

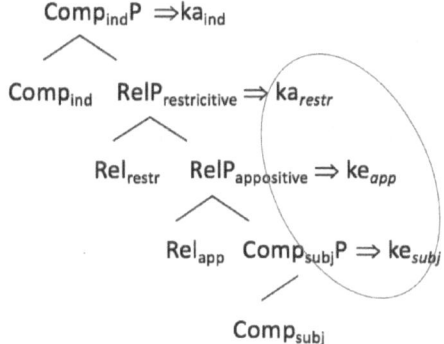

b. Sonnino

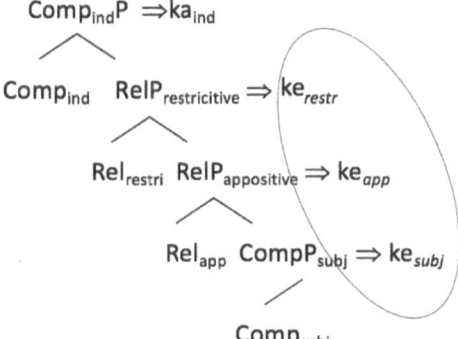

Note that the Villa San Giovanni dialect, which exhibits syncretism for the two Rels, crucially spells out Comp$_{subj}$ and Comp$_{ind}$ as different morphemes:

(17) Villa San Giovanni dialect (Reggio de Calabre) [A. Idone, pc.]

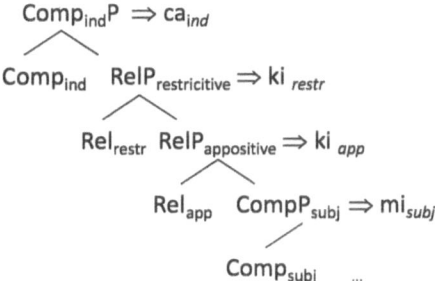

Since French and Italian show syncretism all the way down, each XP lexicalizes *que*. Given the hierarchy (15b) that we adopt, we propose the following structure for the complementizer system:

(18) French and Italian

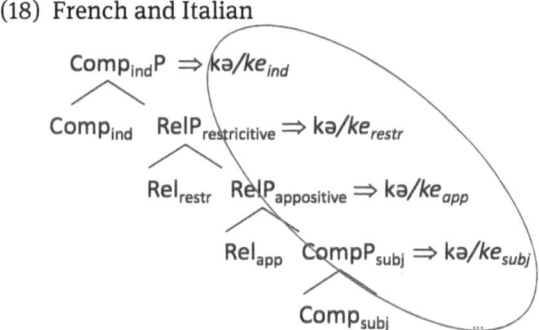

4 The emotive factor

The question that naturally arises is what triggers the choice/realization of these different sizes of complementizers. We adopt a strict locality approach, and assume that Comp is directly selected by the matrix predicate. Therefore, some component of this predicate must be active in the licensing of the features that make up indicative or subjunctive Comps. We propose that the key to mood choice lies in the (lexical) semantic decomposition of the selecting verb. Building on Baunaz and Puskás (2014), Baunaz (2017), we argue that the matrix external arguments of verbs taking the subjunctive share some property crucial to mood selection, which we identify as an **"emotive"** property. This property is licensed by a specific feature of the subjunctive selecting predicate. Typically, external arguments of verbs taking the indicative lack this construal, because these verbs lack the emotive feature.

To show this, we examine the properties of French predicates that exhibit mood alternation, instantiated in (19), and claim that their various forms are syncretic.

(19) *comprendre* 'understand', *espérer* 'hope, expect', *rêver* 'dream', *accepter* 'accept', *admettre* 'admit'

We show that these verbs coincide with systematic grammatical differences, such as mood alternation and adverb modification.

Our analysis then extends to the classes of French (non-syncretic) verbs given in (20), of which verbs of saying and epistemic verbs select for indicative embedded clauses and emotive factives, desire and directive verbs select for subjunctive embedded clauses.

(20) a. Verbs of saying: *dire* 'say', *observer* 'observe'...
 b. Epistemic factives: *réaliser* 'realize', *se rappeler* 'remember'...
 c. Emotive factives: *regretter* 'regret'...
 d. Desire: *préférer* 'prefer', *souhaiter* 'wish', *vouloir* 'want'...
 e. Directive: *suggérer* 'suggest', *insister* 'insist'...

4.1 Predicates with mood alternation

We start our exploration with a prototypical case, that of *comprendre* ('understand'). Predicates like *comprendre* come with mood alternation correlating with a difference in meaning, as illustrated in (21):

(21) a. Léon comprend que Georges écrit des romans de gare.
 Léon understands that Georges writes.IND dime novels
 'Léon understands that Georges writes dime novels.'

  b. Léon comprend que Georges écrive des romans de gare.
    Léon understands that Georges writes.SUBJ dime novels
    'Léon understands why/sympathizes with the reasons why Georges writes dime novels.'

The verb *comprendre* in (21a), which selects an indicative clause, involves some cognitive exercise. In other words, the activity of understanding is an intellectual achievement, which requires cognitive abilities; in addition, (21b), the version that selects a subjunctive clause, contains some kind of subjective position: Léon, the subject of the matrix clause, is emotionally involved in the process of 'understanding'. In nanosyntactic terms, *comprendre* in (21a) and *comprendre* in (21b) are **syncretic**.

4.2 Adverb modification

In addition to mood choice, verbs like *comprendre* exhibit systematic differences in adverb modifications: (i) agent-oriented modifiers like *par déduction* ('by deduction') can only modify the subject of *comprendre* + indicative, as in (22a); (ii) degree adverbs like *tellement* ('so much/well') can only modify *comprendre* + subjunctive, (23b):

(22) a. Léon comprend par déduction que Georges écrit la nuit.
    Léon understands by deduction that Georges writes.IND at night.
  b. #Léon comprend par déduction que Georges écrive la nuit.
    Léon understands by deduction that Georges write.SUBJ at night.

(23) a. #Léon comprend tellement que Georges écrit des romans.
    Léon understands so well that Georges writes.IND novels.
  b. Léon comprend tellement que Georges écrive des romans.
    Léon understands so well that Georges write.SUBJ novels.

What (22, 23) reveal is that the attitude of the **external argument** is crucial to distinguish between the two syncretic verbs. If we can identify the common property of external arguments of subjunctive selecting verbs, and contrast it with those of indicative selecting verbs, we will be in a position to distinguish between the two types of predicates in terms of some mood-related core feature.

4.3 Dowty (1991): The semantics of arguments

In order to identify the relevant property, we consider Dowty's (1991) work on the semantics of arguments. Dowty argues that the semantic roles of arguments should be viewed as prototypical concepts, as listed in (24) for Proto-agent, rather than discrete categories.

(24) Dowty's (1991) categories of Proto-Agents:
 – Volition : volitional involvement in the event or state
 – Sentience (and/or perception)
 – Cause: causing an event or change of state in another participant
 – Movement (relative to the position of another participant)

Note that in Dowty's list, *sentience* is a cover term used for a cognitive state, emotion or perception, translating into "S is conscious of p" and that *Cause* here indicates causing an event or change of state in another participant.

As such, Dowty's distinction of the properties of (Proto-)Agents in terms of sentience, volition and cause does not account for the distinction between external arguments of verbs taking the subjunctive vs indicative. We therefore refine the notion.

4.3.1 Sentience and Emotion

Following the idea that semantic properties match syntactic features, we propose that the semantic licensing of Proto-Agents requires a feature built in the syntactic fseq of the predicate. We observe that the verbs selecting embedded clauses, listed under (20) above (be they indicative or subjunctive), all license sentient external arguments. They are therefore all associated with a *sentient* property.[13] Indeed, all of these verbs involve a consciousness on the part of the subject. In (25), the predicate *screech* may have an external argument both of the inanimate and the animate kind.

(25) a. The tire screeched loudly.
 b. #**The tire** screeched that the bend was too tight.
 c. **John** screeched that the bend was too tight.

---

[13] Verbs that do not select embedded clauses may or may not involve sentient subjects.

The inanimate external argument is not compatible with an embedded clause (25b). Only the animate and *sentient* external argument is felicitous with an embedded clause (25b). The latter expresses the content of the conscious mental process of the agent.

In addition, desire and directive predicates license a volitional external argument. The volitional component only appears with desire and directive predicates (20d,e) as obviously, the other classes do not require "volitional involvement in the event or state" denoted by the predicate.

Finally, among the classes of predicates we are considering, only directives (20e) involve a causing external argument, and we tentatively propose that they are associated with a cause feature.

In Table 5, the vertical black line indicates the divide between predicates selecting subjunctive embedded clause vs. those selecting the indicative clause.

Tab. 5: Classes of embedding verbs, Proto-agent licensing features and mood selection I

	Saying	Epistemics	Emotive factives	Desire predicates	Directive predicates
Sentient	yes	yes	yes	yes	yes
Volitional	no	no	no	yes	yes
Cause	no	no	no	no	yes
	indicative		subjunctive		

As shown, mood does not correspond to a uniform set of features for the proto-AGENT. We need a more fine-grained distinction.

We therefore propose to add a category, the emotive category, to the set of proto-AGENT categories discussed in Dowty. This allows us to make the correct cut: all predicates that license an "emotive" Proto-agent select the subjunctive mood in table 6 (note that all emotive licensing predicates are also sentient, but the reverse is not true). Predicates that are not associated with an emotive feature do not select for the subjunctive mood, but for indicative clauses.

Tab. 6: Classes of embedding verbs, Proto-agent licensing features and mood selection II

	Saying	Epistemics	Emotive factives	Desire predicates	Directive predicates
Sentient	yes	yes	yes	yes	yes
Emotive	no	no	yes	yes	yes
Volitional	no	no	no	yes	yes
Cause	no	no	no	no	yes
	indicative		subjunctive		

5 Decomposing the subjunctive mechanism

5.1 What is "emotive"?

We now need to give a formal account of what the "emotive" component is. Formal semantic accounts associate subjunctive mood with a shift from the speaker's epistemic world to a set of possible worlds associated with the subject (see e.g. Farkas 1992, Quer 1998, 2009 a.o.). We claim that it is the focus on the *emotive* attitude of the subject that induces subjunctive

The nature of "emotive" is discussed in Blochowiak (2014: 173), where she argues that "emotive propositional attitudes (...) provide information about the emotional state of the speaker towards the state of affairs described by the embedded proposition". Note that this is not what is generally associated with e.g. 'emotive factives', nor with a psychological category of 'emotion'. In other words, 'emotive' refers to a category of states that are triggered by a linguistic category of *attitude denoting predicates*.

Blochowiak adds that "[a]ny emotional state has its polarity (negative or positive). This polarity tells us something about the experiencer's wishes, i.e. her bouletic attitude, which inherits the polarity of emotional states (w.r.t. eventuality described by the embedded proposition)" (Blochowiak 2014: 173). A formal definition of the emotive attitude is given in (26).

(26) a. x is in an emotional state *s* towards some eventuality *e*
 b. eventuality *e*
 c. x wishes or not that *e* occurs (cf. bouletic Op)
 d. *e* is desirable or not w.r.t. some corpus of rules (cf. axiological Op)
 (Blochowiak 2014: 177, (274))

We therefore propose that an external argument that has an emotive property is licensed by the class of predicates that denote an eventuality associated with *bouletic* (and *axiological)* operators. We transpose Blochowiak's emotional state of the speaker to 'emotional state of the subject' and we claim that these are the contexts where subjunctive is licensed. Examples (27, 28) below illustrate the contrast:

(27) a. Georges rêve que Léon reçoit le prix Nobel.
 Georges dreams that Léon receive.IND the Nobel prize.
 b. Georges rêve que Léon reçoive le prix Nobel.
 Georges dreams that Léon receive.SUBJ the Nobel prize.

(28) a. Georges regrette que Léon **a** reçu le prix Nobel.
 Georges regrets that Léon has.IND received the Nobel prize.
 b. Georges regrette que Léon **ait** reçu le prix Nobel.
 Georges regrets that Léon has.SUBJ received the Nobel prize.

While (27a) expresses an external (speaker's) description of the subject's mental state/activity, (27b) involves a shift to the subject's point of view, and indicates the subject's emotional state. This emotional state corresponds to the subject's attitude towards the eventuality of the embedded clause (namely Léon's winning the Nobel Prize), an attitude of desirability, axiologically determined by conventions about the prestige of a Nobel Prize. Similarly, with 'regret', (a so-called 'factive verb'), (28a) in the indicative is equivalent to 'expressing one's regrets', (without necessarily being committed to them). In contrast, (28b) with the subjunctive reveals the subject's emotive expectations (of wishes/desires not coming true) w.r.t to the situation denoted by the embedded clause.

"Emotive" licensing predicates are thus predicates whose external argument (realized as the subject of the matrix clause) denotes an individual having an emotional attitude of wishing, i.e. considering a set of possible worlds with a non-realistic modal base, for which she has (positive or negative) *expectations* about an eventuality, ranked according to a set of rules, etc. We claim that these are the contexts where subjunctive is licensed.

5.2 The internal structure of selecting predicates

Recall Table 6 above. The organization of the features suggests that these subject-related properties are hierarchically organized. Disregarding for now the fine-grained distinctions between the different classes of predicates listed in (20), we propose a hierarchy based on semantic containment: verbs of saying and epistemic verbs have a feature [sentient], emotive factive predicates, desire verbs and directive verbs have (at least) a [sentient] and a [emotive] feature. The containment relations appear as follows:

(29) ... > ... > emotive > sentient

Recall also that we consider verbs like *comprendre, rêver* etc. as being syncretic between predicates with pure [sentient] and [emotive] + [sentient] features. Given NS assumptions about the syntactic encoding of features, we propose that each of the properties discussed here is syntactically encoded within the *fseq*. We therefore propose a syntactic representation of the relevant predicates as follows.

All verbs selecting an embedded clause license a sentient argument. The relevant feature occurs in the fseq of all embedding verbs, as the head of a *v*sentientP (30). Verbs licensing an emotive sentient argument, as discussed above, also include a bouletic component. We propose that the bouletic operator is the head of a higher $v_{emotive}$P (31).[14]

(30) **Verbs of saying** (*penser*), *comprendre 1* :
 [$v_{sentient}$P v [...V

(31) **Emotives** *comprendre 2,* emotive factives (*regretter*),desire verbs (*vouloir*), directives (*suggérer*):
 [(...) [$v_{emotive}$P v_{boulOP} [$v_{sentient}$P v [...V

Predicates selecting for the indicative contain only a sentient component. They mainly denote individuals associated with mental activity, but without any emotional component. They refer to entities entertaining intellectual/logical/cognitive capacities in that they express knowledge or access to/loss of knowledge.

Predicates selecting for the subjunctive all contain minimally a 'sentient' component and an 'emotive' component, and they may additionally contain

---

[14] We also assume a more complex structure for different classes of 'emotive sentient' verbs, which we do not detail here, but see Baunaz and Puskás (submitted).

other properties. They denote individuals who have an emotive (subjective) reaction towards the event described by their predicate (see also Portner and Rubinstein 2012). These emotions may include *volition, desire, worry, fear, urge, sadness*....

(32) a. Léon suggère que... (directive)
 = Emotion: **strong desire** that X do P
 b. Léon regrette que... (emotive factive)
 = Emotion: **being sorry** that P
 c. Léon souhaite que ... (desire)
 = Emotion: **(weak) desire** that P

A possible objection to such an approach may arise from the observation that subjunctive may be triggered by classes of verbs which do not, at first sight, belong to the group of 'emotive' verbs.[15] We nevertheless contend that emotivity is indeed the relevant feature. First, epistemic modality may trigger subjunctive in the embedded clauses, as illustrated in (33a). And second, impersonal constructions (with a deontic modal meaning) also embed subjunctive clauses (33b):

(33) a. Je doute qu'il soit honnête.
 I doubt that he be.SUBJ honest
 (Gosselin 2016: 158)
 b. Il est nécessaire que Georges parte.
 It is necessary that Georges leave.SUBJ

Although both matrix predicates have some modal semantic dimension, we argue that this is not what triggers subjunctive. Rather, a more fine-grained analysis of these predicates shows that they are both 'emotive' in our sense, in that they involve an emotive participant. *Douter* licenses an external argument which needs to be [+sentient], but also [+emotive], in that the individual denoted by this argument entertains some negative expectation with respect to the eventuality described by the embedded proposition. As for *necessaire*, the emotive component is rather transparent, but obviously, no external argument seems to be involved. We propose that in this case, the emotive property is associated with the Speaker, who takes over the emotive feature. A detailed account of these cases is developed in Baunaz and Puskás (submitted).

---

[15] We thank a reviewer for pointing this out to us.

5.3 Selecting complementizers

Since emotive arguments are licensed by given classes of predicates, we will consider that these predicates are *sentient emotive* predicates. We propose that these predicates will select the smallest Comp, Comp$_{subj}$, which licenses embedded subjunctive clauses. Similarly, pure sentient arguments are licensed by *sentient* predicates, which will select Comp$_{Ind}$, which in turn licenses embedded indicative clauses. Crucially, these features stand in a containment relation which means that 'bigger' structures necessarily include 'smaller' ones.

Coming back to the Italo-Romance (and Italo-Greek) dialects we started with, we claim that the same distinction between predicates holds. Recall the data in (8–13) above, repeated here:

(34) a. Pensu **ca** vèni. (S. Calabria)
(=8) 'I think that he'll come.'
    b. Vogghiu **mu** (mi) imanga.
       'I want that$_{MOOD}$ he eat.'

(35) a. Pistèo **tí** pái. (Calabria, Bova)
(=9) 'I think that he will go.'
    b. θèlo **na** pái.
       'I want that$_{MOOD}$ he go.'

(36) a. 'm ɔnnə 'dəttə **ka** vɛ 'krɛ (Guglionesi, Molise)
(=12) to me they.have said that he.comes tomorrow
    b. 'vujjə **kə** vɛnnə 'krɛ
       I.want that he.come tomorrow

(37) a. 'm anta 'nau **ka** eniði ɣraza (Ardaùli, Sardinia)
(=13) me they.have told that he.comes tomorrow
    b. 'kɛrdzɔ **ki** 'ɛndzɛðɛ ain'nɔɣɛ
       I.want that he.comes here

The predicates *pensu, pistèo, 'dəttə, 'nau* are bare sentient predicates, while *vogghiu, θèlo, 'vujjə, 'kɛrdzɔ* are sentient emotive predicates. The licensing of the Comp$_{subj}$ in (34b, 35b, 36b, 37b) is attributed to the presence of the bouletic component of the sentient emotive predicates.

6 Conclusions

In this paper, we argued that the selection of a (subjunctive) embedded clause is necessarily local, and mediated by the complementizer. We started with two questions we intended to address:
i. What role do complementizers play in the selection of the subjunctive mood (vs. indicative) in embedded clauses?
ii. What licenses these complementizers?

As an answer to question (i), we claimed that Comps may be syncretic. They come as a hierarchically organized set of different properties. The realization of a subset of the properties may result in different lexical items, as is the case in some Italo-Romance dialects, or may be syncretic with the realization of the maximal set of properties, as in French or Standard Italian.

Answering question (ii) led us to making a crucial distinction among embedded clause selecting predicates. We argue that predicates are also decomposed into organized sets of features. We proposed that the modal property associated with subjunctive is licensed on Comp by a bouletic operator present on one of the heads of the structurally complex predicates. It is responsible for the *emotive* interpretation of the matrix predicate, that is, for the presence of an emotive external argument. The bouletic component licenses $Comp_{subj}$, which, in turn selects for subjunctive (modal) clauses.

Clearly, what has not been addressed in this paper is the relation between the complementizer and the embedded clause itself. While some research has put forth the idea that clauses may vary in the richness of their internal structure depending on their mood/modal characteristics (see a.o. Sočanać 2017 and references therein), the exact selecting properties of different complementizers remains to be analyzed, especially in the light of work by Ledgeway 2009, 2016 (a.o), Schifano 2018 on the position of Romance verbs in the clausal spine.

Acknowledgement: We would like to thank Natascha Pomino, Eva-Maria Remberger, and Marc Hinzelin as well as the organizers and participants to the XXXV Romanistentag held in Zürich (October 8–12, 2017). This work also benefited from the comments and questions put forward by the audience of the TEAM 2018 event in Padua (June 14–15, 2018). In particular, we thank Emanuela Sanfelici and M.R Manzini. We also thank Eric Lander, Fredérique Berthelot, Kevin Mulligan, Ur Shlonsky and Elisabeth Stark for useful comments on various versions of this paper. Special thanks to the anonymous reviewers whose relevant observations helped us sharpen some of our points.

7 References

Baunaz, Lena. 2015. On the various sizes of complementizers. *Probus* 2(2). 193–236.
Baunaz, Lena. 2016. Deconstructing complementizers in Serbo-Croatian, Modern Greek and Bulgarian. In Christopher Hammerly & Brandon Prickett (eds.), *Proceedings of NELS* 46(1), 69–77.
Baunaz, Lena. 2017. French predicates selecting the subjunctive mood under the microscope: The emotive factor. In Sílvia Perpiñan, David Heap, Irtziri Moreno-Villamar & Adriana Soto-Corominas (eds.), *Romance languages and linguistic theory 11. Selected papers from the 44th Linguistic Symposium on Romance Languages, London, Ontario*, 9–31. Amsterdam: John Benjamins.
Baunaz, Lena. 2018. Decomposing complementizers: The Fseq of French, Modern Greek, Serbo-Croatian and Bulgarian complementizers. In Lena Baunaz, Karen De Clercq, Liliane Haegeman & Eric Lander (eds.), *Exploring nanosyntax*, 149–179. New York: Oxford University Press.
Baunaz, Lena & Eric Lander. 2017. Syncretism with nominal complementizers. *Studia Linguistica*. 1–27.
Baunaz, Lena & Eric Lander. 2018a. The basics of nanosyntax. In Lena Baunaz, Karen De Clercq, Liliane Haegeman & Eric Lander (eds.), *Exploring nanosyntax*. 3–56. New York: Oxford University Press.
Baunaz, Lena & Eric Lander. 2018b. Deconstructing categories syncretic with the nominal complementizer. *Glossa: a Journal of General Linguistics* 3(1). 1–31.
Baunaz, Lena & Eric Lander. 2018c. Cross-categorial syncretism and the Slavic containment puzzle. In Illeana Krapova & Brian Joseph (eds.), *Balkan syntax and (universal) principles of grammar*, 219–247. Berlin: Mouton de Gruyter.
Baunaz, Lena, Karen de Clercq, Liliane Haegeman & Eric Lander. 2018. *Exploring nanosyntax*. New York: Oxford University Press.
Baunaz, Lena & Genoveva Puskás. 2014. On subjunctives and islandhood. In Marie-Hélène Côté & Eric Mathieu (eds.), *Variation within and across Romance languages. Selected papers from the 41st Linguistic Symposium on Romance Languages* (LSRL), Ottawa, 5–7 May 2011, [CILT 333], 233–254. Amsterdam: John Benjamins.
Baunaz Lena & Genoveva Puskás. Submitted. A Cross-linguistics approach to the syntax of subjunctive mood.
Blake, Barry. J. 1994 [2004]. *Case*. Cambridge: Cambridge University Press.
Blochowiak, Joanna. 2014. A theoretical approach to the quest for understanding. Semantics and pragmatics of whys and becauses. PhD dissertation. Geneva: University of Geneva.
Caha, Pavel. 2009. The nanosyntax of case. PhD dissertation. Tromsø: University of Tromsø.
Caha, Pavel. 2010. The parameters of case marking and spell out driven movement. In Jeroen van Craenenbroeck (ed.), *Linguistic variation yearbook 2010*, 33–77. Amsterdam/Philadelphia: John Benjamins.
Caha, Pavel. 2013. Explaining the structure of case paradigms by the mechanisms of nanosyntax: The classical Armenian nominal declension. *Natural Language and Linguistic Theory* 31(4). 1015–1066.
Calabrese, Andrea. 1993. The sentential complementation of Salentino: A study of a language without infinitival clauses. In Adriana Belletti (ed.), *Syntactic theory and the dialects of Italy*, 28–98. Turin: Rosenberg and Sellier.

Cinque, Gugliemlmo. 1999. *Adverbs and functional heads*. Oxford: Oxford University Press.
Cinque, Guglielmo & Luigi Rizzi. 2008. The cartography of syntactic structures. In Vincenzo Moscati (ed.), *CISCL Working Papers on Language and Cognition 2*, 43–59.
Cinque, Guglielmo & Luigi Rizzi. 2010. The cartography of syntactic structures. In Bernd Heine & Heiko Narrog (eds.), *The Oxford Handbook of Linguistic Analysis*, 51–65. New York: Oxford University Press.
Cotfas, Maria Aurelia. 2011. A closer look at (lack of) obviation phenomena in Romanian subjunctive complements. *Bucharest Working Papers in Linguistics* 13. 27–48.
De Clercq, Karen. 2013. *A unified syntax of negation*. Doctoral dissertation. Ghent: Ghent University.
De Clercq, Karen. 2018. Syncretism and the morphosyntax of negation. In Lena Baunaz, Karen De Clercq, Liliane Haegeman & Eric Lander (eds.), *Exploring Nanosyntax*, 180–204. New York: Oxford University Press.
Damonte, Federico. 2002. The complementizer layer in Saramaccan. In Manuel Leonetti, Olga Fernàndez Soriano & Victoria Escandell Vidal (eds.), *Current issues in generative grammar. Tenth colloquium on generative grammar: Selected papers*, 31–50. Madrid: Universidad Alcalà de Henares, Servicio de Publicaciones.
Dowty, David. 1991. Thematic proto-roles and argument selection. *Language* 67. 547–619.
Fábregas, Antonio. 2009. An argument for phrasal spellout: Indefinites and interrogatives in Spanish. *Nordlyd: Special Issue on Nanosyntax* 36. 129–168.
Farkas, Donka. 1992. On the semantics of subjunctive complements. In Paul Hirschbuehler (ed.), *Romance languages and modern linguistic theory*, 69–105. Amsterdam: John Benjamins.
Giannakidou, Anastasia. 2009. The dependency of the subjunctive revisited: temporal semantics and polarity. *Lingua* 119(12). 883–1908.
Gosselin, Laurent. 2016. Les modes expriment-ils des modalités? L'alternance indicatif/subjonctif dans les complétives objet. *Lingvisticæ Investigationes* 39(1). 143–189.
Kayne, Richard S. 2005. *Movement and silence*. Oxford: Oxford University Press.
Lander, Eric. 2015. The nanosyntax of the Northwest Germanic reinforced demonstrative. Doctoral dissertation, Ghent University.
Lander, Eric & Lilian Haegeman. 2018. Syncretism and containment in spatial deixis. In Lena Baunaz, Karen De Clercq, Liliane Haegeman & Eric Lander (eds.), *Exploring nanosyntax*, 116–148. New York: Oxford University Press.
Ledgeway, Adam. 2005. Moving through the left periphery: The dual complementizer system in the dialects of Southern Italy. *The Philological Society* 103(3). 339–396.
Ledgeway, Adam. 2006. The dual complementiser system in Southern Italy: Spirito Greco, Materia Romanza? In Anna Laura Lepschy & Arturo Tosi (eds.), *Rethinking languages in contact: The case of Italian*, 112–126. Oxford: Lengenda.
Ledgeway, Adam. 2009. Aspetti della sintassi della periferia sinistra del cosentino. In Diego Pescarini (ed.), *Studi sui dialetti della Calabria* (Quaderni di lavoro ASIt n.9), 3–24. Padua: Unipress.
Ledgeway, Adam. 2013. Testing linguistic theory and variation to their limits: The case of Romance. *Corpus* 12. 271–327.
Ledgeway, Adam. 2016. Complementation. In Adam Ledgeway & Martin Maiden (eds.), *The Oxford guide to the Romance languages*, 1013–1028. Oxford: Oxford University Press.
Lefebvre Claire & Anne-Marie Brousseau 2002. *A grammar of Fongbe*. Berlin/New York: Mouton de Gruyter.

Manzini, Maria Rita & Leonardo Savoia. 2003. The nature of complementizers. *Rivista di Grammatica Generative* 28. 87–110.
Manzini, Maria Rita & Leonardo Savoia. 2011. *Grammatical categories*. Cambridge: Cambridge University Press.
Pantcheva, Marina. 2011. *Decomposing path: The nanosyntax of directional expressions*. Ph.D. dissertation. Tromsø: University of Tromsø.
Portner, Paul & Aynat Rubinstein. 2012. Mood and contextual commitment. In Anca Chereches (ed), *The Proceedings of SALT 22*, 461–487. Chicago: CLC Publications,
Quer, Josep. 1998. *Mood at the interface*. Ph.D. Dissertation. Utrecht: University of Utrecht.
Quer, Josep. 2009. Twists of mood: The distribution and interpretation of indicative and subjunctive. *Lingua* 119(12). 1779–1787.
Ramchand, Gillian. 2008. *Verb meaning and the lexicon*. Cambridge: Cambridge University Press.
Rohlfs, Gerhard. 1969. *Grammatica storica della lingua Italiana e dei suoi dialetti. III. Sintassi e formazione delle parole*. Turin: Einaudi.
Rizzi, Luigi. 1997. The fine structure of the left periphery. In Liliane Haegeman (ed.), *Elements of grammar: A handbook of generative syntax*, 281–337. Dordrecht: Kluwer.
Rizzi, Luigi. 2004. Locality and left periphery. In Adriana Belletti (ed.), *Structures and beyond. The cartography of syntactic structures Vol. 3*, 223–251. New York: Oxford University Press.
Rizzi Luigi. 2013. Syntactic cartography and the syntacticisation of scope-discourse semantics. In Anne Reboul (ed.), *Mind, values and metaphysics – Philosophical papers dedicated to Kevin Mulligan*, 517–533. Dordrecht: Springer.
Roussou, Anna. 2010. Selecting complementizers. *Lingua* 120. 582–603.
Schifano, Norma. 2018. Verb placement in Romance: A comparative study. Oxford: Oxford University Press.
Starke, Michal. 2009. Nanosyntax. A short primer to a new approach to language. In Peter Svenonius, Gillian Ramchand, Michal Starke & Knut Tarald Taraldsen (eds.), *Special issue on nanosyntax*, 1–6 [Nordlyd 36.1]. Tromsø: CASTL.
Starke, Michal. 2011. Towards an elegant solution to language variation: Variation reduces to the size of lexically stored trees. Manuscript. Barcelona, Spain.
Sočanać, Tomislav. 2017. Subjunctive complements in Slavic langugages: A syntax-semantics interface approach. Doctoral dissertation. Geneva: University of Geneva.
Taraldsen, Knut Tarald. 2009. The nanosyntax of Nguni noun class prefixes and concords. Manuscript. CASTL. Available at LingBuzz/000876.

www.ingramcontent.com/pod-product-compliance
Lightning Source LLC
Chambersburg PA
CBHW030530230426

43665CB00010B/827